IMMORTALITY
AND THE
UNSEEN WORLD

A Study in Old Testament Religion

W.O.E. OESTERLEY, D.D.

A Reprinti

DEFENDER

CRANE, MO

Immortality and the Unseen World: A Study in Old Testament Religion
By William Oscar Emil Oesterley

Originally published 1921
©2019 this edition by Thomas Horn

Defender Publishing
Crane, MO 65633

A CIP catalog record of this book is available from the Library of Congress.

Cover illustration and design by Jeffrey Mardis.

CONTENTS

THE SPIRITS OF THE DEAD AND THEIR ABODE

THE LIVING AND THE DEPARTED

MOURNING AND BURIAL CUSTOMS

THE DOCTRINE OF IMMORTALITY

Introductory

I

SOME PRELIMINARY CONSIDERATIONS

I. The Subject to be treated on the Lines of Comparative Religion

No department of Israelite religion can be adequately dealt with unless it be studied in the light of the religious beliefs of kindred peoples. It may in these days be regarded as axiomatic that, whether it be Israelite religion as a whole, or whether it be some particular part of that religion, the subject cannot be properly understood nor adequately appreciated unless it be studied on the comparative method. No scholar has done more to show the need of this than Robertson Smith. "No positive religion," he says, "that has moved men has been able to start with a *tabula rasa*, and express itself as if religion were beginning for the first time; in form, if not in substance, the new system must be in contact all along the line with the older ideas and practices which it finds in possession. A new scheme of faith can find a hearing only by appealing to religious instincts and susceptibilities that already exist in its audience, and it cannot reach these without taking account of the traditional forms in which all religious feeling is embodied, and without speaking a language which men accustomed to these old forms can understand. Thus, to comprehend a system of positive religion thoroughly, to understand it in its historical origin and form as well as in its abstract principles, we must know the traditional religion that preceded it."[1] The profound truth of these words is only enhanced when applied to the Israelite belief in Immortality. We find in the Old Testament a mass of antique conceptions regarding the life beyond the grave which the Israelites shared with other peoples, and which had been handed down from time immemorial; but these antique conceptions, though, as a rule, fully discernible, are nevertheless often blurred; many appear as remnants of earlier belief; to understand them the Old Testament is not sufficient; we must seek the parallel ideas, beliefs, and customs as these appear among other Semitic peoples in order to realize their significance. Not only so; for since in some instances these conceptions have come down from a time when man was in a lower stage of culture than the Semites were at any time of which we have cognizance, it follows that the origin and history of an idea must sometimes be studied in its form among savage men. The scope of the present study does not permit of our extending our inquiries beyond the Semitic domain, but here and there references will be made to the ideas and customs of non-Semitic peoples.

We are not blind to the dangers involved in treating our subject on the comparative method. The student of Comparative Religion is, as all the world knows, not infrequently tempted to see parallels which are such only in appearance, not in essence; there are many pitfalls. While we have taken pains to keep this danger in view, we are far from feeling assured that in dealing with subjects which are at times very intricate we have always succeeded in avoiding these pitfalls. But however insidious the danger, it would never do on that account to forget that many undoubted parallels between the Israelite beliefs and conceptions about Immortality and those of other peoples do really exist; and these parallels concern not only beliefs and conceptions, but also customs and usages to which they have given birth. There are still many people who claim for the religion of Israel absolute uniqueness and originality from its beginnings onwards, and who therefore refuse to recognize parallels of any kind among the beliefs, and possibly also the customs, of other peoples; to such be it said that if religious development took place in a more pronounced degree within the limits of one nation—or, what comes to the same thing, if the response to divine inspiration was more intensive, and therefore fuller, on the part of Israel's religious thinkers—that does not imply that the divine solicitude was unmindful of, or left itself without witness among, the peoples of other races. The religious faculty has been accorded to all men; the capacity for apprehension has varied immensely among them, whatever the reasons for this may have been; but all have in greater or .less degree responded to what has, in effect, been a divine revelation to them. It may be that some would describe it as folly to contend that the crass ideas of early man are to be looked upon as a response to divine revelation; or, indeed, that a divine revelation was possible to man in such a low stage of culture; but however crass those ideas may be to the modern thinker, they were not so to early man; and if they represented the utmost that the savage mind could rise to, is it not in accordance with all our belief in God that the divine interest in man should be such as would have consideration even for the most childlike efforts towards truth? We smile commiseratingly, and with justice, at the *naive* conceptions of the men who lived, say, 50,000 B.C.[2]; but what right have we to suppose that our conceptions will be less *naive* to the men of, say, 50,000 A.D.? To an omniscient God the advance in thought from the time of the dawn of man's understanding to the present day may not be so great as it appears to us. When St. Paul in Athens told how he had seen an altar to an unknown god, he frankly recognized that the worshippers at this altar had been seeking after God, though in ignorance.[3]

It is, therefore, both on scientific and religious grounds that the Israelite ideas and customs which we are to consider should be illustrated by the parallels among other peoples.

II. Inconsistent Ideas in the Old Testament

We come now to another preliminary consideration. The study of the Old Testament belief in Immortality often appears very puzzling because such inconsistent ideas are met with in close proximity. We find there at times crass and childish ideas, and we find there distinctly advanced conceptions; and sometimes these occur mixed up together. How are we to account for this? The answer is, we believe, two-fold:

In dealing with things religious, and especially when it is a question of teaching, men are influenced, generally speaking, by two tendencies, either consciously or unconsciously; these tendencies may be described, roughly, as retrospective and prospective; there is, mostly, an inclination to view things in accordance with a set mode, and to teach accordingly; what has been handed down, what has been received, is regarded as authoritative, and must therefore be treated with respect. That is altogether fit and proper. But traditional ideas and traditional teaching are again and again seen to be at variance with the new points of view, and therefore with the new ideas, which press themselves into the minds of the thinking. Hence arises this two-fold tendency of looking back upon the old and looking forward to the new. These tendencies are strikingly illustrated in the Old Testament. With some, at all events, of the writers of the Old Testament respect for tradition induced a disinclination to discard any part of the venerable records of the past, and therefore the ideas and teachings embodied in them. On the other hand, these writers were faced with the fact that thought advances, widens, develops; owing to one cause and another new points of view arose; some of the old ideas were seen to be untenable, for it was recognized that they were based upon misconceptions; they had, therefore, to be modified, or in some cases altered altogether. Consequently we find that in the Old Testament the spirit of compromise has been at work; and the form that this has again and again taken has been that the old wording has been kept as far as possible, only that which was thought to be absolutely necessary having been altered. At the same time certain things demanded by the development of thought and conception were added. We may sometimes wonder why this process was not carried farther; we may also wonder how the redactors of the books could be content to leave what, upon occasion, amounts to a glaring inconsistency without a more heroic attempt to soften it down; the attempt is at times made, but the inconsistency remains. One must, however, remember that the oriental is not very logical in his ideas; an inconsistency which is a veritable worry to the Western does not trouble the Eastern. Thus, the Old Testament has within it the marks of compromise. This applies emphatically to the subject with which we are to deal, the belief in Immortality. Things are said in regard to this belief which are inconsistent with each other; and, therefore, the attempt has been made to compromise. But as the compromise is by no means always satisfying, the subject appears at times very puzzling.

III. Two Beliefs Regarding Immortality in the Old Testament

But there is a second and more deep-seated reason for these inconsistencies. Indeed, in dealing with the belief in Immortality in the Old Testament it is found that not only do inconsistencies exist, but conceptions are met with which are of an entirely contradictory character; we may go so far as to say that they are mutually exclusive. The presence of these can, we believe, only be satisfactorily explained upon one hypothesis, and that is that the Old Testament has preserved two sets of ideas and beliefs regarding the future life. The details of these will be found in the following pages, and therefore we shall not deal with them here. But the hypothesis may be briefly stated thus:

Speculation regarding the departed, the place of their abode, their powers, their desires, their requirements, their activities, their relationship to the living—all these things have exercised the minds of men of all races from the earliest times. Various beliefs concerning the departed, some of them fundamentally identical in character, took shape independently among the most diverse races. We are not, for the moment, concerned with the subject of how and why these beliefs arose, but only with the fact that they did arise. The Semitic race shared these beliefs with other races; and though the Semites moulded them in accordance with their special genius, most of them, so far as their fundamental essence was concerned, were the same as the beliefs of other races. Now the Israelites shared these beliefs with the rest of the Semites; and among them the belief, which developed in course of time, in what was called by the Israelites "Sheol," a lugubrious place to which men went when they had finished their ordinary life. Among the Israelites this belief underwent a fundamental change because it was found to be incompatible with the belief in Jahwe; the essence of this change consisted in the teaching that they who went to Sheol could never leave it; they were tied to it forever. This had not been held hitherto. But the official exponents of the religion of Jahwe found it not only difficult, but quite impossible, to root out the ancient traditional belief which was held by the people. For centuries, therefore, two beliefs existed in Israel regarding Sheol—the ancient popular belief, and what came to be the official belief and doctrine. These two forms of belief are to be found over and over again in the Old Testament. Other beliefs which centered around that of Sheol, and which were expressed by various prac-tices, were also found to be incompatible with the religion of Jahwe; but in spite of penal enactments against the perpetrators of these practices, they continued until long after the Exile.

The existence of two diametrically opposed Sheol-beliefs, a popular and an official, illustrated in a variety of ways in the Old Testament, is amply sufficient to account for inconsistent and contradictory elements regarding belief in the future life.

Details of what has been said are dealt with in the following pages.

IV. PLAN AND METHOD OF DEALING WITH THE SUBJECT

A few words are called for in order to set forth the plan and method which have been adopted in dealing with the subject of belief in Immortality in the Old Testament.

We begin with a brief consideration of the Hebrew ideas regarding the various parts of which man is made up. This is required; for, to the ques-tion, "What part of man continued to live after death?" the answer given by the ancient Hebrew is uncertain. It was obvious that he distinguished between the soul and the body; and at first we should be tempted to say without hesitation that the belief was that the soul continued to live after death, while the body went to corruption. But there are some considerations which suggest that this does not represent what was really believed. Why was there such a horror among the Hebrews at the idea of a dead body being burned? Why was it regarded as such a grievous punishment for a body to be buried in foreign soil? Why, above all, was it considered such a dreadful thing for a body not to be buried? To this last question there are two obvious answers: one is that since a dead body was unclean it was necessary to bury it lest contact with it should cause contamination; the other is that the natural feeling of respect for the dead would demand decent burial. Probably, however, these two answers do not exhaust the subject. At any rate, the two other questions suggest that the body was not done with at death. We referred just now to the "popular" Sheol-belief, according to which that part of man which after death went to Sheol was able to leave it, on occasion, temporarily; the reason it wished to do so was its intimate relationship with the body, even after death. The great care expended on graves may be supposed to have had something to do with this. Embalming was not, it is true, in vogue among the Israelites, and it is very uncertain to what extent they were influenced by Egyptian belief concerning the life hereafter; but there are some grounds for believing that the Israelites put spices within the grave-clothes with the primary object of preserving the body. Then there is another consideration. We draw attention later on, but it requires mention here, to the inscription of Eshmunazar, in which it is said: "…I lie in this coffin and in this grave, in the place which I built.…I adjure every prince and every man that they open not this resting-place…I adjure every prince and every man that they open me not, nor uncover me, nor carry me from this resting-place, nor take away the coffin of my resting-place, lest these holy gods deliver them up, and cut off that prince and those men, and their seed, forever!" Other similar sepulchral inscriptions are not wanting; and though they are not Israelite, they are Semitic, and there is every reason to believe—as will be seen in the following pages—that the Israelites shared the beliefs about the hereafter common to the rest of the Semites. As to this inscription, and others like it, it is evident that the solicitude evinced has reference to the body. And once more, what is the purpose of placing food, utensils, arms, ornaments, lamps, etc., in tombs by the side of, or in close proximity to, the body? When this kind of fact is taken into consideration it is quite evident that one cannot say off-hand that the Israelite belief regarding the component parts of man's body was simply that the soul lived on and that the body went to corruption. Above all, we have the definitely expressed belief that life resided in the bones, and that they would flourish and sprout again. It will, therefore, be seen that some discussion upon the component parts of man is a necessary preliminary in dealing with the subject of the Old Testament belief in Immortality.

Then we come to consider the Israelite belief in supernatural beings. It needs no insisting on the fact that belief in supernatural immortal beings must of itself have some influence upon the belief in the immortality of man; and in what a variety of respects this is so we hope to show. We divide this part of our study under three heads: first a brief general survey of Semitic Demonology; the fact that among the various classes of demons some were believed to be the spirits of the dead is sufficient to show the appropriateness of dealing with the subject of Demonology here. Then we come to the more restricted Demonology of the Old Testament. So far as the evidence goes, Israelite Demonology was not systematized in the way that Babylonian and Arabian Demonology were; but that the Israelite belief in demons was of a more extensive character than the comparatively meagre indications in the Old Testament would lead one to suppose is probable. Knowing what we do about Semitic Demonology in general, *any* references to the subject in the Old Testament suggest a more extended belief in demons than appears upon the surface; for in other respects there are so many points of similarity between Israelite belief and that of the rest of the Semites that it is difficult to believe that in this particular similarity was altogether wanting. The difference that undoubtedly did exist, was, we venture to think, in its want of systematization among the Israelites. This, however, came later, and was very elaborate—a fact which in itself supposes a preexisting mass of unsystematized beliefs. The third division is devoted to Angelology. The appropriateness of dealing with this in the present connexion is, we confess, not great; but when once the question of supernatural beings is raised one cannot well omit some reference to angels. It must also be remembered that in view of later developments of belief some consideration of Angelology is useful.

Then we enter more directly into our main subject. Here we consider in some detail what is said in the Old Testament about the *Rephaim*, usually rendered "Shades," in reference to the departed; and it is seen that the word occurs, apparently, in two connexions there; but the attempt is made to show that the name *Rephaim*—applied originally to "the sons of the gods" who, according to an ancient myth, were, on account of their wickedness, destroyed by the gods and cast down into the under-world—came to be used of all the inhabitants of the under-world, i.e. of the departed. Further, it is surmised that this word *Rephaim*, which is usually explained as the "weak ones," this being supposed to be descriptive of the shades of the departed, is rather to be derived from the root meaning "to heal"; it is then explained why this term should have been originally applied to the inhabitants of the underworld. And lastly, the significance of this name being given to a valley near Jerusalem is shown.

The abode of the departed, Sheol, is then considered; and from this inquiry it comes out that while the official teaching about this place in the Old Testament is clear and consistent, it cannot be reconciled with much that is said about the *Rephaim*, the inhabitants of this place.

We shall repeatedly point out that the various subdivisions of our subject cannot be treated in isolation; the different matters dealt with depend so much on one another, and each has to be considered in the light of factors which occur in some other subdivision. Therefore we must insist strongly on the fact that agreement or disagreement with any particular contention put forward here should be withheld until all the facts have been weighed. This applies particularly to the subject of the *Rephaim*; the whole of that division of our inquiry entitled "The Spirits of the Dead and their Abode" must be read and judged in the light of the division that

follows, "The Living and the Departed," in which we deal with Ancestor-worship and the cult of the dead, and ultimately with the subject of
Necromancy. The chapter that follows then, "Mourning and Burial Customs," lengthy though it is, touches upon such a variety of topics connected with our general subject that we have been compelled to leave
unsaid much that ought to be dealt with; indeed, it became evident as we
proceeded that the subject of this chapter, if adequately treated, would
require a separate volume.

The last two chapters deal respectively, in the light of what has gone
before, with the Old Testament doctrine of Immortality, and the Development of Belief which appears in some of the later books, and especially
in some of the later Psalms.

A certain amount of repetition in quoting passages from the Old Testament cannot well be avoided, since it often happens that passages contain references to more than one subject.

II

THE OLD TESTAMENT TEACHING
ON THE CONSTITUENT
PARTS OF MAN

I. Basar, Flesh

Obviously, in dealing with the subject of Immortality in the Old Testament it is indispensable that we should get some clear and definite ideas as to what the Old Testament teaches regarding the constituent parts of man and their different functions.

We are met at the outset with the real difficulty that so many people have in envisaging things from the standpoint of the Old Testament writers. The development of thought and conception during the ages, as well as the manner of expressing them, make it a matter of no slight difficulty for us to get into the mental environment of the ancient Hebrew and to look out upon things from his circumscribed point of view. Nevertheless, it is quite necessary that this difficulty should be overcome; and it can be overcome to a large extent in this way: in the first place it must be realized that the differentiation between what is material and what is immaterial or spiritual, a thing that comes so natural to us, was entirely unfamiliar to the people of antiquity. In the second place, it is necessary for us to remember that when, as was the case with the Israelites of old, ideas have not been logically thought out nor formulated with precision, the words used to express these ideas will, as a consequence, often be used loosely and ambiguously. And it is the fact that there is confusion of thought and want of consistency in some things which the Old Testament teachers said regarding the component parts of man. This fact must be allowed for.

According to Old Testament teaching man is made up, firstly, of flesh (*basar*). Here there is no difference between man and the animals; the word is used indiscriminately of man and beast; in Gen. vi. 17, for example, it is said: "I do bring the flood of waters upon the earth, to destroy all flesh, wherein the breath of life is"; and in Gen. vii. 15: "And they went in unto Noah into the ark, two and two of all flesh wherein is the breath of life"; and so in many other passages. Equally numerous are the places in which the word is used in reference to man; in one case, in order to make the reference to man more definite, we get the phrase, "the spirit of the flesh of man" (Job xii. 10; the R.V. renders "the breath [marg. 'spirit'] of all mankind"). As far as this word is concerned, then, there is no ambiguity.

II. NEPHESH, SORN,

Next we come to the part of man called *nephesh*, which is translated "soul"; and so long as we do not understand "soul" here in the modern sense, this translation will stand. The word is mostly used to denote the individual life as distinct from the body or flesh; that is, the nephesh is the inner, while *basar* is the outer, part of man. Like *basar*, however, *nephesh* is used in reference to animals too, though not so generally as is the case with *basar*, see Gen. i. 20, etc.; this may be ultimately due to the fact (which cannot, however, be said to have been proved) that *nephesh* in its original signification meant "breath," by means of which every living being, animal as well as human, lives. Although it is undeniable that this meaning of *nephesh* had almost entirely disappeared at a comparatively early time, we find the verb from the same root used in the sense of refreshing oneself, i.e. taking in breath (the *niphal* form, see Hebrew of Exod. xxiii. 12, xxxi.

17, 2 Sam. xvi. 14); the cognate roots in Assyrian and Arabic also have this meaning. Once in the Old Testament nephesh is used of "breath," viz. Job xli. 13 (E.V. xli. 21): "His breath kindleth coals, and a flame goeth forth from his mouth." These remnants in the Old Testament of the original signification of *nephesh* are interesting, for it is probable that in its original conception *nephesh*, regarded as a material part of man dwelling within the body, announced its presence there by means of the breath; when a man died and his breath ceased, this was because the *nephesh* had left the body. Since, therefore, the life of man ceased with the exit of the soul, this latter was regarded as his breath; and one can understand why the word is frequently used in the sense of "life," e.g. in Exod. xxi. 23, "life for life," cp. Lev. xxiv. 18, Judges xii. 3, 1 Sam. xix. 5, 2 Sam. xiv. 7, etc.; as such it is conceived of as residing in the blood: "But flesh with the life (*nephesh*) thereof, which is the blood thereof, shall ye not eat"(Gen. ix. 4); indeed, it is sometimes looked upon as identical with the blood: "For the life (*nephesh*) of the flesh is in the blood, and I have given it to you upon the altar to make atonement for your souls[4] :for it is the blood that maketh atonement by reason of the life (*nephesh*)" (Lev. xvii. 11, see also Deut. xii. 23, 24). When the blood of a man is poured out he dies, but that is because the *nephesh* has left the body with the blood. When the blood was seen to "smoke" the ancient Israelite believed this to be the breath.

So far we have briefly indicated the more or less official and orthodox teaching regarding the *nephesh*. But there were, in addition, some popular conceptions about it which must be spoken of. How far these conceptions were shared by the more responsible religious teachers depended upon the particular age; originally, and in the earlier ages of Israel's history, there can be little doubt but that the popular conceptions were held by all; later, especially in post-exilic times and onwards, the official teaching on the subject departed from that of the people, and everything was done to eradicate the popular ideas.

Like many other peoples of antiquity, the ancient Israelites believed that the soul could slip in and out of the body at will. How this belief in the "external soul" arose originally cannot be said with absolute certainty;

but it probably owed its origin to dreams. When man in a primitive stage of culture dreams, he believes that he lives through an actual experience, but that it is his other self, or *nephesh*, that does so; the soul-part of him slips out of the body-part of him and experiences literally the occurrences in the dream.[5] As the *nephesh*, though material, is a very fine and subtle substance, it has no difficulty in thus slipping out of the body and slipping back again. This belief with regard to the nephesh appears several times in the Old Testament; in Gen. xxxv. 18, for example, it is said, in reference to Rachel: "And it came to pass, as her soul was in departing (for she died), that she called his name Ben-oni...." Another interesting case is that in 1 Kings xvii. 21, where Elijah prays for the widow's dead child, saying: "O Lord, my God, I pray Thee, let this child's soul come into him again. And the Lord hearkened unto the voice of Elijah; and the soul of the child came into him again, and he revived." This belief in the material character of the soul, or *nephesh*, may be further illustrated by the curious idea of its tangibility referred to in 1 Sam. xxv. 29, where Abigail says to David, "And though man be risen up to pursue thee, and to seek thy soul, yet the soul of my lord shall be bound in the bundle [more correctly "bag"] of life with the Lord thy God; and the souls of thine enemies, them shall He sling out, as from the hollow of a sling." As Driver has pointed out, the word "with" has the force of "in the care and custody of," as in Lev. v. 23, Deut. xv. 3, Isa. xlix. 47.[6] This idea that God has a bag in which He keeps souls is very quaint; it belongs to the circle of ideas connected with the belief that the soul can be detached from the body for short or long periods. It has been amply proved that this belief has been, and is, held by men in a primitive stage of culture in many parts of the world.[7] Quite possibly Frazer may be right in his conjecture that "the houses of the soul" mentioned in Isa. iii. 20 (the R.V. renders "perfume boxes," evidently following the Vulgate) were "amulets in which the soul of the wearer was supposed to lodge"; in the text these words are followed by "and the amulets." Certain it is that the Egyptians, according to Flinders Petrie, put miniature houses on their tombs in which the souls of the departed were supposed to take up their abode.[8] However this may be, it is quite clear from a passage in Ezekiel that as late as his time the Israelites believed in the possibility of losing their souls much in the same way as they might lose anything they carried about with them; the passage in question is the following: "And thou, son of man, set thy face against the daughters of thy people, which prophesy out of their own heart: and prophesy thou against them and say, Thus saith the Lord God; Woe to the women that sew pillows[9] upon all elbows [or "joints of the hands"], and make kerchiefs for the head of persons of every stature to hunt souls! Will ye hunt the souls of My people, and save souls alive for yourselves? And ye have profaned Me among my people for handfuls of barley and for pieces of bread, to slay the souls that should not die, and to save the souls alive that should not live, by your lying to My people that hearken unto lies. Wherefore thus saith the Lord God: Behold I am against your pillows, wherewith ye there hunt the souls to make them fly, and I will tear them from your arms, and I will let the souls go, even the souls that ye hunt to make them fly. Your kerchiefs also will I tear, and deliver My people out of your hand, and they shall be no more in your hand to be hunted; and ye shall know that I am the Lord. Because with lies ye have grieved the heart of the righteous, whom I have not made sad; and strengthened the hands of the wicked, that he should not return from his wicked way, and be saved alive; therefore ye shall no more see vanity, nor divine divinations: and I will deliver My people out of your hand; and ye shall know that I am the Lord" (Ezek. xiii. 17–23).[10]

III. NESHAMAH, BREATH

However varied the conceptions of the soul were,[11] both the popular and the official beliefs agreed in this, that the *nephesh* continued to exist after the death of a man; and that is the point of prime importance. We shall refer again to the *nephesh* in speaking of other component parts of man, as these were conceived of according to ancient Hebrew belief.

We have already seen the close connexion there was between the *nephesh*, and the "breath" of man; there are a few things about the breath

(*neshamah*), according to Old Testament teaching, which need notice. In
Gen. ii. 7 it is said that God breathed into man's nostrils "the breath of
life, and man became a living soul"; with this we may compare the expression "the breath of the spirit of life" (Gen. vii. 22). The breath is thus the
principle of life which is the common possession of all living and is the
same in every living creature; the soul (*nephesh*) is individual in character
and is a different thing in each person. The breath is given by God, and
man lives thereby (cp. Job xxxiii. 4); when it is withdrawn man dies (cp.
Job xxxiv. 14, 15), but this does not affect his *nephesh*, The breath, or
neshamah, is thus something which God gives from His own Being to
man (and the same is true of the beasts) by means of which the *nephesh* is
(temporarily) joined to the body, made of dust. The pre-existence of the
nephesh would seem to be implied; but this is nowhere definitely stated in
the Old Testament.[12]

IV. RUACH, SPIRIT

We come next to the "spirit" (*ruach*).[13] Here again we must guard ourselves against applying to this word its modern connotation; in its root
signification it means "wind,"[14] and it is so used in describing wind in
the ordinary sense of the word, as well as when it refers to the "wind" in
man, i.e. his breath, and when it means a component part of man, his
second *ego*. It was regarded as a material substance, though intangible,
and invisible itself, but the result of its action could be seen, and it could
be heard. That is to say, all that was true of the wind proper was applied
to the spirit of man. There is probably no word in the Old Testament
which has gone through such development in the Old Testament itself
as this word *ruach*; but we are here concerned with it only in so far as
it refers to one of the component parts in man according to the ancient
Israelite conception. Man's spirit was conceived of as composed of the
same light aerial substance as the wind; like the *nephesh* it could enter
and leave the body at will; it is given by God, and returns to God when

a man dies (see e.g. Ps. civ. 29). It is not easy to see how *nephesh* was differentiated from *ruach* in the minds of ancient Israelites; probably they themselves were not clear upon the subject; certain it is that the two are synonymous in quite a number of passages (e.g. Isa. xxvi. 6); and both are used of any living creature, though it is most likely that there was an instinctive idea that in animals it was not quite the same kind of thing as in human beings. Speaking generally, we may perhaps say that, upon the whole, so far as there was any adumbration of a differentiation between matter and spirit, *nephesh* was thought of rather in the former direction, *ruach* in the latter; what lends colour to this supposition is the fact that nowhere is *ruach* thought of as being specially connected with any part of the body as *nephesh* was with the blood, with which it was, indeed, identified, as we have seen.

V. DAM, BLOOD

This leads us to say a further word about blood as one of the component parts of man. The Israelite belief in its identity with the life or *nephesh* was the same as that of the Arabs. Among these "*nafs* (= the Hebrew *nephesh*) is used of the life-blood. When a man dies a natural death his life departs through the nostrils (*mata hatfa anfihi*), but when he is slain in battle 'his life flows on the spear-point' (*Hamasa*, p. 52)....To the use of *nafs* in the sense of blood, the Arabian philologists refer such expressions as *nifas*, childbirth...."[15] The identity between blood and the life explains why it was necessary to cover over blood with earth (Lev. xvii. 10–12, 13, 14,[16] Gen. ix. 45, Jer. ii. 34), and why it was forbidden to be eaten (Lev. iii. 17, vii. 26 f., xvii. 10 ff., Deut. xii. 16, 23, 24, etc.). The word is frequently used in the plural in the Old Testament in order to express its abundance. Among many peoples blood was offered to the dead for the purpose of giving them more of "life."[17] We are only thinking here, however, of blood as a component part of man, and cannot, therefore, touch upon the big subject of its use in sacrifice.[18]

VI. AZAMOTH, BONES

The human bones as constituent parts of man occupied a peculiarly important place, difficult for the modern mind to understand. The expression "bone and flesh," often used to express kinship, where we should say "flesh and blood," shows that the bones were conceived of in a special way; in Gen. xxix. 14, e.g., Laban says to Jacob: "Surely thou art my bone and my flesh," cp. Judges ix. 2, 2 Sam. v. 1, xix. 12, 13, 1 Chron. xi. 1. In Gen. ii. 21–23, the account of Eve's creation, the, woman is made of one of Adam's bones, a rib, whereupon the man says: "This is now bone of my bones, and flesh of my flesh . . ." Here it is something more than kinship; indeed, we have passages in which it seems as though the bones were regarded as synonymous with man (cp. Job xx. 11), and that not merely in a physical sense, but as identified with his personality; in Ps. xxxv. 10, e.g., the psalmist says: "All my bones shall say, Lord, who is like unto Thee?" and in Job iv. 14 it is said: "Fear came upon me, and trembling, which made all my bones to shake," cp. Jer. xxiii. 9. Further, we find in a number of passages that importance is attached to the burying of bones; in Gen. I. 25 it is said that "Joseph took an oath of the children of Israel, saying, God will surely visit you, and ye shall carry my bones from hence," see the sequel in Exod. xiii. 19 and in Josh. xxiv. 32; cp. 1 Sam. xxxi. 13, 2 Sam. xxi. 13, 14, 1 Kings xiii. 31; that in all these passages "bones" is not used in a loose way for "body" is evident when one sees from certain other passages the importance which bones, as such, had in the eyes of men. Thus, the direst punishment that can be inflicted on a man is not only to leave his body unburied, but also his bones, long after the flesh has decayed; an example of this is seen in 2 Kings xxiii. 16: "And as Josiah turned himself, he spied the sepulchers that were there in the mount; and he sent, and took the bones out of the sepulchers, and turned them upon the altar, and defiled it...." But of the bones of the man of God he says: "Let no man move his bones. So they let his bones alone, with the bones of the prophet that came out of Samaria" (see I Kings xiii. 31). And again in Jer. viii. 1, 2: "...they shall bring out the bones of the kings of Judah, and the bones of his princes, and the bones of the priests, and the bones of the prophets, and the bones of the inhabitants of Jerusalem out of their graves: and they shall spread them before the sun, and the moon, and all the host of heaven, whom they have loved, and whom they have served, and after whom they have walked, and whom they have sought, and whom they have worshipped: they shall not be gathered, nor be buried...." It was not only the burning of bodies, but also of the bones, as distinct from the flesh, which was looked upon as a dreadful thing; hence the prophet says: "For three transgressions of Moab, yea, for four, I will not turn away the punishment thereof; because he burned the bones of the king of Edom into lime," Amos ii. I. The reason why this importance was attached to the bones, as distinct from the flesh, is nowhere directly stated in the Old Testament; but it is hinted at in such a passage as Ezek. xxxvii. (the vision of the dry bones), and in Isa. lxvi. 14, where, in speaking of the comfort and happiness of the Messianic Kingdom, the prophet says: "And ye shall see it, and your heart shall rejoice, and your bones shall flourish like the tender grass...." (cp. lviii. 11, but the text is doubtful). Thus, there was the belief that life resided in the bones long after death, indeed permanently; and it is a striking thing that this belief is directly expressed by such a one as Ben-Sira, who says: "And also the twelve prophets, may their bones sprout beneath them"(*Wisdom of Ben-Sira* [*Ecclesiasticus*], xlix. 10; so, too, in xlvi. 11, 12: "Also the judges...may their bones flourish again out of their place, and may their name sprout afresh for their children." In the *Testament of Job*[19] there is a curious reference to the bones of Job's children; in chap. ix. Job's wife begs the king to allow the bones of her dead children to be dug out from among the ruins of the house, and to be placed in a tomb; but Job says it is useless. It then continues: "And the king answered and said, 'Who will gainsay that he is out of his mind, and raves? For while we desire to bring the bones of his children back he forbids us to do so, saying, they have been taken and placed in the keeping of their Maker." The context of this passage shows that an advanced doctrine of the resurrection was held, but the reference to the bones clearly echoes an ancient conception.[20]

Two other words describing constituent parts of man are *leb* and *lebab* ("heart"), and *me'im*. ("inward parts," lit. "intestines"); both are used in figurative as well as literal meanings. The former is often used as being the seat of the understanding, the latter as the seat of the emotions. Neither of these has any direct bearing upon our present subject, so that we need not enter into any details here concerning them.

Belief in Supernatural Beings

III

THE DEMONOLOGY
OF THE SEMITES

I. Semitic Demonology in General

Some consideration of this subject, so far as it concerns the Israelites
and kindred nations of the Semitic race, is demanded here, for it cannot
be separated from the subject of Ancestor-worship and the cult of the
Departed, which we shall consider later. Moreover, anything that has to
do with superhuman, and therefore immortal, beings requires to be taken
into consideration in our study of Immortality in the Old Testament.
And then there is a further important fact which is of itself sufficient to
demand some attention to what may not at first appear directly concerned
with the subject in hand—the fact, namely, that with the development of
the belief concerning Immortality there arises the question of the fate of
men hereafter as conditioned by their life on earth; and with this arises
the belief in the Kingdom of Satan, the head of the demons. This has
its ultimate roots in primitive Israelite Demonology. However much it
may owe to extraneous influences, there was an indigenous Demonology
in Israel, very distinct indications of which are to be found in the Old
Testament. The belief in harmful spirits (not that they are *all* or always

harmful) is characteristic of a certain stage in the evolution of the religious beliefs of, as far as is known, every race of men. It is so ineradicable an element in popular superstition that even among the most civilized nations of the present day there are numerous practices which are remnants of the universal belief in the activity of demons which existed even within quite recent times. If this is so in modern times, how much more is it likely that that belief flourished three or four millennia go among less civilized nations! So that although the references to Demonology in the Old Testament are, comparatively speaking, not numerous (nevertheless, in reality, they are more numerous than many people realize), this must be due not to the fact that it did not exist, but to some other cause.

Again, among those nations which are, racially, closely connected with the Israelites we find a very extended belief in demons. The Canaanites at the time of the Israelite invasion were in the stage of Polydaemonism; they also practiced Ancestor-worship, venerating the ancient tribal heroes at their traditional tombs, as well as under holy trees and beside holy wells.[21] Like other Semites they recognized the activity of a spirit, sometimes kindly disposed, at other times harmful, in the storm, in the desert, in the tree, well, and stone, in the heat of summer and cold of winter, in the clouds and stars, as well as in animals. They did not make the distinction between gods and demons, whether in nature or animal, that was made in later times.[22] In the same way, the Phoenicians, although owing to special causes they had attained a higher culture than the other Canaanite nations, practiced a religion which had a like origin, a religion which, like that of the Canaanites, was developed from conceptions of a primitive character, and whose content was most probably very similar to that which the early Arabs practiced.[23] The belief of the Arabs concerning spirits and demons is particularly significant, for the great Arabian peninsula was the primeval home of the Semitic race;[24] and Arab belief and practice, even as found at the present day, go back to very ancient times; Muhammadanism scarcely affected the popular superstitions concerning the *Jinn* at all. Lastly, the demonology of the Babylonians and Assyrians was of a very elaborate character, and, owing to the far reaching influence which Babylonian thought and practice had upon the ancient Israelites as well as upon the Jews of the exilic and postexilic periods, Babylonian demonology is of great importance in connexion with our present investigation. So that the fact that an elaborate demonology existed among the Canaanites, the Arabs, and the Babylonians, all closely connected with the Israelites racially, and living either in their midst or in the lands around them, and having constant intercourse with them, raises the natural presumption that these latter had their beliefs regarding spirits and demons, and that we should therefore expect to find traces of them in the Old Testament.

Then again, in the Judaism of post-biblical times we find a system of demonology which is simply colossal. One would reasonably suppose that this had its roots in the beliefs of earlier times within the nation itself; but it is objected that the demonology of later Judaism is really the product of neo-Babylonian, Persian, and Greek influence. Nobody would for a moment doubt that these influences have been very strong, and that Jewish Demonology owes much to them; but the question is whether *all*— Babylonian, Greek, and Persian—do not trace their beliefs on this subject back to a common very early source, of which the ancestors of all these nations possessed a common stock, varying of course greatly in details, but identical in fundamentals? It seems difficult to doubt this in view of what we know of the beliefs and practices of ancient Phoenicia and of the Canaanites generally, and especially in view of what we know of Arab Demonology. While there is great similarity both in belief and practice in many respects among these peoples, there is yet sufficient difference in the systems of the Babylonians, Arabs, and Jews to admit of a certain amount of matter proper to each, sufficient individuality in each of the systems to warrant the belief that each has an independence of its own. And if this is so, if the demonology of later Judaism can in any way lay claim to a character of its own, then there is, at any rate, some justification for believing that it is based in part upon earlier belief.

II. Some Details of Semitic Demonology

We shall now indicate some beliefs and practices in reference to demons which are common to Arab, Babylonian, and Jewish Demonology; other points in these systems will come before us later on in this chapter. All three systems teach that immense numbers of demons and other spirits exist in the world. The Arabic term *Jinn* is a collective word implying, therefore, multiplicity.[25] Among the Babylonians the large number of proper names for demons is enough to show how numerous they were; but in one text it is said that the demons cover the whole world; in another that "they cover the earth like grass."[26] The Rabbis taught that the demons gather themselves together in companies (*Berakhoth* 51*a*), and according to *Tanchuma, Mishpatim* 19, the whole world is full of "harmful spirits" (*Mazzikin*); the number is given by one Rabbi as seven and a half millions, and elsewhere it is stated that every man has ten thousand of them at his right hand, and a thousand at his left.[27]

According to Arab teaching the *Jinn* (= the "dark" or "concealed" ones) were the ghostly shadows of nations that have perished; certain ruined sites, such as Higr and Nicibin, were pointed out as being inhabited by the spirits of those who in days gone by had lived there. All burial places, excepting of course the tombs of saints, were believed to be full of demons.[28] The connexion between demons and the spirits of the departed is likewise a strongly marked characteristic in Babylonian belief; here it was taught, for example, that the demons were the messengers of Ereshkigal, queen of the realm of the dead. Namtaru, one of the worst demons, issued, it was said, from the netherworld, the abode of the departed. Utukku, "who harms those who abide in the wilderness," is also a spirit of the dead; and closely connected with him is Ekimmu, "the departed soul," as he is called, who for some reason or other can find no rest, and wanders over the earth injuring men whensoever opportunity offers; his anger is especially directed against those with whom he has had any relations while on earth, and it is supposed to be partly their fault (see below) that he is unable to re-enter the realm of the dead and find rest.[29] If for any reason the spirits of the departed are unable to enter the realm of the dead, they have to wander about the earth until the hindrance is taken away; while thus banished from their rightful abode they make it their business to harm all those with whom they had had any intercourse while on earth, especially relatives; for, according to Babylonian belief, it was owing to the neglect of those who were left behind that the departed spirits are unable to get to rest. Ekimmu would thus appear to be a kind of general representative or embodiment of a class. Among the causes which hindered departed spirits from entering into rest were neglect of the prescribed burial rites, more especially when a body remained unburied, or lay in foreign soil; neglect to bring the proper offerings for the dead would also, doubtless, have been considered another cause of the restlessness of departed spirits.

That Jewish belief regarding the connexion between the departed and demons ran on the same lines may be presumed from the fact that cemeteries were looked upon as one of the favorite spots in which demons congregated; in the *Sibylline Oracles*, Proem. 20–22, it is stated that the people will be punished because they have ceased to worship the one true God, and because "they offer sacrifice to demons in the underworld," who are the spirits of the departed. Again, all sickness was regarded as being due to demons; thus the Arabs believed that fainting fits, epilepsy, gout, fever, and epidemics of every sort were the result of the harmful activity of demons; madness is described as being the effect of a demon taking up his abode in a man and "possessing" him.[30] The same is found in the Babylonian and Jewish systems; thus, among the Babylonians there was a demon who was the cause of headache; Labartu and Namtaru were pest-demons, and there were many storm-demons by whom men were harmed. Ashakku was the demon of burning fever, and Dimetum was "the evil curse."[31] Among the Jews Shabiri was the demon who brought blindness, while there was another demon of leprosy, another of heart disease, another of fever; and there was also a storm-demon.[32]

All three systems agree that at night the power of demons is greatest; for this reason the Arabs were in the habit of covering up the children's faces when they went to bed; every vessel was covered over, lights were lit, and the doors were locked. It was only at the rising of the morning star that the demons dispersed. Among the Babylonians it was the demon Alu who wandered about at nights; he is to be found especially in ruins, where he hides, waiting to fall upon any luckless passerby; he also creeps into bedrooms and robs the weary of their sleep; he is described as running about at nights "like a dog." In the same way the demon Gallu sweeps through the streets after dark, making every place insecure.[33] So, too, in the Jewish system it is taught that demons are most harmful from dusk until cock crowing; at nights they surround houses and injure everyone who falls into their hands; they kill children if found out after dark. As soon as the cock crows their power is at an end (Midr. *Bereshith Rabba*, c. 36).[34]

Again, according to all three systems, it was believed that demons had a special predilection for certain places. As we have already seen, the Arabs held that desert places, burial grounds, thickets where beasts gather, and ruined sites where men used to live were the special kinds of places where demons loved to congregate; they believed that the weird moaning of the wind in the wilderness and bleak, bare spots was the voice of demons, which "caused the locality to speak"[35] (cp. "the howling wilderness," Deut. xxxii. 10). With this Babylonian teaching agrees; Namtaru, it is said, "rushes over the wilderness like a storm-wind"; Utukku and Ekimmu with their followers hover about in desert places and in mountainous regions, they are also to be found near tombs and in cemeteries.[36] This is entirely in accordance with Jewish belief on the subject; they gather in shaded spots on moonlight nights, in waterless spots, near ruins, and in cemeteries, and harm people who come within their reach; they are especially to be found in the wilderness and other desert places; they are particularly hurtful at nights; it is supposed to be unsafe to salute a person in the dark, for it might be a demon.[37]

Further, the Arabs taught that demons have the power of becoming visible or invisible at will; they have also the power of assuming various forms, especially those of snakes, lizards, scorpions, and other creeping things (see further below).[38] Among the Babylonians it is said that

"Ashakku places himself by the side of a man, and nobody sees him"[39]; all demons could render themselves invisible; when they appeared in visible form it was usually in the shape of some animal[40] (see below). This power of becoming invisible and of assuming various shapes, whether animal or human, is likewise true of Jewish Demonology. Satan, the head of the demons, is said to appear in the form of a beautiful woman, or of a beggar[41]; Sheija appears in the shape of a bull.[42] One is never safe from demons, on account of their sudden appearing; apparently the presence of a demon is entirely unsuspected while all the time some animal close by is a demon in disguise.[43] This relationship believed to exist between the demons and animals is a feature common to all three systems. According to Arab belief some animals scent out the approach of demons when as yet men are unaware of their presence; thus, when a donkey brays or a cock crows it is a warning of the approach of a demon (presumably the cock crowing in the early morning, on the other hand, was a note of warning to the demon!). Demons appear in the form of wild beasts in the wilderness[44]; even domestic animals are sometimes in league with them. Between some birds and demons there exists quite a friendship; e.g. such birds as crows, woodpeckers, owls, and others. Owls, moreover, were regarded as incarnations of departed spirits; ostriches[45] were believed to be used by demons for riding upon; this is also true of foxes. But the closest connexion of all is that between demons and serpents. *Jann* and *Ghul* are synonyms for "serpent"; this applies also to *Shaitan* (= Satan).[46] It is no exaggeration when Wellhausen says that "the zoology of Islam is at once a demonology." Then, as regards Babylonian belief on this point, it was held that Utukku, Ekimmu, and Alu appeared in the form of bulls; the same applies to Shedu, one of the foremost demons. Indeed, all demons were conceived of as normally dwelling in animals; it was the way in which the Babylonians explained the problem as to where the permanent abode of the demons was, seeing that, according to them, the demons were excluded from the realms of the dead. Among such animals those were chosen which were the most likely to inspire sudden fear, more especially serpents (op, Ps. xci. 13), which appeared suddenly, one knew not whence, and disappeared as suddenly, one knew not whither; or again, scorpions, which were very injurious and hid in spots where they could not be noticed until too late. Many demons were also supposed to appear in the form of birds, or they were conceived of as hybrid monsters, birds with the heads of lions or donkeys, and the like.[47] In the Jewish system it was taught that bulls,[48] mosquitoes, donkeys, and above all, serpents, were in league with the demons. Satan is, of course, identical with the serpent in the Garden of Eden[49]; indeed, it is said that the demons (*Shedim*) were originally serpents, and became what they are by a process of evolution.[50]

Lastly, a very significant trait common to all these systems was the belief in different *species* or classes of demons. The Arabs regarded them as being divided into clans and tribes much in the same way as they themselves were.[51] "Though the *Jinn* have no individuality, they fall into various classes, and certain of these are sometimes mentioned as particularly harmful. The most dangerous kind of all is the *Ghul* (a feminine noun), of which the plural is *Ghiliin* or *Aghwal*; this word comes from the root signifying 'to destroy,' perhaps originally 'to assault.' The *Ghul* is supposed to lie in wait at some place where men are destined to perish; she also entices them thither, especially by night. 'The *Ghul* has carried him off' is sometimes merely a poetical expression meaning 'he has perished.'… The poets also mention a kind of female demon called Si'lak, of which the plural is Sa'ali; this term scarcely ever occurs except as a simile for the purpose of describing swift horses or camels, formidable warriors, or frightful women."[52] Examples of the same kind of thing among the Babylonians are the followers of Utukku, who form a different category from the followers of Ekimmu. So, too, in the Jewish system various species of demons are recognized, viz. the *Shedim*[53] (from a root meaning "to be violent"), the *Lilin* (from *Lilith*, "the night-hag," whose followers they were; see further on this below); and the *Ruchin* (from the root *ruach*, "wind"); all, however, come under the general term *Mazzikin*, which includes all the "harmful" spirits.[54]

These details form a very brief *resume* of elements common to Arab, Babylonian, and Jewish Demonology; other points will be mentioned when we deal with the demons and spirits referred to in the Old Testament. They offer, it is believed, some grounds in support of the contention that in spite of superficial appearances there must have been a widespread belief in these spirits among the Israelites, to which the Old Testament bears witness. Such a belief, and all that it involves, is an element in the Old Testament teaching on Immortality, hence the need of devoting some attention to a subject which would otherwise come more appropriately under the head of Folk-lore.

IV

THE DEMONOLOGY OF THE OLD TESTAMENT

From what has been said in the previous chapter it is evident that an extended belief in demons was common to all the Semites. To this the Israelites formed no exception. It is true that in their case there was not the elaborate classification such as we find among the Babylonians and Assyrians, and, to a rather less degree, among the ancient Arabians; but that does not necessarily imply that belief in the activity of demons was any the less real among the Israelites. The fact is that the Old Testament is not the kind of literature in which we should expect to find much information on the subject of Demonology; the Israelites had nothing parallel to the great body of literature represented by the Babylonian magical texts. For one thing the far more ancient and more advanced civilization of the Babylonians would naturally presuppose a much larger body of scribes who could commit these things to "writing." Nevertheless, the signs in the Old Testament of an Israelite Demonology, elaborate if not yet reduced to a system, are, we believe, more numerous than is generally supposed. This we must now proceed to show.

I. Theriomorphic Demons

Although this class of demons only remotely concerns us, a brief reference to them is required on account of their connexion with the general subject of demons.

(*a*) *The Seraphim.*—Our ideas about the Seraphim are so colored by the description and function of them given in Isa. vi. 1 ff., and their mention in the "*Te Deum*," in conjunction with the Cherubim (who belong, however, to the angelic order), that it is likely to come as a shock to some to find them reckoned among theriomorphic demons. But in early Semitic belief, as will be seen, it is evident that the Seraphim were originally regarded as a species of harmful beings of demonic nature. The name comes from a root *saraph*, meaning "to burn"; and the name "burning ones" (Seraphim) was in all probability given on account of their burning bite[55]; this is suggested by such passages as the following: Num. xxi. 6, "And the Lord sent fiery serpents (lit. seraphim serpents) among the people, and they bit the people; and much people of Israel died." In verse 8 it is said: "And the Lord said unto Moses, Make thee a seraph, and put it on a pole; and it shall come to pass, that everyone that is bitten, when he seeth it, shall live." Deut. viii. 15, "…who led thee through the great and terrible wilderness wherein were seraph serpents and scorpions…." Cp. also Isa. xiv. 29: "…for out of the serpent's root shall come forth a viper, and his fruit shall be a fiery flying serpent (lit. a flying seraph)"; similarly in Isa. xxx. 6. We have already seen, in the preceding chapter, the close connexion between serpents and demons, according to general Semitic belief; and it is impossible to separate early Israelite belief on the subject from that of kindred nations. A striking parallel to the Hebrew flying seraph serpent is mentioned by Wellhausen[56]; among the ancient Arabs there was the belief that demons (*Jinn*) flew out of the burning grove of al Quraija in the form of white serpents. Herodotus (ii. 75) says: "There is a place in Arabia, situated very near the city of Buto, to which I went, on hearing of some winged serpents; and when I arrived there, I saw bones and spines of serpents in such quantities as it would be impossible to describe....It is reported that, at the beginning of spring, winged serpents fly from Arabia towards Egypt, but that ibises, a sort of bird, meet them at the pass, and do not allow the serpents to go by, but kill them; for this service the Arabians say that the ibis is highly reverenced by the Egyptians; and the Egyptians acknowledge that they reverence these birds for this reason." Herodotus does not say whether these flying serpents were regarded as demons, but, knowing what we do about Arab belief in the connexion between demons and serpents, it can scarcely be doubted that they were so regarded. Parallels of this kind, which could be multiplied, strengthen the impression, already suggested by various passages in the Old Testament, that originally the name Seraphim was applied to serpents who were looked upon as demons.

(b) *The Se'irim.*—In writing about the beliefs of the heathen Arabs concerning the *Jinn*, or demons, Robertson Smith says that these demons "are not pure spirits, but corporeal beings, more like beasts than men, for they are ordinarily represented as hairy, or have some other animal shape, as that of an ostrich or a snake....Like the wild beasts, they have, for the most part, no friendly or stated relations with men, but are outside the pale of man's society, and frequent savage and deserted places far from the wonted tread of men. It appears from several poetical passages of the Old Testament that the northern Semites believed in demons of a precisely similar kind."[57] Among these he mentions the "hairy beings," called *Se'irim*, who haunted waste and desolate places. That the mention of these in the Old Testament is found in comparatively late passages does not affects, since they only echo beliefs of much earlier times. In Isa. xiii. 21, 22, for example, where the desolation of Babylon is described, it is said that "wild beasts of the desert shall be there; and their houses shall be full of doleful creatures; and ostriches shall dwell there, and satyrs (lit. *se'irim*) shall dance there...." The translation of this word as "satyrs" is misleading if by it we are intended to think of the Greek satyrs who were spirits of the woodland in the train of Dionysus, and who were represented as being in semi-human form and as having bristling hair and goat like ears, and with short tails; this is not the Semitic idea of the *sa'ir*, which was a hairy creature in the form of a calf, and was worshipped among the Assyrians and Phoenicians[58] as well as by the ancient Israelites[59]; in Exod. xxxii. 4 ff. we have the well-known worship of the golden calf, see also Lev. xvii. 7, Deut. ix. 21, and 2 Chron. xi. 14–16, and recent excavations have illustrated this form of worship in a very interesting way, for on the site of ancient Gezer many remains of cow- or calf-statuettes were discovered which point indubitably to the worship of a god or goddess of flocks and herds. In later days, when the worship of Jahwe had asserted itself, these gods and goddesses were degraded to demons, and as such were fully believed in. Under this heading we naturally think of what in the Authorized Version is called the "scapegoat" (Lev. xvi. 8–10), i.e. *Azazel*. It will be remembered that after the two he-goats had been taken from the congregation of Israel for a sin-offering, Aaron "set them before the Lord at the door of the tent of meeting"; then it goes on to say that" Aaron shall cast lots upon the two goats; one lot for the Lord, and the other lot for Azazel." From these words it is quite obvious that Azazel was regarded quite as much as a personal being as the Lord; so that to make Azazel equivalent to the scapegoat is an offence against the plain reading of the text. It is said further that the goat upon which the lot for Azazel fell was to be sent away for Azazel into the wilderness; from this it is clear that Azazel dwelt in the wilderness like the *Se'irim*. It is thus highly probable that the Azazel ritual was a development of what was originally an offering to the denizens of the waste. Azazel was originally (the name itself is late, see below) a Semitic god of the flocks, like Ashtoreth-Karnaim (see Gen. xiv. 5 and compare Dent. vii. 13, "He will bless the Ashteroth of thy flock"). With the growth of Jahwe-worship a compromise was effected, since the religious leaders found it impossible to eradicate the ancient ritual; and ultimately this god of the flocks was degraded to a demon of the wilderness just as many other demons who were believed to inhabit waste places. In the Book of Enoch Azazel appears as a leader of evil angels (vi. 7, cp. ix. 6, "Thou seest what Azazel hath done, who hath taught all unrighteousness on earth . . .," see also x. 4–6). As to the meaning of the name, regarding which there are all kinds of theories, it must be said that Cheyne's view is at once the simplest and the most probable; it is a corruption, purposely made by the Jewish religious leaders of the name עֻוֵּאל, "God strengthens"; the name as it now appears in the Hebrew text is עֲזָאזֵל, which is supposed to be derived from the root עזל, and would thus mean "complete removal," i.e. of sins; but an abstract term of this kind does not commend itself. Cheyne's view, which was also that held long ago by Diestel, has also this in its favour, that the epithet "strong" applied to a god conforms to the general usage in regard to Semitic deities, whose chief characteristic is almost invariably that of strength, implying power to help.[60]

(c) In a passage quoted above (Isa. xiii. 21, 22) mention is made of various other strange creatures, in addition to *Se'irim*, which, we believe, may justly be included in the category of theriomorphic demons. It will be remembered that this passage is preceded by a prophecy of the permanent desolation of Babylon: "It shall never be inhabited, neither shall it be dwelt in from generation to generation; neither shall the Arabian pitch tent there, neither shepherds make their flocks to lie down there." It is important to recall here the points referred to in an earlier chapter, namely, that demons were believed to exist in great numbers, that they had a special predilection for desert places, and above all for ruined sites where men used to dwell; and that many wild beasts, especially those that inhabited the waste and wilderness, were identified with demons. The site just described in the passage from Isaiah is just such a one as popular imagination would regard as the haunt of demons. Therefore a brief examination of the creatures spoken of will not be inappropriate. First, there are the "wild beasts" or *Ziyyim*; the word comes from a root meaning "to be dry," and the noun therefore presumably would mean something connected with a dry place, an inhibitor of the desert. Reference to the various passages in which the word occurs shows that these "wild beasts" cannot be identified with any known animals, that they are always spoken of as dwelling in desert places and ruined sites, and, with one exception,[61] that they are always mentioned in connexion with other strange beasts, to be referred to below.

Next occurs the expression "doleful creatures," *Ochim*. This word, which is parallel to *Ziyyim* and is likewise used only in the plural, comes from the root meaning "to howl."[62] According to Delitzsch[63] *ahu* is the Assyrian for "jackal," but this is disputed by other scholars; no help is gained from the Versions; its indefiniteness and uncertainty are perhaps significant. The next creature, translated "ostrich" in the Revised Version, means literally "daughters of greed" (*benoth ya'anah*), and is, with two exceptions, used only in the plural. It is reckoned among the unclean animals in Lev. xi. 16, Deut. xiv. 15; no doubt it came to be used of the ostrich, but it is striking that in the passage before us the Septuagint renders it σειρῆνες[64] and makes it parallel to δαιμόνια. According to Arab belief demons have the hunger of a lion, an idea which may conceivably be connected with these "daughters of greed"! Whether the word in Hebrew originally meant something other than ostrich it is impossible to say; but in any case, ostriches were looked upon as being connected with demons. The Arabs said that demons used them for riding on (see above); they believed also that demons appeared in the form of ostriches.

The "satyrs" (*Se'irim*), which occurs next, we have already dealt with. There remain the "wolves" (*Iyyim*) and "jackals" (*Tannim*). It is very difficult to say what the first of these means; the root from which the word comes means "to howl" or "screech" (a word for "hawk" comes from the same root); in view of the fact that many birds were regarded as the incarnations of demons it may be that a bird of prey of some kind is intended. The Septuagint renders ὀνοκένταυροι, which shows to what straits the translators were driven, though the word is interesting as illustrating the belief that hybrid monsters were among the forms in which demons appeared. The parallel word in our passages, "jackals," would indeed favour the rendering "wolves"; but it cannot be said that we have any certainty regarding the meaning of *Tannim*, "jackals"; the Septuagint gives six different renderings of the word in the fourteen instances in which it occurs in the Hebrew Bible, and in one case omits it altogether. In studying this passage[65] the conviction is forced upon one that it refers from beginning to end to what were believed to be demons, or, more strictly speaking, animals which were looked upon as the incarnations of demons; the demon part was supernatural and not subject to death like human beings. In the case of the *Se'irim* the demonic character admits of no doubt; so that where we have these other creatures enumerated together with the *Se'irim*, it is obvious that they too were reckoned among the demons.

II. Demons of Human Form

We have next to consider some demons of human, or quasi-human, form. The references to these in the Old Testament are not many; but when considered in the light of certain Babylonian parallels it will be seen that the mention of them is not without significance.

(*a*) *Lilith*.—In Isa. xxxiv. 11–15, a passage of somewhat similar import to Isa. xiii. 21–22, but in reference to Edom, there occur these words in verse 14: "And the wild beasts of the desert (*Ziyyim*) shall encounter the wolves (*Iyyim*), and the *sa'ir* (singular of *Se'irim*) shall meet with his fellow; there, in truth, shall Lilith repose, and shall find a resting place for herself." The Revised Version translates Lilith by "night-monster," but it is a proper name. The fact that Lilith, represented at one time as a female demon, at another a male one, was well known among the Assyrians supports the belief that Lilith played a part in Hebrew Demonology in pre-exilic times; the Assyrian beliefs regarding this demon were greatly developed by the Babylonians, as we shall see in a moment. According to later Jewish teaching, which may well, however, have been handed down for many centuries previously, Lilith was a night-hag, and got her name from *Lay-elah*. ("night"); the etymology was false, but Lilith was, nevertheless, the night-demon *par excellence*. The connexion was suggested by the similarity of the two words, as well as by the fact that Lilith was believed to be active at nights. There is an evident reference to this demon, though her name is not mentioned, in Ps. xci. 5: "Thou shalt not be afraid because of the night-terror, nor because of the arrow that flieth by day." In the Midrash to the Psalms (Midrash *Tehillim*) on this verse occurs the comment: "Rabbi Berechya said, 'There is a harmful spirit that flies like a bird and shoots like an arrow"[66]; while it is a mistake to suppose that only one demon is referred to in this verse, the Rabbi is doubtless right in picturing Lilith as one who flies, for the Jewish conception regarding this demon is likely to have corresponded with the Babylonian which also pictured Lilith as flying at nights. In Babylonian Demonology a demon-triad was formed by Lilu, Lilitu, and Ardat Lili; the male, the female, and the hand-maid; the Old Testament Lilith would correspond to the second of these, Lilitu. The three are spoken of particularly as storm-demons[67] who rush about at night seeking what harm they can do to men. They are spoken of as flying, and were therefore, though not necessarily, conceived of as having wings. Ardat Lili is once spoken of as "flitting in through a window" after a man.[68] In later Jewish belief, which is, however, largely traditional, Lilith appears as the head of one of the three great classes into which the demons are divided, viz. the *Lilin*; who take their name from her. They are described as of human form, and have wings; they are all females; children are their chief victims. Lilith was conceived of as a beautiful woman, with long, flowing hair; it is at nights that she seeks her prey; she is dangerous to men, but does not appear to molest women.

(*b*) *Keteb*.—It is in Ps. xci. 6 that this proper name of a demon occurs, and to understand its significance it must be read in the light of its context. In verse 5, as we have just seen, it is highly probable that the demon Lilith is referred to, although not named; the text of verse 6 is partly corrupt and must be emended on the basis of the Septuagint; it must then be translated thus:

"Nor because of the pestilence that goeth about during the dark,
Nor because of Keteb or the midday demon (δαιμονίου μεσημβρινοῦ)."

The Hebrew for "pestilence" is *Deber*, and if this is not a proper name, the word implies at any rate the existence of a pest-demon. We are reminded of the well-known Babylonian pest-demon Namtar; he is often spoken of as "violent Namtar," and he comes among men as the pest-bringing envoy from the realms of the dead, like a "raging wind"; his action is described in a Babylonian text thus: "Wicked Namtar, who scorches the land like fire, who approaches a man like Ashakku,[69] who rages through the wilderness like a storm-wind, who pounces upon a man like a robber, who plagues a man like the pestilence, who has no hands, no feet, who goes about at night...."[70] The words remind one forcibly of "the pestilence that goeth about in the dark." That pestilence, and sickness of every kind, were believed to be due to the action of demons is too well known to need illustration. It is in this context that the name *Keteb* occurs. The word is usually translated "destruction"; it is only mentioned three times elsewhere, viz. in Deut. xxxii. 24, Isa. xxviii. 2, Hos. xiii. 4, and in the first two of these the underlying thought of demons is fairly obvious. In Rabbinical literature *Keteb* is used as the proper name of a demon; whether he was the "midday demon" himself, or whether two demons are referred to in the text, one cannot say for certain. That a special midday demon, whatever his name, was believed in is highly probable; the burning rays had to be accounted for somehow. In later Judaism it was believed that midday was one of the times during which demons were specially busy,[71] and in some Babylonian texts there are some suggestive passages.[72] The Midrash to the Psalms (Midrash *Tehillim*) on this verse has the following in reference to *Keteb*: "Our Rabbis said, 'It is a demon (*Shed*).'... Rabbi Huna, speaking in the name of Rabbi Jose, said, 'The poisonous *Keteb* was covered with scales and with hair, and sees only out of one eye, the other one is in the middle of his heart; and he is powerful, not in the darkness nor in the sun, but between darkness and sun(shine). He rolls himself up like a ball and stalks about from the fourth to the ninth hour, from the 17th of Tammuz (July) to the ninth of Ab (August); and everyone who sees him falls down on his face.'"

(c) *'Alukah*.—In Prov. xxx. 15 the Revised Version has:

"The horseleach (mg. vampire) hath two daughters, crying (mg. called) Give, give."

The Hebrew for "horseleach" is a proper name, '*Alukah*; very little is known of this creature excepting that she was a female demon of the Lilith type. From the context in Proverbs it is clear that she was insatiable in her desires. Among the ancient Arabs there was a corresponding female demon called '*Alukah*.[73] The Septuagint and Vulgate renderings imply that she was a blood-sucker.

(*d*) *Satan*.—This name is derived from a root meaning "to oppose." In such an early passage as Num. xxii. 22 ff. the noun is used without any idea of a proper name; we read there: "…and the angel of the Lord placed himself in the way for an adversary (lit. "a satan") against him"; the same word is used as "a foe" in the ordinary sense in 1 Sam. xxix. 4, 2 Sam. xix. 22 (23), 1 Kings, v, 4, xi. 14, 23, 25, Ps. cix. 6,[74] though in this last passage the sense is rather that of "accuser," on account of the words which follow, "when he is judged let him come forth guilty." In Zech. iii. 1, 2, we find that a development has taken place, for here the word is used with the definite article and means the Adversary, *par excellence*, who accuses men before God; this passage is especially instructive because in it the word is used in a two-fold sense: "The Adversary (the satan) standing at his right hand as his adversary (satan)." It is in a similar sense that the word is used in the book of Job (i. 6 ff., ii. 1 ff.); a still further development is probably to be seen in 1 Chron. xxi. 1 (= 2 Sam. xxiv. l), where the word is used without the article, and the context shows that it is not an ordinary foe that is meant; so that here Satan is used as a proper name; he is, moreover, not only an accuser, but one who tempts to evil.

With the further development of Satan as the arch-fiend and head of the powers of darkness we are not concerned here, as this is outside the scope of the Old Testament.

V

THE ANGELOLOGY OF THE
OLD TESTAMENT

I. Semitic Angelology in General

It is a striking fact that among the early Semites generally, so far .as the available evidence shows, the belief in angels is quite overshadowed by the belief in demons. This, however, is not a matter for surprise. For one thing, among the mass of mankind the ills and worries of life outweigh in number the things which are regarded as blessings—and this is especially true of the ancient world; moreover, it lies in human nature to take the good and pleasant things of life as a matter of course, and to exaggerate its ills; so that, in that undeveloped state of culture in which most untoward occurrences are ascribed to the agency of Some malevolent spirit, it was natural that the activity of demons should have been regarded as much greater than that of more kindly disposed spirits. There were plenty of means at hand whereby to counteract the activity of demons—magic and witchcraft—which accounts for the small number of references to the calling upon benevolent spirits for protection. Over and above this there is the fundamental and well-known fact to be reckoned with that in the earliest stages of Semitic religion there is no distinction between angels and demons; this was a later development; there are, it is true, kindly spirits and maleficent spirits, but they all come under one general category. "It is habitually found," says Tylor, "that the theory of Animism divides into two great dogmas, forming parts of one consistent doctrine; first, concerning souls of individual creatures; capable of continued existence after the death or destruction of the body; second, concerning other spirits, upward to the rank of powerful deities."[75] It is within this latter category that all those spirits are included which in course of time developed into the classes of angels and demons; though we also find that among the former (spirits of the departed) there are some who are evil disposed, whether, as was believed, for the want of proper burial, or on account of the omission of burial rites, or what not. We also find, so far as the Arabs are concerned, if (as is probable) we may be guided by present-day custom and belief,[76] that the *weli*, or saint, who is always the real or imagined spirit of a man who once lived on earth, takes the part which very much corresponds to that of angelic protection. This, however, in any case, belongs to a time, comparatively ancient no doubt, in which a development had taken place. The earliest stage of which we have cognisance is one in which there is no distinction between what we now call angels and demons. But it is the more developed stage with which we are here concerned, because the beliefs and practices of this stage are those which throw light upon the Old Testament records, the stage, namely, in which it is seen that a distinction is being made between evil and good spirits.

Now, as far as the Arabs are concerned we have but little direct evidence; but we have a large amount of indirect evidence; and this indirect evidence comes from three sources: ancient Arabic writings wherein are preserved far more ancient traditions; the Koran; present-day custom and belief. In all three sources there is an immense mixture of later and developed doctrine and belief, and it is by no means easy always to sift the later from the earlier; but there is no sort of doubt that, embodied in these sources, a great deal is to be found which illustrates the Old Testament teaching and practice on the subject.

"Besides the gods to whom they devoted a regular cult, the ancient

Arabs recognized a series of inferior spirits, whom they conciliated or conjured by magical practices. In this matter, as in others, Muhammad preserved the ancient beliefs by adapting them to the new religion, in such a way that it is impossible to distinguish which elements in his teaching are sprung from his inward conviction and which are simply a concession to the doctrine of his compatriots."[77] This is perhaps going a little too far, for in some respects it is quite possible to distinguish these elements. Among the Muhammadans there are three classes of supernatural beings: angels, demons, and the *Jinn*, these last form a lower class of demons. Of these the angels are the most important body, a clear mark of development; but what reflects a really ancient trait is the fact that all three classes of supernatural beings partake of the same nature in so far as they are formed from one single substance. This points back to the time when there was no distinction between angels and demons. The function of the angels is two-fold: glorifying God in heaven, and guarding men on earth from the demons and the *Jinn*. The Arabs of the present day offer sacrifices to angels, just as, millennia ago, they sacrificed to demons; this, therefore, is also the development of an ancient and long-preserved custom. According to Doughty, quoted by Curtiss,[78] the Arabs, in sacrificing to angels, cooked part of the flesh of the sacrifices, which was distributed among their friends, while the other part of the flesh "they hung upon the branches of sacred trees, which are the places where angels are thought to reveal themselves."[79] The Arabs, like the rest of the Semites, passed through various stages of belief regarding demons, angels, and gods; first, the stage of Animism, with its hosts of benevolent and, more numerous, maleficent spirits, yet all of one category. Then came a stage wherein some of these spirits developed into gods; side by side with these gods there were the innumerable maleficent spirits who came to be definitely regarded as demons; at the same time the kindly disposed spirits were also believed in, but they occupied only a very subordinate position; it is probable that some of them gradually became looked upon as servants of gods (see below, under "the angel of Jahwe"). Lastly, there was the stage during which, owing to the growth of monotheistic belief (we are thinking especially of the Israelites and later

Muhammadanism), the gods were degraded to demons and were reck-oned among the ordinary demons (Azazel among the Israelites is a case in point); the benevolent spirits issued into the definite category of angels. It is during this last stage that the whole body of spirits finally develops from benevolent and malevolent into good and evil spirits, i.e. angels and demons in the present ordinary sense of the words. It is not to be sup-posed that these different stages were clearly marked; older beliefs contin-ued, of course, during periods of development, other elements also came in, such as Ancestor-worship on the one hand, and evil-disposed spirits of the departed on the other. But, roughly speaking, some such stages as those just outlined seem to indicate the course of development which belief in demons and angels took in ancient times among the Arabs.

The post-biblical Angelology of Judaism, which offers much of great interest, must not detain us; incidental reference will be made to this when we come to the Old Testament doctrine of angels; but it is important and necessary to take a brief glance at Assyrian and Babylonian angelology, since this was contemporary with Israelite belief. As in the case of the Israelites and Arabs, there was amongst the ancient Babylonians originally no belief in angels; indeed, it is true to say that even among the Neo-Babylonians of the post-Assyrian period angels, in the sense of the word as understood among the Jews of the post-exilic period and onwards, played no great part. Nevertheless, we find that the ancient Babylonians had a belief in certain benevolent *genii*, spiritual superhuman beings who were of a lower degree than the gods, and who seem to have occupied a posi-tion somewhat analogous to the later conception of the guardian-angels. The *Shedu*[80] were in the main evil spirits, demons, but among them there were also benevolent guardian-spirits. That these latter were not gods is certain because when their names occur on the ancient texts they have not the determinative which is always found in connexion with the name of a god. Besides the *Shedu* there were the *Lamassu*, or "Colossal forms"; these were represented by huge sculptures—bulls, serpents, lions, and hybrid forms, which were set up at the entrance gates of temples and palaces to drive off "the foes," by which were meant evil spirits and demons. But they were also the guardian-spirits of individuals, as is abundantly shown on various texts of different ages. Both names are generic, but they are also used as proper names. The word Lamassu connotes the idea of "protection"[81]; originally the name was used as that of a god; but in the later texts *Lamassu* appears invariably as a kindly disposed guardian-spirit. As a rule *Lamassu* and *Shedu* are found together on the texts. On a magic text recording a formula, which was uttered to ward off demons, occur the words: "May the good *Shedu* walk at my right hand, may the good *Lamassu* walk at my left hand."[82] The help of these two was sought in various emergencies; thus, in another text, the exorcist who is about to enter the house of one who is ill conjures *Shedu* and *Lamassu* to be at his side when he approaches the patient and lays his hand upon his (the patient's) head. Interesting, too, is the idea contained in another similar text where the petition is offered for the patient: "May the good Shedu and the good Lamassu establish themselves within his body." In another case in which it is believed that the demon Utukku has possessed a man, the goddess of the underworld is besought "to turn her face away" in order that this evil demon may depart from the body of the possessed, and that "the good Shedu and the good Lamassu may take his place there." The same is said in another case in which the demon "Rabisu, who lurks," has taken up his abode in the body of a man. In one text Lamassu is called upon for protection from evils brought about through an eclipse of the moon; and in a prayer for the king supplication is made to *Shedu* and *Lamassu* to protect, for the king's benefit, "all fields, pastures, and rivers." Finally, there is the curious case in which in a supplication made to the god Ea, "the king of the deep," it is said: "O be thou my guardian Shedu, O be thou my guardian Lamassu. "It will thus be seen that these guardian-spirits occupied an important position in the spirit world, and that their help was believed to be obtainable in a variety of circumstances. The texts[83] to which reference has been made belong to different ages, from, roughly speaking, 2500 B.C. to 500 B.C. In some of the latest Assyrian and in Neo-Babylonian texts there are references to benevolent spirits who are to all intents and purposes angels in the ordinary sense of the word. Thus, mention is made of "the messenger of mercy," who is sent by 1the deity to accompany the king when going into battle; there is also the "guardian of life" who stands by the king's side.[84] Regarding Cherubim, and Seraphim in the form of angels, see below, pp. 60 ff.; neither of these names has hitherto been found on the inscriptions, but there are many carved figures which correspond to the descriptions of them given in the Old Testament.

II. THE ANGELOLOGY OF THE OLD TESTAMENT

(*a*) *The First Stage: the "sons of the gods."*—Among the early Israelites there was not the popular belief in multitudes of angels such as existed in regard to demons. The origin of the idea of angels, so far as the Old Testament is concerned, is probably to be sought in the "Beni ha-Elohim," lit. "the sons of the gods," referred to in Gen. vi. 2–4[85]; this conception of angels means, according to linguistic analogy, "beings of the Elohim kind."[86] The passage is a remnant piece of Semitic mythology incorporated in the Hebrew Scriptures to account for the existence of supernatural beings who were believed to be of similar nature and power to Jahwe, but subordinate to Him. The mythological element regarding their relations with the daughters of men was, later on, dropped or ignored, and these "sons of the gods" became, with the development of Jahwe-worship, Jahwe's attendants in the heavenly court, with whom He took counsel[87]; their duties were also to praise Him and His might and glory, and to act as His messengers (hence later the regular name for "angel," *malak*,[88] lit. "messenger"); and to carry out His will among men. These points can be illustrated from the following passages: Job i. 6, "Now there was a day when the sons of God (lit. 'the sons of the gods') came to present themselves before Jahwe...." The context tells of how God discusses with Satan the case of Job in the hearing of the assembled heavenly courtiers; the word for "present themselves" implies that they came to report and to receive further commands (cp. Zech. vi. 5); "Satan," in the context, is wrong; it is not a proper name, but simply "the adversary" (see above). In Job ii. 1ff. the same picture is presented. In Job xxxviii. 1 ff., where there is a reference to the creation of the world, it is said in verse 7, "…When the morning stars sang together, and the sons of the gods shouted for joy" (cp. Ps. xix. 1[2 in Hebr.], xxix. 1, 2). These attendants of Jahwe are thus, in spite of the creation accounts in Genesis, thought of as having been present during the forming of the world. Instructive is the passage Ps. lxxxix. 5–7 (6–8 in Hebr.), where the "holy ones" are the angels and parallel to the "sons of gods": "And the heavens shall praise thy wonders, O Jahwe; thy faithfulness also in the assembly of the holy ones. For who in the skies can be compared unto Jahwe? Who among the sons of gods is like unto Jahwe? A God very terrible in the council of the holy ones, and to be feared above all them that are round about Him?" In this connexion the passage I Kings xxii. 19–22, referred to in the note above, should be read; it is rather too long to quote in full.

(b) *The Second Stage: Jahwe and the "theophanic angel."*—The next step in the Old Testament teaching on angels is concerned with what is known as "the angel of the Lord,"[89] lit. "the messenger of Jahwe," called also "the messenger of God,"[90] i.e. the theophanic angel; here it is essential to distinguish clearly between the two documents which have been amalgamated in the present form of the Hebrew text of the earlier Biblical books, viz. J, the older one, so called because the compiler always speaks of God as "Jahwe," and E, so called because the compiler always speaks of God as "Elohim." The following are a few of the most important passages from the J document, from which it will be seen what is meant by "the angel of Jahwe," Gen. xvi. 7, "And the angel of Jahwe found her (i.e. Hagar) by a fountain of water in the wilderness"; "the angel of Jahwe" is spoken of in verses 9, 10, 11; but when we come to verse 13 we read: "And she called the name of Jahwe that spake with her El roi…." Here it is quite obvious that Jahwe and "the angel of Jahwe" are one and the same. Again, in Exod. iii. 2 it is said: "And the angel of Jahwe appeared unto him (i.e. Moses) in a flame of fire out of the midst of the bush.…And Moses said, I will turn aside now, and see this great sight, why the bush is not burnt"; then it immediately goes on to say: "And when Jahwe saw that he turned aside to see, God called unto him out of the midst of the bush, and said.…" Here again it is clear that "the angel of Jahwe" and Jahwe are regarded as one and the same. On the other hand, we get in Exod. xxxii. 33, 34 (belonging to the same document) a clear distinction between Jahwe and His angel. In the long passage Num. xxii. 20–38, belonging in the main to the same document, there appears to be for the most part a clear distinction made between Jahwe and "the angel of Jahwe"; but in verse 35 it is said: "And the angel of Jahwe said unto Balaam, Go with the men; but only the word that I shall speak unto thee, that shalt thou speak"; but that Jahwe Himself is meant is clear from verse 38, where Balaam says: "The word that God putteth in my mouth, that shall I speak." It is true that the name for the Deity in this verse is Elohim and not Jahwe, but that does not alter the fact that here again Jahwe and "the angel of Jahwe" are one and the same. This is the case, too, in Judges ii. 1–5, where "the angel of Jahwe" says: "I made you to go up out of Egypt . . ."; and in Judges vi. 11–24, where verses 22, 23 are especially clear: "And Gideon saw that he was the angel of Jahwe; and Gideon said, Alas, O Jahwe Elohim! forasmuch as I have seen the angel of Jahwe face to face. And Jahwe said unto him, Peace be unto thee; fear not; thou shalt not die." The same identification is found in the passage Judges xiii., which is too long to quote. On the basis of all these passages the presumption is justified that when in other passages of the J document "the angel of Jahwe" is mentioned, it is Jahwe Himself who is meant, viz. Gen. xviii. 1–33, and also in such cases as Gen. xxxii. 24–32, xlviii. 16, though "the angel of Jahwe" is not spoken of by name.

We turn now to the E document. Here we have the name "the angel of God (Elohim)" in place of "the angel of Jahwe." In the version of the Hagar story contained in this document we read (Gen. xxi. 8–21): ". . . And God heard the voice of the lad; and the angel of God called to Hagar out of heaven, and said unto her, What aileth thee, Hagar? Fear not; for God hath heard the voice of the lad where he is. Arise, lift up the lad, and hold him in thine hand; for I will make him a great nation. And God opened her eyes . . ." (verses 17–19). In this passage it is evident that God and "the angel of God" are thought of as one and the same.[91] Again, in Gen. xxxi. 11–13 we read: "And the angel of God said unto me in a dream, Jacob; and I said, Here am I. And he said, Lift up now thine eyes....I am the God of Bethel...." Here again "the angel of God" is identified with God. In another passage (Exod. xiv. 19) the identity is not so distinct, though it is certainly implied: "And the angel of God, which went before the camp of Israel, removed and went behind them"; it is so frequently said elsewhere that it was God who led the children of Israel out of Egypt that in this passage it is evidently God Himself who is thought of when "the angel of God" is mentioned. In Judges vi. 20 (see above) "the angel of God" is identified with Jahwe, the God of Israel. And lastly, there is complete identification between "the angel of God" and God in the passage (too long to quote) Judges xiii. 2–9, but compare together especially verses 6 and 9.

The passages cited or referred to include all in which "the angel of Jahwe" and "the angel of God" are mentioned. There are a few others where one or other of these titles is implied, but not expressed, viz. "the angel" (Gen. xlviii. 16); "an angel" (Exod. xxiii. 20, xxxiii. 2, Num. xx. 16, cp. Hos. xii. 5); "my angel" (Exod. xxiii. 23, xxxii, 34); "his angel," Gen. xxiv. 7, 40, and cp. Acts xii. 15, "it is his angel," in reference to St. Peter. In all these passages the context shows whether "the angel of Jahwe" or "the angel of God" is intended.

The study, then, of all these passages leads to the conclusion that in pre-exilic times there was no clear distinction between Jahwe, the God of Israel, and His angel. And this seems to be the faint and dying echo of the much earlier stage of belief in which it was held that supernatural beings existed, indeed, but were all of one category, without head or leader, still less without a deity of a different and higher order; this only arose with the development of Jahwe-worship.

Before we leave the subject of "the angel of Jahwe" it is worth pointing out that in later times the idea arose that there *was* a distinction between Jahwe and His angel, i.e. a special angel; for, although the expression "angel of Jahwe" does not occur again (nor yet "angel of God" in its original con-notation), we get "the angel of his presence" (Isa. lxiii. 9), where the context shows that it is a reference to ancient times, and also "the angel of the covenant" (Mal. iii. 1); "the covenant," again, refers back to ancient times.

(c) *The Third Stage: "God's Messengers."*—The next stage in the development of Old Testament angelology is that in which the angels are quite clearly and distinctly God's messengers, who only exist for the purpose of praising God and carrying out His will among men. A few passages illustrative of their functions and nature may be given. Primarily their duty is to wait upon God (e.g. Gen. xxviii. 12) and to praise Him; ever greater stress is laid upon this as time goes on, and as one would expect, it is in the Psalms that this receives fullest expression, e.g. Ps. ciii. 20, 21: "Bless the Lord, ye angels of His, ye mighty in strength that fulfil His word, hearkening unto the voice of His word. Bless the Lord, all ye His hosts; ye ministers of His that do His pleasure," cp. Ps. cxlviii. 2, etc. Only second in importance is their function of succoring men, and this is always associated with the carrying out of the will of God. The two angels who come to warn Lot and his family of the impending destruction of the cities of the plain, and to save them, are the emissaries of God, as the context shows, and are therefore carrying out His will (Gen. xix. 1, 15, 16).[92] Again in 1 Kings xix. 5 ff. Elijah is succored by an angel sent by God; the angel of Jahwe mentioned in verse 7 must not be understood as "the angel of Jahwe" (the theophanic angel) spoken of above; this also applies to Ps. xxxiv. 7 (8 in Hebr.) and other passages: "The angel of Jahwe encampeth round about them that fear Him, and delivereth them." In Ps. xci. 11, 12 we have another example of angels as the protectors of men: "For He shall give His angels charge over thee, to keep thee in all thy ways. They shall bear thee up in their hands, lest thou dash thy foot against a stone."

There are quite a number of cases in which superhuman beings are spoken of who are not called angels, but are such nevertheless; for example, in Isa. x. 3, 4: "The voice of one that crieth, Prepare ye in the wilderness the way of Jahwe. Make straight in the desert a highway for our God." Here the voice is that of an angelic being, who calls to his fellows to make a highway straight through the desert (instead of the ordinary journey first to the northwest and then to the south) in order that God may lead His exiled people back to their home from Babylonia. In other cases angels are referred to under different names; we have already seen that they are several times spoken of as "gods"; in Ps. lxxviii. 5 they are called *Abirim*, "mighty ones"; in Ps. lxxxix. 5 (6 in Hebr.) *Kedoshim*, "holy ones," cp. Job v. I; in Job xxxiii. 22 *Memithim*, "the destroyers," lit. "killers." But however described, their function is to serve God and help man. As the servants of God they are sometimes called to execute judgement on the wicked; thus in Ps. xxxv. 5, 6 it is said: "Let them be as the chaff before the wind, and the angel of Jahwe driving them on; let their way be dark and slippery, and the angel of Jahwe pursuing them." They even punish the Israelites in extreme cases, see 2 Sam. xxiv. 16, 17 (= 1Chron. xxi. 12 ff.). ·

(*d*) *The nature and characteristics of the angels.*—As is to be expected, the conceptions regarding angels differed in the various stages of belief concerning them, although certain characteristics were common to all stages. Thus, the might and strength imputed to angels, owing to the belief in their origin from the gods (the root meaning of *El* is "strength"), are always characteristic of them. This is already reflected in the mythological fragment Gen. vi. 4: "…when the sons of the gods came in unto the daughters of men, and they bare children to them; the same were the mighty men which were of old, the men of renown." The idea of their strength occurs in other passages; and the same is found in the Psalms, e.g. ciii. 20: "Bless Jahwe, ye angels of His, ye mighty in strength that fulfil His word," etc.

It is probable, from the analogy of Babylonian ideas on the subject, and apart from the mythological passage quoted above, that the angels were at one time conceived of as neither good nor bad; the idea of their goodness or otherwise did not arise; they were non-moral; it was rather a question of whether they were kindly disposed or maleficent.[93] But at a comparatively early time they .were regarded as good (1 Sam. xxix. 9) and as wise (2 Sam. xiv. 17, 20, xix. 27 (28 in Hebr.). In appearance they were clearly believed to resemble men (Gen. vi. 4), since they are spoken of as such (Gen. xviii. 2 ff.); and Ps. xci. 12 shows that this was the case, too, in later times, "…they shall bear thee up in their hands."

(*e*) *Special classes of angels.*—The origin of the *Cherubim* is obscure; "so far as can be seen at present, the early Hebrew cherub came nearer to the griffin, which was not divine, but the servant of the deity, and the origin of which is now assigned to the Hittites of Syria.[94] The idea of this mythic form is the combination of parts of the two strongest animals of air and land— the eagle and the lion—and a reminiscence of this may perhaps be traced in the reference to these animals in Ezek. i. 10. It was adopted by various nations, but to understand its true significance we must go, not to Egypt nor to Greece, but to the Hittites, whose originality in the use of animal forms is well known. The Hittite griffin appears almost always, in contrast to Babylonian representations, not as a fierce beast of prey, but seated in calm dignity like an irresistible guardian of holy things."[95] This reminds one of the account of the cherubim on the mercy-seat (Exod. xxv. 18–22); these have wings, and presumably this was thought to be the case with the cherubim who guarded the Tree of Life in the Garden of Eden (Gen. iii. 24).[96] The Assyrian and Babylonian representations of genii who guard palaces and temples always have wings, and though the corresponding word for cherubim has not yet been found on the inscriptions, it is evident that these sculptures do represent the Assyrian conception of the cherubim; this is brought home to anyone who compares these sculptures with the description of the cherubim in Ezek. i.

As to the meaning of the cherubim we have no certainty, but there is some support for the theory that they represent storm-clouds rushing on "the wings of the wind"; in Ps. xviii. 10 (11 in Hebr.) we have: "And he rode upon the cherub, and did fly; yea, he flew swiftly upon the wings of the wind"; and again in Ps. civ. 3 (cp. Deut. xxxiii. 26, Isa. xix. 1, Hab. iii. 8): "Who maketh the clouds His chariot, who walketh upon the wings of the wind"; in Ezek. i., where the "four living creatures" (= cherubim, see x. 2, 16–22) practically form the divine chariot, which is at the same time the throne of God. This is, however, a developed idea of the cherubim, though probably based on an ancient conception of the cherubim being the storm-clouds personified. Whether or not the horsemen of the air, the angelic riders, are to be in any way connected with the cherubim is uncertain; these occupy a prominent position in the book of Zechariah (see i.

8 ff., vi. 1–8, cp. 2 Kings vi. 17), where they appear as God's messengers, bringing in their reports to Him. These angelic riders remind one irresistibly of the *Walkure* in Teutonic Mythology.

(*f*) *The Seraphim.* —As these have already been enumerated under theriomorphic demons, it will appear strange that they should be mentioned here. As angels they occur once only in the Old Testament, in the well-known passage Isa. vi. 1–7, where they appear as attendants upon Jahwe, and praise Him, and carry out His behests. They are described as having six wings; they are very mighty, so much so that the doorposts of the temple shook at the sound of their voice. Presumably they had the appearance of men, since they had feet and hands (verses 2, 6).

That the early conception of the Seraphim as demons should have developed into the belief of their being angels is not so strange as may appear at first sight. There is something parallel to this in the fact that the demon saraph-serpent of Num. xxi. 6 became a god who was worshipped, see 2 Kings xviii. 4. That in later times the Seraphim, reckoned among the angels, were still conceived of as being in the form of serpents is clear from one or two passages in the book of Enoch; in xx. 7 it is said of Gabriel, one of the holy angels, that he is "over Paradise and the serpents and the cherubim"; that by "the serpents" the Seraphim are meant is clear from lxi. 10, where it says: "And He will summon all the host of the heavens, and all the holy ones above and the host of God, the Cherubim, Seraphim, and Ophannim [another order of angels in the developed Angelology of Judaism], and all the angels of power...." (See also lxxi. 7.)

We are not here concerned with the later Jewish Angelology, but only with the references on the subject in the Old Testament. Enough has been said to show the reality and strength of the belief in these superhuman, spiritual beings. As has already been pointed out, all belief in the existence of beings in the unseen world strengthens the conviction that man, too, will have a *role* to play in that world. And it needs no words to show that this will have been one of the elements that fostered the hope of Immortality among the Israelites of old.

The Spirits
of the Dead
and Their Abode

VI

THE REPHAIM

The *Rephaim* is the name given in the Old Testament to what would nowadays be called the spirits of the departed. In order to get some clear ideas about the meaning of this word we must briefly examine the passages of the Old Testament in which it occurs; these are not very many in number, so we can refer to them all.

I. THE REPHAIM A NAME GIVEN TO THE DEPARTED

We will take first those passages in which the word is applied to the departed:—

Job xxvi. 5: "The Rephaim (R.V. they that are deceased, marg. *the shades*) tremble beneath the waters and the inhabitants thereof"; see also verse 4.

Ps. lxxxviii. 10 (11 in Hebr.): "Wilt thou show wonders to the dead? Shall (the) Rephaim (R.V. as above) arise and praise thee?" Op. Ps. cxv. 17. Note that "the dead" and the Rephaim are parallel terms.

Isa. xiv. 9, 10: "Sheol from beneath is moved for thee to meet thee at thy coming; it stirreth up (the) Rephaim (R.V. the dead, marg. as above)....All they shall answer and say unto thee, Art thou also become weak as we? Art thou become like unto us?"

Isa. xxvi. 14: "They that are dead, they shall not live; (the) Rephaim (R.V. they that are deceased, marg. as above) shall not rise."[97]

Prov. ii. 18, 19: "For her house (i.e. the house of the strange woman) inclineth unto death, and her paths unto (the) Rephaim (R.V. the dead, marg. as above). None that go unto her return again…." Op. vii. 27.

Prov. ix. 18: "But he knoweth not that (the) Rephaim (R.V. the dead, marg. as above) are there (i.e. in the house of folly), that her guests are in the depths of Sheol."

Prov. xxi. 16: "The man that wandereth out of the way of understanding shall rest in the congregation of (the) Rephaim (R.V. the dead, marg. as above)."

To these may be added two quotations from Phoenician inscriptions in which the word Rephaim occurs in reference to the departed.[98] The Tabnith inscription (Sidon, circa 300 B.C.) contains the following: "And if thou do at all open me (i.e. my coffin), and at all disquiet me, mayest thou have no seed among the living under the sun, nor resting-place among the Rephaim." In the inscription of Eshmunazar, King of Sidon, belonging to about the same date as the preceding, it says: "For every prince and every man who shall open this resting-place, or who shall take away the coffin of my resting-place, or who shall carry me from this resting-place, may they have no resting-place with the Rephaim…."

All these Biblical passages are post-exilic; they are the only ones in the Old Testament in which the Rephaim are referred to by name when the word is intended to apply to the departed. From them we gather the following points as to the beliefs regarding the Rephaim: they have emotions, since they tremble because of God; it is assumed that they are unable to arise and praise God; they recognize those who come into their abode and speak to them; they speak of themselves as being "weak"; there is no return from the place to which they go; the foolish man has his lot among them. The two inscriptions show that it was regarded as a punishment not to have a resting-place among them, and therefore that to be among them after death was a thing to be desired. It is clear that we have here some ideas which are incompatible with each other. Let us turn to some other passages in which the Rephaim are referred to, though not mentioned by name; we will take first some that are generally recognized either as exilic or post-exilic:

Isa. xxxviii. 18: "For Sheol[99] cannot praise Thee, death 1 cannot celebrate thee; they that go down into the pit cannot hope for Thy truth."

Job iii. 11–19: "Why died I not from the womb?...For now should I have lien down and been quiet; I should have slept; then had I been at rest with kings and counsellors of the earth....There the wicked cease from troubling, and the weary are at rest. There the prisoners are at ease together; they hear not the voice of the taskmaster. The small and the great are there; and the servant is free from his master."[100]

Job xxxviii. 17: "Have the gates of death been revealed unto thee? Or hast thou seen the gates of the shadow of death?" Cp. Job xxvi. 6.

Ps. vi. 5 (6 in Hebr.): "For in death there is no remembrance of thee; in Sheol who shall give thee thanks?"

Ps. xxx. 9 (10 in Hebr.): "What profit is there in my blood, when I go down to the pit? Shall the dust praise thee? Shall it declare thy truth?"

Ps. xlix. 17–19 {18–20 in Hebr.): "For when he dieth he shall carry nothing away; his glory shall not descend after him....He shall go to the generation of his fathers; they shall never see the light."

Ps. lxxxviii. 5 (6 in Hebr.): "Cast off among the dead, like the slain that lie in the grave, whom thou rememberest no more, and they are cut off from thy hand."

Ps. cxv. 17: "The dead praise not Jah, nor they that go down to silence."

Ezek. xxxii. 17–32: this passage, a prophetic denunciation and of coming woe upon Egypt, is too long to quote in full, but a few verses may be given: "The strong (lit. gods) of the mighty shall speak to him out of the midst of Sheol with them that help him; they are gone down, they lie still, even the uncircumcised, slain by the sword "(verse 21). Again: "And they shall not lie with the mighty that are fallen of the uncircumcised [we should read with the Septuagint: "And they shall not lie with the mighty, the giants (i.e. Nephilim, see Gen. vi. 4) of old"],[101] who went down to Sheol with their weapons of war; and they laid their swords under their heads, and their iniquities [this is a text corruption, we should read, "their shields"][102] are upon their bones" (verse 27). And once more: "Pharaoh shall see them, and shall be comforted over all his multitude" (verse 31). There are other verses in this chapter which are instructive, but those cited must suffice.

It is clear that here again we have ideas about the dead which are quite incompatible. In the passages from the Psalms, as well as in that from Isaiah, the dead are thought of as pitiable, and leading a silent aimless existence; God does not remember them, nor they Him; and they are therefore without hope for His truth and all that this implies; they cannot praise Him nor give thanks to Him; they are altogether profitless, for God has nothing to do with them or with the place where they are. With this contrast what is said about them in the Job and Ezekiel passages; the place where the dead are is a place of rest, where the ordinary man is in the company of kings, who retain their rank there; there is no annoyance there; those who are prisoners are at ease; though master and servant are there, "the small and the great," there is no oppression. The dead are to be envied. From Job xxxviii. 17 it is evident that God knows all about the place where they are, and therefore presumably about them too (see the whole context of this passage). The Ezekiel passages are very striking; they represent the dead as recognizing newcomers into their abode and as speaking to them; so that according to this view the dead are neither in darkness nor yet silent. From verse 27 we gather that the prophet recognizes a kind of aristocracy in the abode of the dead; and he describes how that in Sheol the mighty heroes of old still have their swords and shields.

Now let us briefly examine two pre-exilic passages (others will come before us later). In Isa. viii. 19[103] the prophet, though inveighing against the practice, testifies to the existence of a prevalent custom which shows that the dead were regarded as anything but powerless shades: "On behalf of the living (should men seek) unto the dead? "This custom, and the belief which it implies, must have been ancient, for centuries before these words were spoken we have the episode recounted in 1 Sam. xxviii. In the time of Saul, and owing to the activity of the prophet Samuel, the worship of Jahwe had grown so powerfully that all alien cults had been vigorously fought, and to a large extent rooted out; among these cults was that of the dead,[104] who were consulted through the medium of those who were believed to be specially initiated[105]: "And Saul had put away those that had familiar spirits, and the wizards, out of the land" (verse 3). But it shows how ingrained the practice of consulting the dead must have been when Saul himself, in an hour of dire necessity, has recourse to it. He is in great stress on account of his people's hereditary foes, the Philistines; he therefore seeks guidance and help from Jahwe, but in vain: "And when Saul enquired of Jahwe, Jahwe answered him not, neither by dreams, nor by Urim, nor by prophets" (verse 6); thereupon he tries the old method once more, and determines to consult a woman who had a familiar spirit and who dwelt at Endor. "And Saul disguised himself, and put on other raiment, and went, he and two men with him, and they came to the woman by night; and he said, Divine unto me, I pray thee, by the familiar spirit, and bring me up whomsoever I shall name unto thee" (verse 8). After some hesitation on the part of the woman, she says: "Whom shall I bring up unto thee? And he said, Bring me up Samuel." The ritual of "bringing up" is not described, but the narrative goes on: "And when the woman saw Samuel, she cried with a loud voice; and the woman spake to Saul, saying, Why hast thou deceived me? For thou art Saul" (verse 12); there is some difficulty about this verse as it stands now in the Hebrew text, for why should the woman cry with a loud voice when she beholds Samuel, seeing that she expected his appearance? If when Saul bade her bring up Samuel (verse 11) she had suspected who the visitor was, there would have been nothing surprising. We should probably read, "And when the woman saw (i.e. looked at) Saul" (in Hebrew the names Samuel and Saul look very similar, and could quite easily be interchanged by mistake), which is the rendering of four Septuagint manuscripts; .i.e. when Saul asked her to bring up Samuel, the request induced her to look scrutinizingly at the stranger, for it was a bold thing to ask for the man who had been the moving spirit in championing the cause of Jahwe and abolishing the very practice with which she was now occupied; then on looking carefully at this visitor she recognized Saul, and cried aloud in fear lest she should be punished for being caught red-handed in the forbidden practice. Saul, however, reassures her. Then the narrative continues; Saul says: "What seest thou? And the woman said unto Saul, I see a god (*elohim*) coming up out of the earth. And he said unto her, What form is he of? And she said, An old man cometh up; and he is covered with a robe. And Saul perceived that it was Samuel, and he bowed with his face to the ground, and did obeisance. And Samuel said to Saul, Why hast thou disquieted me, to bring me up? And Saul answered, I am sore distressed...and God is departed from me, and answereth me no more, neither by prophets, nor by dreams; therefore I have called thee, that thou mayest make known unto me what I shall do. And Samuel said, Wherefore dost thou ask of me, seeing Jahwe is departed from thee and is on the side of thy neighbor?" (so the Septuagint, the Hebrew text is corrupt; by "thy neighbor" is meant David). Samuel then announces Saul's impending ruin.

These two pre-exilic passages, then, present us with a very vivid belief in the understanding and activity of the dead on the part of the people of Israel; and this will be further illustrated when we deal with the subject of Necromancy[106] What these passages say about the departed agrees with what is said on the same subject in some of the passages given above, while disagreeing *in toto* with others. We have, therefore, to recognize two diametrically opposed sets of ideas regarding the dead: there were the primitive popular ideas which had existed from time immemorial, according to which the dead were of superior understanding and power to mortals; hence the custom of consulting them whenever occasion arose. That they are spoken of as "elohim," "gods," raises further questions which are dealt with below. On the other hand, there was the official belief regarding the dead; this is represented in the other set of passages given above. According to this the dead were to all intents and purposes nonexistent, at any rate in so far as dealings with them on the part of the living were concerned; they were thought of as having no life in them in the ordinary sense of the word, no parts nor passions, mere shadows of what they once were, incapable of action of any kind. Now it is very necessary to note that wherever this official view of the dead is represented it is always in post-exilic passages, while in a few cases pre-exilic passages have been emended or altered in order to harmonize a little more with the later ideas. The rise of this official point of view was due to the growth of the worship of Jahwe. It must soon have become apparent to the religious leaders in Israel that the popular beliefs and practices in regard to the dead were incompatible with the belief in, and worship of, Jahwe; and the imperative need not only of rooting out the former, but of putting something else in their place presented itself forcibly. But the success with which these efforts were attended was for long very moderate; this will be further illustrated when we come to consider the subject of Necromancy; and this is why in the pre-exilic literature what may be termed the reformed doctrine of the dead never occurs, excepting in passages where it is evident that a redactor has been at work. For in exilic and post-exilic times, when the people were taken from their land, all intercourse (or supposed intercourse) with the departed necessarily ceased, because for them to leave their own land would have been a thing unheard of. Then it was that the reformed doctrine really came to its own, and hence the stress laid upon it in the post-exilic literature. But how deep-seated were the popular beliefs can be realized when we find them reflected in such a passage as Ezekiel xxxii., and those from Job quoted above.

The reformed doctrine concerning the Rephaim can be illustrated in an interesting way by turning to Isa. xiv. 9, 10; here the Rephaim are spoken of, and are represented as saying to the king of Babylon on his entry into their abode: "Art thou also become weak as we?"[107] The root for "to be weak" here is not the same as that from which the Rephaim is usually supposed to come, which, however, also means "to be slack," or "feeble," or "weak"; hence the meaning "the weak ones" usually given to the Rephaim; and this accords with the reformed teaching regarding the Rephaim. Therefore this Isaiah passage is often quoted to support the contention that the word Rephaim comes from the root רפה (*raphah*), "to be weak."[108] But, as we have seen from passages which reflect the ancient and popular view about the Rephaim, there is nothing "weak" about them;

and, as we shall see in dealing with Necromancy, the dead were regarded as possessing knowledge superior to that of mortals. If the word Rephaim occurred only in post-exilic literature, and if it were never used excepting in reference to the dead, its derivation as given above could scarcely be challenged; but we have now to consider the word Rephaim in another connexion.

II. The Rephaim, the Name of an Ancient Race of Giants

A very ancient race of giants, believed to have existed in Palestine "of old," were known by the name of Rephaim. They are referred to quite a number of times in the Old Testament; some of the passages are worth examining. These giants are mentioned for the first time in Gen. xiv. 5, where it is said that among those who were overcome by Chedorlaomer and the kings that were with him were "the Rephaim in Ashtaroth-Karnaim" (cp. Gen. xv. 18–20); in Josh. xii. 4 it is also said that they dwelt in Ashtaroth; they lived in the forest land, according to Josh. xvii. 15. In the very early history of Israel they were looked upon as a "remnant"; Josh. xiii. 12 ff., though a late passage, echoes an old tradition that in the time of Moses these people were driven out of the land: "All the kingdom of Og the king of Bashan, which reigned in Ashtaroth and in Edrei (the same was left of the remnant of the Rephaim); for these did Moses smite, and drave them out" (cp. Deut. ii. 20); in Deut. iii. 11 also it is said: "For only Og the king of Bashan remained of the remnant of the Rephaim" (cp. Deut. iii. 13). Another ancient notice is preserved in Deut. ii. 10, 11: "The Emim dwelt therein aforetime, a people great, and many, and tall, as the Anakim; these also are accounted Rephaim, as the Anakim; but the Moabites call them Emim." Once more, it is said in Deut. ii. 20, 21 regarding the land of Ammon, "that also is accounted a land of Rephaim; Rephaim dwelt there aforetime; but the Ammonites call them Zamzummim; a people great, and many, and tall, as the Anakim."

It is worth noting, first of all, that of the twenty times that the name Rephaim occurs it is written fourteen times without the article, and six times with the article; probably men originally spoke only of "Rephaim," the addition of the article having only arisen later when it was thought that once a race existed who were called "the Rephaim." If this was so, then "Rephaim" was not a gentilic name. Further, it will be seen that in comparing the various passages in which the Anakim (or "sons of Anak"), Emim, and Zamzummim (= Zuzim) occur, these were all other names for, or branches of, Rephaim; the same is true of Nephilim (see Gen. vi. 4, Num. xiii. 33, and cp. Ezek. xxxii. 27 quoted above); none of these are gentilic names. The Nephilim were "mighty men of old"; of the Emim nothing is known, but there is some justification for Schwally's contention that they were believed to be serpent spirits[109]; of the Zamzummim (Zuzim being probably a shortened form) the same authority points out that it is an onomatopoetic word connected with a Semitic root "to hiss," used of "the hissing, whistling sound made by the Jinn of the desert in the night."[110] All these names, then, are enshrouded in mystery, the only certain point about them being that they are all to be included under "Rephaim." Now as this word is exactly the same as that used for the departed, it is not unnatural to ask if there is possibly any connexion between them. One is led to this especially when one remembers the diametrically opposed conceptions regarding the departed (Rephaim) in the Old Testament, the older passages representing them as being anything but "weak" or as "shades." More than a century ago the theory was put forward[111] that "Rephaim" referred to the giants (equivalent to "the sons of the gods" and the Nephilim in Gen. vi. 1–7) who were destroyed by God from the earth and cast down into the underworld[112]; then, in course of time, when this ancient myth had been gradually toned down, the name of Rephaim was used as a general designation of all the departed in the underworld. But the question still remains as to why they received this name, the ordinary derivation of it from the root meaning "to be weak" (*raphah*) does not fit in with the facts. It is conceivable that it comes from a very similar root (*rapha*) which means "to heal." But why should the departed (supposing there is any justification for this derivation) be spoken of as "healers"? The subject will come before us again in dealing with that of Necromancy; here it must suffice to quote the words of a high authority: "If one bears in mind the close ties which united divination and therapeuty among the ancients, and that men sought from the gods above all things the revelation of the remedies required, one will not be disinclined to regard the Rephaim as 'the healers' *par excellence*, an extension of the ἥρως ἰατρός of Athens."[113] To realize the significance of this theory one must take into consideration the question of Ancestor-worship; this subject is dealt with in Chapters VIII., IX.

III. The Valley of Rephaim

Among the twenty references to Rephaim mentioned in the preceding section, there are a certain number which speak of "the valley of Rephaim"; there are also some others in which mention is made of parts of the country supposed to have been inhabited by Rephaim. It is probable that in some cases the information given is unreliable on account of the belief of later times that Rephaim was a gentilic name; but it will be seen that in other cases there is considerable significance regarding the localities supposed to have been inhabited by Rephaim. One set of passages points to Bashan, together with the countries of Ammon and Moab; the two latter lie to the south of Bashan all three are on the east of the Jordan. Ammon and Moab are mentioned only incidentally in connexion with Rephaim, and are not of importance; the fact that to the east of each of them lies the desert may possibly be of significance. But as to Bashan (or rather, parts of it) something must be said, especially that portion of it which touches Ammon and to the southeast of which lies the desert; this is the part of the country wherein, in all probability, Ashtaroth and Edrei lay. In Deut. iii. 4 mention is made of "threescore cities, all the region of Argob, the kingdom of Og in Bashan" (cp. 1 Kings iv. 13). Now, as to all this region Driver says: "There are the remains of many ancient towns and villages in these parts, especially in the Leya, and on the sloping sides of the Jebel Hawan; according to Wetzstein, for example (*Hawan*, 42), there are three hundred such ancient sites on the E. and S. slopes of the Jebel Hawan alone. The dwellings of these deserted localities are of a remarkable character. Some are the habitations of Troglodytes, being caverns hollowed out on the mountainside, and so arranged as to form separate chambers; these are found chiefly on the E. of the Jebel Hawan. Others are subterranean abodes entered by shafts invisible from above; these are frequent on the W. of the Zumleh range, and at Edrei the dwellings thus constructed form quite an underground city."[114] It is not difficult to picture the effect that these cave-dwellings and underground abodes and their inhabitants must have had upon the Israelite nomads when first seen; and one can understand that extraordinary stories would have sprung up among an imaginative people who had from time immemorial believed in the possibility of the dead appearing from their abode "under the earth." what more natural than that, these stories having become traditional, later ages should have believed that these districts had in times past been one among the spots in which the "giants of old," the Rephaim, were wont to appear? This would, at all events, account for those Old Testament notices which point to these parts as having been inhabited by Rephaim in days gone by.[115]

But there is another set of passages which speak of "the valley of Rephaim"; this can be accurately located from the indications given. It lay immediately to the southwest of Jerusalem, between Jerusalem and Bethlehem, but much closer to the former.[116] Why was it called the valley of Rephaim? It may be taken for granted that all places originally got their names for some reason; and though no reason has been preserved as to why this valley was called the valley of Rephaim, common sense suggests that it must have been on account of something connected with Rephaim. In any case this word was applied either to the giants of old or else to the departed; whichever may have come into consideration when the valley was given this name, it is evident that men believed there was something "uncanny" about it. Therefore it is significant that the two outstanding things which we know of regarding this valley are just the kind of things which would be described as "uncanny." First we have the narrative in 2 Sam. v. 17–25 (= 1 Chron. xiv. 8–17), but more especially verses 22–25:"And the Philistines came up yet again, and spread themselves in the valley of Rephaim. And when David enquired of Jahwe, he said, Thou shalt not go up: make a circuit behind them, and come upon them over against the mulberry trees [marg. balsam trees; cp. Ps. lxxxiv. 6 (7 in Hebr.)]. And it shall be, when thou hearest the sound of marching in the tops of the mulberry trees: for then is Jahwe gone out before thee to smite the host of the Philistines...." Here is a strange piece of folklore. Jahwe is supposed to come into the trees, or upon the tree-tops, so that David may receive a sign for beginning his attack. Was this really believed of Jahwe? It is possible; but we doubt it. It seems more likely that the action was imputed to Jahwe in later times, incongruous as it was, in order to tone down the heathen practice which was originally referred to. The numberless instances on record even at the present day of the belief that spirits of the departed come into trees, and are there ready to help (over and over again for the purpose of healing) those by whom they are revered, suggests the high probability that something of the same kind was believed to have taken place on this occasion; it would have tallied with the valley's repute.

Next we have the passage Josh. xv. 8: "...and the border went up by the valley of the son of Hinnom unto the side (or "shoulder") of the Jebusite southward (the same is Jerusalem): and the border went up to the top of the mountain that lieth before the valley of Hinnom westward, which is at the uttermost part of the valley of Rephaim" (a similar notice occurs in xviii. 16). The description of the position of the valley of Rephaim, therefore, agrees with what is said in the other passages. The special point to notice here is that the valley of the son of Hinnom is part of the valley of Rephaim. Although there is diversity of opinion among experts as to the exact position of the valley of the son of Hinnom, this does not affect the present inquiry, for all seem agreed that it formed part of, or the extension of, the valley of Rephaim; "whatever view is taken of the position of the valley of Hinnom, all writers concur in its extending to the junction of the three valleys of Jerusalem below Siloam i.e. there must be one spot below Siloam which all agree in making a portion of the valley of Hinnom" (Warren).[117] The evil repute of this valley is referred to in Jer. vii. 31, 32: "And they have built the high places of Topheth, which is in the valley of the son of Hinnom, to burn their sons and their daughters in the fire!...Therefore, behold, the days come, saith Jahwe, that it shall no more be called Topheth,[118] nor the valley of the son of Hinnom, but the valley of slaughter; for they shall bury in Topheth, till there be no place to bury," cp. xix. 6; also xix. 12, 13: "...and the houses of Jerusalem, and the houses of the kings of Judah, which are defiled, shall be as the place of Topheth, even all the houses upon whose roofs they have burned incense unto all the host of heaven, and have poured out drink offerings unto other gods." Different cults are referred to here; but among them, one may surmise, was the cult of the dead (Rephaim); it is certain, from, e.g., Isa. lvii. 6, that drink offerings were poured out to the dead (see further, pp. 100–112). But the really significant point about the valley of Hinnom from our present point of view is that it became a symbol of the place of the wicked departed; or perhaps it would be more strictly true to say that the idea of the valley of Hinnom was transferred to the next world. The name of this place is more familiar in its abbreviated Hebrew form, "Gehenna" (*Ge* means "valley"). The "ever ascending smoke" from it was pointed to as its being the entrance to the place of torment beneath the earth.[119]

From the various *data*, then, that have been given we believe there is some justification for the contention that at one time there was in the minds of the Israelites a direct connexion between the Rephaim conceived of as "the giants of old" and the Rephaim as used of the "shades" of the departed; and that the valley of Rephaim originally received its name from the belief (the reasons for which it is now no more possible to trace) that the souls of the departed were in some way directly connected with it.

VII

SHEOL, THE PLACE OF
THE DEPARTED

In dealing with this subject, which is so closely connected with the Rephaim, it is inevitable that there should be some little repetition in the matter of references to passages from the Old Testament; but we think it is better to give references and quotations, even at the risk of some repetition, than to be constantly referring the reader back to the preceding chapter. Before, however, coming to the Old Testament belief in Sheol we shall briefly touch upon the Babylonian conceptions concerning the underworld; these will, we believe, be found to be both interesting and instructive.

I. BABYLONIAN CONCEPTIONS CONCERNING THE UNDERWORLD

The varied information that has been preserved in the cuneiform inscriptions about what the Babylonians believed regarding the place of the departed must belong to different ages. This conviction is forced upon one on account of the conflicting ideas and contradictory things that are told us in these ancient documents about the underworld.[120]

The Babylonians believed in special gods of the underworld; they were subordinate to the great gods of the Babylonian Pantheon, but they were nevertheless gods. The netherworld gods had their palace in the abode of the dead. Foremost among the rulers of the underworld was the goddess Erishkigal, "the mistress of the great place"; she is also known as Allatu, "the mighty one"; together with her is her husband, Dergal, called "Lord of the great land"; their wedding is referred to on the Tel-el-Amarna tablets.[121] The Sumerians, who lived in the country of the Babylonians before these latter drove them out, also had their ideas about the place of the departed; and the Babylonians evidently got from them some of these ideas. The Sumerians called the place of the departed Kurnugea, which means "the land without return," and this name figures in Babylonian poetry.[122] Thus, in the account of Ishtar's descent into the realm of the departed this place is spoken of as "the abode which whosoever enters never leaves again; the path from which there is no return." While this place is sometimes conceived of as a great hollow mountain,[123] it is more usually thought of as an immense city which could not be measured for size; the way to it was across the ocean westward, towards the sinking sun, for it was situated beyond the waters that are beneath the earth. This great city of the dead is described as being enclosed by seven walls, and there are seven gates with ponderous bolts; and when a newcomer has entered one of these gates the guardian who keeps watch by it closes it again and makes it secure with bolts and bars. It was, according to the Babylonians, "a house of darkness," and they who lived there were shut out from the light. No ranks were recognized in that underworld; there all men were equal. And in that place of darkness dust covers all things; dust is upon bolt and bar, and dust covers the shades of men as they silently glide along the dust-laden streets of the city. The food of these weird inhabitants is dust, and black, murky water is their drink. In that place there is neither love nor hate; only sorrow and wailing; monotonous moaning echoes along those streets of dust; that is the only sound in the surrounding silence, the only occupation of the dusty shades of men.[124] The following from "The Descent of Ishtar" gives a graphic picture:

"Ishtar, the moon-god's daughter,
Bethought her of the Land without return, the land [. . .],

The daughter of the moon-god bethought her
Of the house of darkness, the abode of Irkalla (i.e. Nergal),
Of the house which whosoever enters never leaves again,
Of the path from which there is no return,
Of the house which whosoever enters is taken from the light,
Of the place where dust is their food and earth their nutriment.,
Where they behold no light, but dwell in darkness,
Where they are clad like birds in garments of wings,
Where dust is spread on door and bolt."[125]

But there is another side to the Babylonian conception of the abode of the dead which is quite incompatible with those just spoken of; these also demand a little notice. In spite of the repeated emphasis laid on the fact that the dead enter a land from which there is no return, there are clear indications of a belief in the possibility of leaving it. Whether such indications are the expression of later and developed thought or not does not greatly matter, since in any case they date from a time prior to the seventh century B.C. The belief in the possibility of being able to "bring up" the spirits of the dead from the underworld, as the witch of Endor brought up Samuel, is a clear indication of the belief that the shades of the departed were not necessarily nor inexorably always confined to their abode.[126] Further, this possibility is also indicated in the Epic of Gilgamesh, where we read of Ishtar entering the realm of the dead to seek the water which shall heal her lover. Elsewhere in the same poem Ishtar threatens to destroy the entire city of the dead, and to bring up all the dead on to the earth again to associate with the living once more. Such conceptions, however quaint, and even if they were metaphorically employed (which may be doubted) or poetically, contain the idea that the realm of the dead was not necessarily a land without return, although absence might only be temporary. But there was more than this in the Babylonian belief about the Hereafter. "Diogenes Laertes appears to have reported rightly when he credits the Chaldaean schools of philosophy (better, schools of the priests) with a belief not only in immortality, but also with a certain kind of belief in resurrection. The Babylonian Noah, after having described the inevitability of death, speaks of the 'god of Fate,' to whom alone it has been granted to shield men from death"[127]; for it is said in the "Descent of Ishtar," already referred to, that there is, under the "eternal palace" (the holy of holies of the underworld) a spring containing the water of life; this is guarded by the demons of the underworld, called the Anunaki. This water can be obtained only by means of pronouncing a magic word known only to the god Ea. Here we have, though in a naive and quaint form, the idea expressed of the possibility of rising from the underworld. Further, we have in the annual Tammuz Festival also both the idea of liberation from the realm of the dead as well as that of resurrection. "If scholars are right in deriving the name of Tammuz from a Sumerian phrase meaning 'true son,' or, more fully, 'true son of the deep water,'[128] we must conclude that the Semites of Babylon took over the worship from their predecessors the Sumerians.... Be that as it may, we first meet with Tammuz in the religious literature of Babylon. He there appears as the youthful spouse or lover of Ishtar, the great mother goddess, the embodiment of the reproductive energies of nature. The references to their connexion with each other in myth and ritual are both fragmentary and obscure, but we gather from them that every year Tammuz was believed to die, passing away from the cheerful earth to the gloomy subterranean world, and that every year his divine mistress journeyed in quest of him 'to the land from which there is no returning, to the house of darkness, where dust lies on door and bolt.' During her absence the passion of love ceased to operate: men and beasts alike forgot to reproduce their kinds; all life was threatened with extinction. So intimately bound up with the goddess were the sexual functions of the whole animal kingdom that without her presence they could not be discharged. A messenger of the great god Ea was accordingly dispatched to rescue the goddess on whom so much depended. The stern queen of the infernal regions, Allatu or Ereshkigal by name, reluctantly allowed Ishtar to be sprinkled with the Water of Life and to depart, in company probably with her lover Tammuz, that the two might return together to the upper world, and that with their return all nature might revive. Laments for the departed Tammuz are contained in several Babylonian hymns, which liken him to plants that quickly fade. His death appears to have been annually mourned[129] to the shrill music of flutes, by men and women about midsummer in the month named after him, the month of Tammuz. The dirges were seemingly chanted over an effigy of the dead god, which was washed with pure water, anointed with oil, and clad in a red robe, while the fumes of incense rose into the air, as if to stir his dormant senses by their pungent fragrance and wake him from the sleep of death."[130]

Although this myth, which, however, to the Babylonians meant a living reality, concerned the gods, one sees from it that there existed the belief in the possibility of release from the realm of the dead, provided the right remedy, the Water of Life, could be procured; the myth also contains the germs, at least, of a belief in resurrection.

One other point in Babylonian belief must be referred to. The term "awakeners from the dead" is one applied to quite a number of Babylonian deities. Originally this "awakening" had reference to the "resurrection" of nature, but the conception is also at times distinctly applied to man. Of the sun-god Shamash it is said: "It is in thy power to make the dead alive, and to release those who are bound"; the god Nebo is praised as being one "who can lengthen the days of life, and who can awaken the dead." Of Marduk it is said that he is "the merciful one, who loves to awaken the dead"; he is also called "the awakener of the dead." Similar power is ascribed to his spouse, Gula; she is called "the Mistress, the awakener of the dead."[131]

Babylonian conceptions regarding the realm of the dead were thus varied and contradictory; probably this is to be accounted for because of the illogical train of thought which on this subject is to be found among so many ancient peoples; in part it is also due, no doubt, to the amalgamation of conceptions belonging to different ages; even when a development of thought has taken place the old ideas are often impossible to eradicate. Upon the whole, Babylonian belief regarding the realm of the dead is gloomy and hopeless; but a brighter conception sometimes emerges, and the hope of better things is contemplated.

A word may here be added regarding the beliefs of the ancient Arabs about the departed and their condition. Very little, it is true, is known of these beliefs, because Mohammedanism has almost entirely obliterated them; but some remnants are left which show that at one time the Arabs did not differ from the rest of the Semites in holding very definite conceptions about the departed. The cry which is uttered at graves, "Be not far off," though officially declared to be useless, must be the echo of some real expression of belief which at one time obtained, especially as it is known that the Arabs have all manner of ways of keeping up, as they believe, relationships with the departed. They furnish the dead with everything which he may require for his journey into the unknown land, they greet him when they visit his tomb, and even swear by his life. They believe that the departed, therefore, are alive, and that they have needs of various kinds; water is believed to be one of their special needs, hence the custom of pouring water on graves.[132] It is believed that the spirits of the departed appear in the form of birds, especially owls, and that in this form they come to their graves and pour forth lamentations. They are also believed to inhabit cemeteries and desolate districts in the capacity of *Jinn*. The belief is vague and undefined, but the conviction is there that the departed are living in some form or another.

II. THE OLD TESTAMENT CONCEPTIONS OF SHEOL

As the Babylonians had their underworld, the Greeks their Hades, the Romans their Orcus, so too the Hebrews had their Sheol. The meaning of this word is still a matter of dispute among scholars. Some hold that it comes from the root meaning "to ask" (שאל), and that the word means "the place of inquiry, or scrutiny"; in support of this the story of the witch of Endor can be pointed to, for Saul comes to ask of Samuel, the inhabitant of Sheol, the information he desires. Assyrian scholars point out also that this is the meaning of the Assyrian equivalent to the Hebrew Sheol, viz. "the place where oracles are obtained" (Jastrow).[133] Then the numerous references in the Old Testament to the practice of having recourse to the dead for help and guidance seem to support this theory. Moreover, in the later Egyptian belief it is taught that the soul of the dead man, after having gone through various vicissitudes, at last reaches the judgement hall of Osiris, where he undergoes an examination concerning his life while on earth, and where finally his heart is weighed in the balance of the goddess of justice. But this theory of the meaning of Sheol is too complex to have been primitive; it is quite possible that as representing a development of ideas it has a good deal to commend it. The ancient Israelite belief was, however, we imagine, of a much simpler character; there was, moreover, no differentiation until a much later—post-biblical—time between the good and the evil in the Hereafter, such as is contemplated in Egyptian belief. A more widely accepted theory is that the word Sheol comes from the root meaning "to be hollow," Sheol being conceived of as a great hollow place deep down under the earth; one recalls the Babylonian idea of the underworld as being a huge hollow mountain. This idea is a simple one, and it is that which commends it, for one expects simple ideas among a comparatively uncultured people such as the ancient Hebrews were.

As we have seen, Sheol was pictured as being situated under the earth. The earth itself being the abode of living men, the skies being the abode of the gods, as the stars showed (according to primitive ideas), there was no alternative other than that of conceiving the realm of the departed to be under the earth; more strictly, under the waters that are under the earth; hence also the idea of the Babylonians that the journey to the underworld led by the way of the ocean; and this is implied when in Job xxvi. 6 it is said: "The Rephaim tremble beneath the waters and the inhabitants thereof." Then, again, it is taught that Sheol is a place from which there is no return: "As the cloud is consumed and vanisheth away, so he that goeth down to Sheol shall come up no more; he shall return no more to his house, neither shall his place know him any more" (Job vii. 9, 10, cp. x. 21).[134] We have seen that the Babylonians called the realm of the departed the "land without return." Further, the Babylonian conception of it as a great city with gates and bars is graphically illustrated in the Old Testament, where a similar conception is found; thus, in the Psalm of Hezekiah

(Isa. xxxviii. 10) the king says: "In the noontide of my days I shall go into the gates of Sheol," and in Ps. ix. 13 (14 in Hebr.), where Death is used as a synonym for Sheol, it is said: "Thou that liftest me up from the gates of death," cp. Ps. cvii. 18, Job xxxviii. 17. Its "bars" are spoken of in Job xvii. 16, where Job says of his hope: "It shall go down to the bars of Sheol." This idea of Sheol being a city would have arisen very naturally, since it was in the cities that people were gathered together; and that Sheol was conceived of as a place in which crowds assembled comes out clearly in Job xxx. 23: "For I know that thou wilt bring me to death, to the house of assembly of all living," cp. Job xvii. 13. We recall in this connexion the expressions "gathered into his fathers," "sleeping with his fathers," "gathered into his people." The idea of the realm of the dead being a city points to Babylon as its place of origin; for this idea was certainly held in Babylonia while the Israelites were still nomads. On the other hand, we get the idea of crowds in Sheol presented by a picture which would suit an agricultural people in Ps. xlix. 14 (15 in Hebr.), conceivably an echo from ancient times: "As a flock they are put in Sheol; Death shall be their shepherd, they shall go down to the grave with the upright."[135] A different idea is expressed by the words "the snares of death" or "the snares of Sheol"; the Revised Version renders more literally and more correctly, "the cords," the idea being that Sheol has the power of dragging men down (Ps. xviii. 4, 5 [5, 6 in Hebr.]). Again, the Babylonian description of everything being covered with dust in the realms of the dead seems to have its counterpart in the Hebrew conception, for in Ps. xxii. 15 (16 in Hebr.) it says: "Thou hast brought me into the dust of death," and Ps. xxx. 9 (10 in Hebr.):"What profit is there in my blood, when I go down to the pit? Shall the dust praise Thee? shall it declare Thy truth? "We are reminded of the words: "Dust thou art, and unto dust thou shalt return" (Gen. iii. 19). Further, Sheol is a place of darkness; in, e.g., Job x. 22 it is called "the land of darkness," and in Ps. cxliii. 3 the psalmist's enemy is spoken of as one who "hath made me dwell in dark places, as those that have been long dead," and in Ps. xlix. 19 (20 in Hebr.) it is said: "He shall go to the generation of his fathers, they shall never see the light"; cp. the expression "the valley of the shadow of death" (Ps. xxiii. 4). Sheol is also a place of silence: "the dead praise not thee, Jahwe; neither they that go down into silence" (Ps. cxv. 17); "Unless Jahwe had been my help, my soul had soon dwelt in silence" (Ps. xciv. 17, cp. Isa. xlvii. 5), and Ps. xxxi. 17 (18 in Hebr.): "Let the wicked be ashamed, let them be silent in Sheol." It is also the land of forgetting: "Shall Thy wonders be known in the dark? And thy righteousness in the land of forgetfulness? "(Ps. lxxxviii. 12 [13 in Hebr.]).[136]

Sometimes we find Sheol personified, thus in Isa. v. 14 it is depicted as an all-devouring monster: "Therefore Sheol hath enlarged her desire, and opened her mouth without measure; and their glory, and their multitude, and their pomp, and he that rejoiceth among them, descend into it"[137]; and in Ps. cxli. 7 it says, "Our bones are scattered at the mouth of Sheol." Again, in Isa. xxviii. 18 Sheol is personified in the words: "And your covenant with Death shall be disannulled, and your agreement with Sheol shall not stand."

Sheol is the ordinary word used in the Old Testament for the abode of the departed; but there are three other words, found only in late passages, which are sometimes used for this; as they express some of the latest ideas about the underworld before the development of belief began, a word or two on them will be useful. In Isa. xiv. 15 occur the words: "Yet thou shalt be brought down to Sheol, to the uttermost parts of the Pit (*Bor*)"; in Ps. lxxxviii. 4 (5 in Hebr.), "I am counted with them that go down into the Pit"; so, too, in Ps. xxviii. 1, xxx. 3 (4 in Hebr.), cxliii. 7, etc., where it is also used synonymously with Sheol. In Isa. xiv. 19 the curious expression occurs of going down to "the stones of the Pit"; the thought is evidently that of the walls surrounding the city of the dead (cp. the Babylonian idea of the seven walls encircling the realm of the dead). Although this word is generally used as parallel with Sheol, it is possible that in the minds of the writers there existed the idea of its being a special spot in Sheol reserved for the worst enemies of Jahwe; this is the impression gained especially from such passages as Ezek. xxxii. 23, 25, 28–30. If this is so, then we are perhaps justified in seeing the beginnings of the idea of some differentiation between the dwellers in Sheol; the conception of a difference of condition there in accordance with what men's life on, earth had been. It is at the most only a very slight adumbration of what was to come; but seeing that the word occurs only in comparatively late passages, there may be something in this idea.

Then there is the word *Shachath*, which means "corruption" or "destruction"; it is used of the underworld in Isa. xxxviii. 17: "For thou hast kept my soul back from the corruption of non-existence"[138]; again in Isa. li. 14 we read, "…and he shall not die (going down) to corruption," cp. Ii. 14. A very instructive passage is Job xvii. 13–16, which is worth quoting in full as it so well illustrates the use and connotation of the word: "If I look for Sheol as mine house; if I have spread my couch in the darkness; if I have said to corruption (*Shachath*),[139] thou art my father; to the worm, thou art my mother, and my sister; where then is my hope? And as for my hope, who shall see it? It shall go down to the bars of Sheol, where once there is rest in dust." In this passage the full significance of the term is clearly brought out; it has reference to the decay of the body in the grave, but is used as a parallel to Sheol; nothing could more graphically describe the hopeless condition in Sheol. The word occurs also in the passage, already quoted, Ps. xxx. 9 (10 in Hebr.): "What profit is there in my blood when I go down to corruption? Shall the dust praise Thee? shall it declare Thy truth?" Were it not for its parallelism with "the dust," which is often synonymous with Sheol, one might say that *Shachath* referred to the grave only. In Ezek. xxviii. 8 it is said of Tyre: "They shall bring thee down to corruption; and thou shalt die the death of them that are slain, in the heart of the seas"; and lastly, in Jon. ii. 6 (7 in Hebr.) we have a case where the word is obviously meant for Sheol and nothing else: "I went down to the bottoms of the mountains; the earth with her bars closed upon me forever; yet Thou hast brought up my life from corruption (*Shachath*), Jahwe my God." These include all the passages in which *Shachath* is used of the underworld. It is clear that its use emphasizes the belief that Sheol is the end of all things for man.

Finally, we have the word Abaddon, from the root meaning "to perish," which further illustrates what was said about Shachath. It occurs only four times in the Old Testament; in Job xxvi. 6 it is used as a parallel to Sheol: "Sheol is naked before him, and Abaddon hath no covering"; so, too, in Prov. xv. 11. It is personified in Job xxviii. 22: "Abaddon and Death say . . ."[140]; it occurs as a parallel to the grave in Ps. lxxxviii. 11 (12 in Hebr.): "Shall Thy lovingkindness be declared in the grave? Or Thy faithfulness in Abaddon?" These three words, then, which occur only in comparatively late passages, point to the high water mark of the "official" conception regarding the abode of the departed reached before the development of doctrine began.

III. Sheol and the Rephaim

It will thus be seen that the teaching on Sheol in the Old Testament is clear and consistent. If it could be separated from much that is said about those who dwell in Sheol the whole subject would be fairly simple; but it is impossible to do this. We have seen that much that is said about the Rephaim cannot be reconciled with the doctrine of Sheol; and we shall see that this irreconcilability is emphasized by the conviction that the departed could be resorted to for help and counsel (see the chapter on Necromancy); we shall also see that there were some mourning customs which run entirely counter to the normal Sheol belief (see the chapter on Mourning Customs). We are thus led again to the conclusion, already formed with regard to the Rephaim, that the ancient Sheol-belief underwent much modification in the interests of Jahwe-worship. It was necessary to try to convince the people that there was nothing to hope for from the phantoms of men who went down to Sheol, for it was a land from which there was no return; having once entered it there was no possibility of emerging from it; they who were there were incapable of further action; there was an entire end to them so far as the living were concerned. The thoroughgoing way in which this point of view was inculcated has been illustrated.

When we compare the Babylonian beliefs of the underworld and its inhabitants with those of the Old Testament one or two interesting facts present themselves. The extraordinary similarity in many particulars suggests the likelihood of one system borrowing from the other; and as the highly cultured Babylonians were scarcely likely to have borrowed from an insignificant and despised little nation such as the Hebrews must have appeared to them, we must suppose that the borrowing was the other way round; and this is the more likely to have been the case in that we know the Israelites to have been much influenced by the Babylonians in other respects.

Further, there is another interesting fact to consider. We have just seen (and the point is to be further illustrated) that the Old Testament doctrine of Sheol does not fit in with much that we read there about the departed. That is precisely the case (see § I of this chapter) with the Babylonian teaching about the realm of the dead when compared with much that we read of the dead themselves (this, too, will be further illustrated later on). We know the reason of this so far as the Israelites were concerned; may there not have been a cause in some sense analogous to this among the Babylonians? We are unable to say so definitely; but it is possible.

Then one last fact which is also one of interest. Taking the Babylonian doctrine of the departed and the abode of the dead as a whole, there seem to be, from the *data* we have gathered, three stages: there is the ancient belief represented by the story of "The Descent of Ishtar," according to which the distinct possibility is recognized of those who enter the realm of the dead being able to emerge from it; this will be more fully illustrated when we deal with necromancy among the Babylonians. This would correspond with the popular belief of the Israelites which had existed from time immemorial. Then there is the stage in which the realm of the dead is described as "the land without return," dark, silent, and dusty; and this corresponds with the normal Sheol doctrine of the Israelites. Among both peoples there is an overlapping of these stages, resulting in the incompatibilities referred to above. Finally, there is a third stage in which there are distinct adumbrations of a resurrection doctrine, represented by the idea of "awakeners from the dead"; this is clearly a development. The Old Testament presents us with a similar development of doctrine, as we shall see in Chapter XIII.

The Living
and the
Departed

VIII

ANCESTOR-WORSHIP
AND THE CULT OF THE DEAD (I)[141]

It is impossible, when dealing with the subject of Immortality in the Old Testament, to avoid some consideration of the strange old world custom of worshipping the departed.

I. The Origin of Ancestor-worship

How Ancestor-worship and the cult of the dead originally arose is a difficult question, and authorities differ in their views on the subject. The materials for its study are abundant; but the interpretation of the *data* is a different matter. Of one thing there can be no doubt, Ancestor-worship was a development; what it developed from is again a question upon which opinions differ; but Jevons makes out a convincing case for his contention that the natural demonstrations of grief at the death of a relative were the original basis upon which, in the course of ages, the superstructure of Ancestor-worship and the cult of the dead was raised. The simplicity of this theory, remembering that we have to do with primitive man, strongly commends it. Having described the outbursts of sorrow amongst savages on the occasion of a death, Jevons says that while such "spontaneous demonstrations of affection, grief, and desire for reunion with the departed do not amount to worship,"[142] it is possible to trace from them the process by which they developed into Ancestor-worship. "The first condition of any such development," he maintains, "is that the demonstrations, at first spontaneous, should become conventional and harden into custom.... When, then, it has become the tribal custom for relatives to perform certain acts, on the occasion of a death, which were originally spontaneous and now are the conventional expressions of grief, it becomes possible for fear to operate, in support of this as of other tribal customs, though it was not in fear that either it or they originated.... When this demonstration of grief and of affection has become conventional, the neglect of it inevitably comes to be regarded as a want of respect to the deceased, and the performance of it is regarded no longer as a crude attempt to give fresh life to the deceased, but as something done to please him." Proceeding then to discuss the significance of offerings of food, hair, and blood,[143] he points out that these "are elements both of the rites for the dead and of the worship of the gods. But they do not together constitute Ancestor-worship: they are its elements as yet, however, held in suspension and waiting for something to precipitate them. In other words, worship in any proper sense of the word implies worshippers, united either by the natural bond of blood or by the artificial bond of initiation. In the case of Ancestor-worship, the body of worshippers is supplied by the family and united by the natural bond of blood.... When Ancestor-worship is established as a private cult, it, like other private cults, is steadily assimilated in form, in its rites and ceremonies, to the public worship of the gods. The animals which provided the food that the deceased originally was supposed to consume are now sacrificed according to the ritual observed in sacrificing animals to the gods;... When the assimilation of the rites for the dead to the ritual of the gods has proceeded thus far, it naturally happens that in many cases some superhuman powers are ascribed to the spirits of the dead. But it never happens that the spirits of the dead are conceived to be gods.... To speak of the gods as 'deified ancestors,' is to use an expression which covers some ambiguity of thought. If what is implied is that in a community possessing the conception of divine personality, certain ancestors are, by some unexplained process, raised to the rank of gods, the statement may be true, but it does not prove that the gods, to whose rank the spirit is promoted, were themselves originally ghosts which is the very thing that it is intended to prove. What then are these gods? Either they are believed to be the ancestors of some of their worshippers, or they are not. If they are believed to be the ancestors of their worshippers, then they are not believed to have been human[144]: the worshipper's pride is that his ancestor was a god and no mere mortal.... If, on the other hand, a god is not believed to be the ancestor of any of his worshippers, then to assert that he was really a 'deified ancestor' is to make a statement for which there is no evidence.... The fact is that ancestors known to have been human were not worshipped as gods, and that ancestors worshipped as gods were believed not to have been human. This last remark leads us to a generalization which, though obvious, is important: it is that wherever Ancestor-worship exists, it exists side by side with the public worship of the gods of the community. The two systems develop on lines which are parallel, indeed, and therefore never meet; whereas, if they had moved on the same line of development, one would have absorbed the other."[145]

The whole of Jevons' argument, of which we have extracted the salient features, is illuminating, and explains many things in regard to our subject which would otherwise be puzzling. Among the Israelites, judging from the number of direct and indirect references in the Old Testament, Ancestor-worship and the Cult of the Dead must at one time have been widely prevalent. Considering the polemic against them in the interests of Jahwe-worship, considering also the fact that the books of the Old Testament were finally redacted by men who would have been interested in removing all traces of cults other than that of Jahwe-worship from its pages, it is surprising that we find as much reference to the subject there as is actually the case. It is true that most of these references are contained in prohibitions, which doubtless accounts for their having been permitted to remain there; but it is just these very prohibitions which testify to the prevalence of the beliefs and rites connected with Ancestor-worship and the Cult of the Dead. Nothing, however, could illustrate more pointedly the belief in

Immortality than this conviction that men were able by various means to communicate with their departed relatives. That there was endless super-stition and crass folly, and also doubtless some chicanery about it all, must not blind us to the reality of the belief, however mistaken. And when all is said and done, it is only right to remember that it contained one element, at all events, which later ages recognized as true, namely that the departed were living in a real sense, and were not the lifeless shades of Sheol which for centuries the religious teachers taught was the case. But before coming to the Old Testament it will be well to say a brief word again about Baby-lonian belief and custom on the subject, since, as is well known, Israelite belief can in many ways be illustrated by the old culture of the lands that lay to the east.

II. Ancestor-worship among the Babylonians

In speaking of Ancestor-worship Tylor says that it is "one of the great branches of the religion of mankind. Its principles," he continues, "are not difficult to understand, for they plainly keep up the social relations of the living world, The dead ancestor, now passed into a deity, simply goes on protecting his own family and receiving suit and service from them as of old; the dead chief still watches over his own tribe, still holds his authority by helping friends and harming enemies, still rewards the right and sharply punishes the wrong."[146] The earliest records in existence, so far as is known, in which definite reference is made to Ancestor-worship among the ancient Babylonians, witness to a stage of culture in advance of that presupposed by Tylor in this quotation; but they, nevertheless, bear out what he says. Examples of early Babylonian rulers being deified and worshipped are those of Sargon I and Gudea. They lived about 3300 B.C. and in later days were regarded as great heroes of the past to whom divine honours were paid; the same is true of Dungi I, who lived still earlier. On tablets in which their names occur the determinative that is placed before the names of gods is put in front of their names. Festivals were celebrated in their honour, and sacrifices were offered to them; statues of them were placed in temples, where they were worshipped. "In paying honour to deified kings and other great personages, the sons and other descendants would, but naturally and in accordance with an established rule, take the lead, and the people generally would share in the celebrations; so that we have here instances, firstly of Ancestor-worship in the strict sense of the word, and secondly in its wider, if looser, signification as homage paid to the departed kings and fathers of the people."[147] In earlier ages, we may be certain from the analogy of many other peoples,[148] that the same thing was done in the case of tribal chiefs before dynasties became established. Further, "an ancient Babylonian bronze tablet, which represents a funeral sceneexhibits the dead person lying on a bier, attended by priests in fish-like garments, with a stand for burning incense not far from the head of the bier. In much later times we have the case of King Asshurbanipal [he reigned 668–626 B.C.] appearing at the tombs of his ancestors with rent garments, pouring out a libation in memory of the dead, and addressing a prayer to them...." The offering of libations appears, among the Babylonians and Assyrians, to have been one of the most important rites in connexion with the cult of the dead; this was primarily the duty of the son of the departed, who offered them regularly on the anniversary of the death of his father. This day was known as "the day of the festival of the dead," "the day of humiliation," "the day of wailing," "the day of mourning"; all these occur. There was a special priest, known as "the pourer out of water," who performed this rite. On the inscription of Asshurbanipal, just referred to, it is said: "During the mourning ceremony of offering libations for the spirits of my royal ancestors, I put on mourning garments, and accomplished an act of benevolence to God and men, to the dead and to the living." Then there follows a prayer offered to his ancestors by the side of their tombs. The same king tells of how he offered a sacrifice of vengeance on the spot where Sennacherib, his grandfather, was murdered; he tells how he here sacrificed a number of prisoners of war in honour of his ancestor.[149]

These are only a few examples, but the evidence, so far as it goes, shows clearly that even in historical times the Cult of the Dead and the element of Ancestor-worship formed, more or less distinctly, part of the

Babylonian and Assyrian religious observances. "As regards deification of deceased ancestors, sacrifices in the proper sense of the word, and festivals held in honour of the dead, the clear evidence, as was to be expected, relates to the ruling families only. It may, by analogy with the religious development of other races, be assumed that Ancestor-worship and the Cult of the Dead were more prevalent in prehistoric times than later on."[150]

III. Ancestor-worship in the Old Testament

Ancestor-worship, as distinct from the Cult of the Dead is not prominent in the Old Testament; this is what we should expect. Traces of its having once existed in ancient Israel are, however, not wanting. But even if there were not the slightest trace of it there, two considerations would justify us in believing that it was at one time practiced by the Israelites. First, its practically universal existence among all peoples in a certain stage of culture; there is no reason to suppose that the ancient Israelites were an exception to the rule. And secondly, its wide prevalence at the present day in Syria.

The most pronounced trace (it would be no exaggeration to call it proof) in the Old Testament of the existence of Ancestor-worship among the ancient Israelites is the fact that many of the ancestral graves were holy sites, i.e. sanctuaries.[151] Thus, the grave of Sarah, the cave of Macpelah "which was before Mamre" in Hebron (Gen. xxiii.), was a sanctuary, as is shown in Gen. xiii. 18: "And Abram moved his tent, and came and dwelt by the oaks[152] ['oak' in the Septuagint] of Mamre, which are in Hebron, and built there an altar unto Jahwe"; this is shown further in Gen. xviii. 1, where it is said that Jahwe appeared here. Theophanies took place only on holy sites. The two latter passages which belong to the earlier document called J speak of the oaks (originally "oak" as still preserved in the Septuagint) of Mamre, while the first, which is from the document P, and much later, belonging to a time when Jahwe-worship was fully established, leaves out all mention of the oaks, or oak; the reason is that by his time holy trees were regarded as heathenish and incompatible with Jahwe-worship. A holy tree was in ancient Israel one of the necessary adjuncts to an altar. So, too, in the case of Deborah, Rebekah's nurse; she was buried "under the oak; and the name of it was called Allon-bacuth," i.e. "the oak of weeping" (Gen. xxxv. 8); also Joseph's grave in Shechem (Josh. xxiv. 32), for, according to Gen. xii. 6, xxxv. 4, this sanctuary was also marked by a holy tree. In the case of Miriam's grave, Hadesh (Num. xx. I), the name itself, which means "holy," shows that it was a sanctuary; moreover from Judges iv. II it is clear that a holy oak stood here too. Another thing which proves that a grave was a place of worship is when a pillar (*Mazzebah*) is set up on the site, for this, too, in ancient Israel was one of the adjuncts to an altar. In Gen. xxxv. 20 we read of Rachel's grave that "Jacob set up a pillar upon her grave; the same is the Pillar of Rachel's grave unto this day"; it was evidently a well-known spot, from 1 Sam. x. 2. There can be no doubt that in all these cases the graves were places of worship at which an ancestor was at one time worshipped, but which in later days were adapted to the worship of Jahwe. The same is, in all probability, true of a number of other graves of ancestral heroes, though the Hebrew text does not imply this as in the cases cited above. Such are Timnath-serah (Josh. xix. 50, xxiv. 30, Timnath-heres in Judges ii. 9), the burial place of Joshua; Shamir, where Tola was buried (Judges x. 2); Hamon, where Jair was buried (Judges x. 5); Bethlehem, the burial place of Ibzan (Judges xii. 10); Aijalon, the burial place of Elon (Judges xii. 12); Pirathon, the burial place of Abdon (Judges xii. 15); the spot between Zorah and Eshtaol where they buried Samson (Judges xvi. 31). In all these cases, as Moore rightly points out, "we are probably to infer that the tomb of the eponymous ancestor of the clan was in later times shown"[153]; judging from the analogy of the other cases referred to above, we are justified in believing that these were sanctuaries and if so, then the ancestors of the different clans were worshipped there.

IV. Ancestor-worship in Syria at the Present Day

What has been said receives interesting and instructive confirmation from the belief and practice of the peoples of Palestine and Syria generally, as well as Arabia, at the present day. It is a well-established fact, proved by numberless examples, that customs and beliefs in the East, existing at the present day, go back to the dim ages of the past. Men who have spent years in the East studying the religious and social customs of the native dwellers of Syria and Arabia have shown in their writings, where detailed proofs are given, that when one once gets off the beaten track of travelers, and penetrates into the central parts of Arabia, into the wilder parts of Syria, and into Mesopotamia, the conditions of life, the tribal and social customs, and above all, the religious beliefs and practices, are today very much the same as they were millennia before the Christian era. One of the most recent and learned of these travelers writes in a work the importance of which is widely recognized: "The simplicity of the Semitic mind accounts for the survival of ancient customs which have been handed down from the remotest antiquity, notwithstanding the teachings of Islam and Christianity. To the Arab or Syrian, custom is mightier than right; indeed, custom is the only right he knows. Both morality and religion depend upon it. The heavens might sooner fall than custom be set aside. If we can get to the usage of the Semite we shall know what his religion is."[154] Some reference to what this observer and writer says about Ancestor-worship at the present day throw much light on the Old Testament passages on the subject just referred to. "Among most sects of Moslems and Christians, including Bedouins as well as Syrians," says Curtiss, "the worship of saints exists. In the popular imagination they exercise a power far above that of God." "These saints are really departed spirits, connected with some particular shrine, chosen because they revealed themselves there in times past, and where they are wont to reveal themselves now to those who seek their favour." There is a close connexion between the ordinary spirit of the departed and that of the saint "who is supposed to possess superior sanctity and power." "Every shrine, of whatever sort, theoretically presupposes a *weli* or saint. He may have lived within the memory of the generation that does him honour, and many tales may have been preserved in regard to him. Or he may be a mythical character about whom a profusion of folklore has sprung up." They are firmly believed to appear to many of their worshippers. The extraordinarily vivid imagination of the Eastern, coupled with the colossal ignorance regarding many a simple natural phenomenon, are responsible for the conviction among numbers of these mentally primitive people that a saint has appeared to them in bodily form. Theoretically these saints "are worshipped in connexion with the God of all the world; practically many people know no other god."[155] These saints are the spirits of men who used to be living on earth. The local shrines where these spirits of ancestors are supposed to take up their abode at certain times are, thus, of special interest in view of what we read about shrines connected with the name of an ancestor or a clan hero in the Old Testament. Of not less interest, as touching directly upon our subject, is the character of these shrines. And here again Curtiss gives us full information. There are, of course, many shrines which have been specially built in honour of some tribal chief or the like; but by far the greater number are not buildings. First among these are sacred stones; here is an example: "At Haryatan, the last outpost for travelers making the journey to Palmyra… in the vineyard, at the rear of the house of the governor of the town…is a prostrate pillar, by the side of which is a structure of mud about the size and shape of a straw beehive; on the side of this is a small hole, where the vessel is placed in which the oil that has been vowed is burned, when a vow is paid. The shrine consisting in this pillar is called by the Moslems Abu Risha, and by the Christians Mar Risha. It is in honour of a saint of the sect of the Jacobites. The pillar is thought by the Syrian priest to mark the site of an ancient church. It is surrounded by a low wall, leaving an enclosure of about twenty feet square. The practices in making a vow and in payment of it are the same among the Moslems and the Christians. They come to the shrine and make their request; they also tie red and blue silk around the weeds in the enclosure as a sign to the saint that they want help. Payment is made in oil, which is burned at the altar."[156] This is only one of many examples given by Curtiss, to whom the reader must be referred. As in the case of sacred stones and rocks, so, too, the spirits of departed ancestors are believed to dwell close to certain springs and wells; these, also, for that reason partake of the nature of a shrine and are looked upon as sacred. But as important as any of these shrines of ancestors are those marked by sacred trees, which vividly recalls some of the Old Testament instances given above. "Some of these are at shrines, and are sacred merely as the property of the saint. They are as inviolable as anything else that belongs to him, or that has been put under his protection.… There are also many trees apart from shrines, which are believed to be possessed by spirits, to whom vows and sacrifices are made.…. There is no doubt that in the minds of the people sacred trees are places where spirits reveal themselves."[157] Other trees are looked upon as holy because some great man during his lifetime rested under them; and it is believed that he is still present in the spirit there at certain times. In some cases, indeed, he is supposed to take up his abode there permanently. In all these cases these spots are sanctuaries where worship in one form or another is offered to a departed great one, be he ancestor, hero, religious leader, or what not. For further details on the subjects dealt with see, among other works: Doughty, *Travels in Arabia Deserta*, i. 365 ff.; Baudissin, *Studien zur Semitischen Religionsgeschichte*, ii. 145 ff.; Goldziher, *Muhammedanische Studien*, ii. 345 ff.; Stade, *Geschichte des Volkes Israel*, i. 454 ff.; von Gall, *Altisraelitische Kultstiitten*, passim; Stade, *Biblische Theologie des alten Testamentes*, i. 110 ff.; Schumacher, in the *Zeitschrift des Deutschen Paliistina-Vereins*, ix. 206 ff.; Wellhausen, *Reste Arabischen Heidentums*, 104 ff., Robertson Smith, The Religion of the Semites, 166–196, 203 ff.; Frazer, "The Golden Bough," *The Magic and the Evolution of Kings*, ch. viii.; Jevons, *Introduction to the History of Religion*, ch. xvi.

V. A Further Remnant of Ancestor-worship in the Old Testament

Another remnant of Ancestor-worship found in the Old Testament, but in this case restricted to the royal family (cp. what was said above regarding Babylonian usage), is preserved in Jer. xxxiv. 5, where the prophet says in reference to Zedekiah, king of Judah: "Thou shalt not die by the sword; thou shalt die in peace; and with the burnings of thy fathers, the former kings which were before thee, so shall they make a burning for thee." The incense-offering to a departed monarch was thus customary in Israel up to the end of the monarchy. In 2 Chron. xvi. 14, again, it is said of Asa: "And they buried him in his own sepulchers, which he had hewn out for himself in the city of David, and laid him in the bed which was filled with sweet odors and divers kind of spices prepared by the apothecaries' art; and they made a very great burning for him." And, once more, in 2 Chron. xxi. 19 it is said of Jehoram: "And it came to pass in process of time, at the end of two years, that his bowels fell out by reason of his sickness, and he died of sore diseases. And his people made no burning for him, like the burning of his fathers." It is quite probable that by the time Chronicles was written the original meaning of this was not realized, and that it would have been described as merely an act of respect for the departed king. But it is well known how customs are continued long after their real signification has been forgotten, and this is especially true of mourning customs. These "burnings for the dead" were remnants of a time when incense offerings were offered in the firm belief in the continued life of the departed, who was thus propitiated; he was believed to be really present, though invisible to those who stood before his body. We are reminded of the words which occur in the *Descent of Ishtar*: "May the dead rise up [from the underworld] and smell the incense."[158]

VI. THE TERAPHIM

In about a dozen passages in the Old Testament mention is made of the "Teraphim." The word from which this word comes (חרף) means "to nourish" or "to maintain." Its use in the plural form is somewhat analogous to Elohim, which can either mean "God" (e.g. Gen. i. I), or "gods" (e.g. Deut. iv. 28), though as a rule the meaning is singular though the form is plural.[159] But unlike Elohim, Teraphim occurs only in the plural. From this fact we must assume that, properly speaking, the Teraphim were several in number. In 1 Sam. xix. 13, 16, in which a singular sense is implied, Michal had a special reason for putting only one image in the

bed; indeed, the fact that in this case the plural and not the singular form
is used, shows that the word was only known and used in its plural form.

It is probable that the Teraphim were of non-Israelite origin, for in
Gen. xxxi. 20, 24, 47, Laban, the owner of Teraphim, is spoken of as
"Laban the Aramrean" (Syrian).

If, as is probable, the word in its root signification means "nourishers"
or "maintainers," we may ask whom they were supposed to nourish or
maintain. From the fact that they are spoken of as being kept in houses
(Gen. xxxi. 19, Judges xvii. 5, I Sam. xix. 13, 16), it may be assumed that
the family was under their care. It would appear, moreover, that the father
(i.e. the head) of the family looked upon them as belonging especially to
him, see Gen. xxxi.19, "Rachel stole the Teraphim that were her father's";
and in verse 30, "Wherefore hast thou stolen my gods?" That they are
called "gods" is significant. In Judges xvii. it is Micah, the head of the family, who is the owner of the Teraphim, and the same may reasonably be
assumed of David in 1 Sam. xix. 11–17. From these facts we are justified
in seeing in the Teraphim household gods, and that their worship was, in
fact, a remnant of Ancestor-worship. It is interesting to note that Josephus
says that in Mesopotamia it was the custom of the land for people to possess household gods, and to bear them off when journeying.[160]

Though in later times Teraphim were regarded with abhorrence
(2 Kings xxiii. 24, Zech. x. 2), yet in earlier days they were evidently a regular element in worship, and no objection was taken to them (Judges xvii 5,
Hosea iii. 4, and the other passages already cited). In shape and appearance
they looked like a man; this seems clear from 1 Sam. xix. 13, 16.

The special function of the Teraphim, besides that of protecting the
family, seems to have been their use in divining the future, for they are
mentioned several times in conjunction with the Ephod; but on this see
below, pp. 135 f.

So far we have dealt only with Ancestor-worship; closely connected
with this is the Cult of the Dead generally; to this we must devote a separate chapter.

IX

ANCESTOR-WORSHIP AND THE CULT OF THE DEAD (II)[161]

I. THE CULT OF THE DEAD

Ancestor-worship and the Cult of the Dead may be regarded as coming under one and the same category, but they are two distinct things. The Cult of the Dead was practiced for ages before such a thing as Ancestor-worship existed. The former developed into the latter; yet both continued side by side. The attitude of the living towards the dead was largely conditioned by what their relationship towards each other had been on earth. On the death of an ordinary member of a family most of the funeral rites had as their object the providing of the deceased with things he had been accustomed to have when alive, and which it was believed he would still require after death; in such "offerings" there was not necessarily any idea of worship. If the father of a family died the attitude towards him was somewhat different; during his life he had occupied a position of honour as being the head of the family. It was natural, therefore, that after death the homage that had been rendered to him during his lifetime would be continued. This did not necessarily constitute worship, but it was certainly a step towards it. If the head of a clan died there was a nearer approach to worship; he had occupied a unique position when alive, and had been the

99

object of special honour; when this continued after death it is not difficult to see that something akin to worship might very easily arise. As a matter of fact, it is this latter which developed into Ancestor-worship proper, while at the same time care for the ordinary dead continued as hitherto.

But there was another element which entered into the whole subject, and that was the extent to which the spirits of the departed were looked upon as supernatural. The evidence is conflicting and difficult; authorities differ; dogmatism in such case were folly; one can only reach tentative conclusions. *Some* idea of the supernatural was, we believe, always felt in regard to the spirits of the departed; it may have been, it doubtless was, vague; all kinds of thoughts, acts, and wants, analogous to those of the living, might have been, and were, imputed to them; but the very fact of their invisibility was sufficient to suggest instinctively the idea of the supernatural. To urge that the incompatibility of a supernatural spirit having temporal wants upsets the argument would show unfamiliarity with the way of thinking among uncultured peoples. To early man the spirits of the departed partook of the supernatural; and while it was believed that they had natural wants which had to be supplied by the living, and which therefore made them in some respects dependent upon the living, there was another side to it all, in that they possessed powers which mortals did not possess; they had superior knowledge; they could help men and harm them; therefore it was necessary that they should be attended to and propitiated.

Such ideas, with their consequential acts, did not, of course, arise all at once; but in course of time they came into the minds of men as they thought about their departed. Acts of affection, piety, reverence, homage, worship, run into one another almost unconsciously; and it is likely enough that an act which was originally simply one of filial piety might, through having become part of a fixed ritual, develop into an act of worship. In some funeral rites it is not always easy to decide whether it is an act of affection or worship which is offered.

However this may be, there is no question that in the Old Testament we have various references which undoubtedly point to the fact that the

Cult of the Dead was practiced among the Israelites; this bears distinct witness to the belief in the continued life of the departed. To these references we will now turn.

II. THE CULT OF THE DEAD IN THE OLD TESTAMENT; JER. XVI. 5–8

In Jer. xvi. 5–8 we read; "For thus saith Jahwe, enter not into the house of mourning, neither go to lament, neither bemoan them.... Both great and small shall die in this land; they shall not be buried, neither shall men lament for them...neither shall men break bread for them in mourning, to comfort them for the dead; neither shall men give them the cup of consolation to drink for their father or for their mother. And thou shalt not go into the house of feasting to sit with them, to eat and drink." The references here to offerings and drink-offerings to the dead, and to funeral feasts, however much toned down, are sufficiently clear. They are also referred to in other passages; in Deut. xxvi. 14 the funeral feast,[162] with offerings to the dead, is regarded as prevalent since it is evidently thought a righteous act to abstain from partaking of it; it is there said that the righteous man who has given the tithe to the Levite, to the stranger, to the fatherless, and to the widow, has not eaten thereof in his mourning; the text continues; "neither have I put away thereof, being unclean, nor given thereof for the dead," cp. Lev. xxi. 6. Reference to the funeral feast is also contained in Ezek. xxiv. 17; "...make no mourning for the dead, bind thy headtire upon thee, and put thy shoes upon thy feet, and cover not thy lips, and eat not the bread of men"; and in Hosea ix. 3, 4; "They shall not dwell in Jahwe's land; but Ephraim shall return to Egypt, and they shall eat unclean food in Assyria. They shall not pour out wine offerings to Jahwe, neither shall they be pleasing unto Him; their sacrifices shall be unto them as the bread of mourners; all that eat thereof shall be polluted; for their bread shall be for their appetite; it shall not come into the house of Jahwe" (cp. *Ep. of Jer.* 32, *Book of Jubilees* xxii. 17). In spite of the vigorous polemic against the Cult of the Dead in the interests of Jahwe-worship it is not difficult to see that this universal custom in antiquity continued among the Israelites; but the full significance of such passages as those quoted will become apparent if they are illustrated by Babylonian and Arab practice, and more especially by the revelations of recent Palestine excavation, as well as by present-day custom in Syria.

In referring to the practice among the ancient Babylonians Langdon writes; "Each family seems to have made monthly offerings to the shades of its ancestors, which consisted in a communion meal at which images of the departed were present. In official accounts of the early period we find frequent reference to offerings made to the statues of deceased persons.... Entries in official documents occur, stating the items of the monthly sacrifice for the souls of deceased persons whose service to the State had been great. This is especially true of kings and priests. More frequently the documents mention the mortuary sacrifices for all the souls who have died, a Feast of All Souls, occurring monthly and performed by the priests in various temples. The word ordinarily employed in the ancient inscriptions is *kianag* 'place where one gives to drink'; but the notion of place is often lost, and the idea of drinking is made to cover sacrifices of animals, bread, cakes, etc., as well as of liquors.... Another word—also Sumerian, and employed for the *parentalia* less frequently in the early period, but ordinarily by the Semites—is *kisig*, 'breaking of bread,' where the emphasis is laid upon the eating of bread at a common meal."[163] An inscription which is then quoted gives "direct evidence for a communion meal, 'breaking of bread,' for the souls of the dead, permanently adopted by the Semites at any early period." The expression "breaking of bread" is interesting as being identical with what Jeremiah says.

There is evidence of like usage among the ancient Arabs. Wellhausen says that "it cannot be denied that remains of a regular cult of the dead, of Ancestor and Hero-worship, are not wanting"[164]; he refers especially to the drink offerings at the graves of the departed, where the mourners drank to the departed and then poured out what was left in their drinking-vessels on to the grave; we are reminded of Asshurbanipal pouring out a drink-offering at the tombs of his ancestors.[165] The "cup of consolation" spoken of by Jeremiah was thus probably drunk at the grave, the actual funeral feast taking place later on. Doughty says that regular sacrifices *for* the dead are offered by modern Arabs down to the third generation,[166] and this is also borne out by Curtiss;[167] but that there are also sacrifices *to* the dead he also shows; "The sacrifices offered to the saints are, of course, really made to those who were once mortals. It is true of the Nusairiyeh that they sacrifice not to God, but to the *weli* (saint); they pray to the *weli* who did good deeds, and when he died was saved without any punishment." He also shows how the sacrifice *for* a dead man is offered *to* a departed saint; "The animal [that is sacrificed] is a spirit, and the sick person [who eventually dies] is a spirit. The saint accepts one in place of another; that is, the soul of the animal in the place of the soul of the man."[168]

The funeral feasts which, as we have seen, were in vogue among the Israelites and Babylonians, and were held in honour of the departed, may in all probability be illustrated by an interesting discovery made on the site of ancient Gezer. In a burial cave were found the remains of fifteen persons, and with them a number of bronze weapons; "the bodies were not cast in, or fallen in by accident, but were deposited in position by people who descended with them into the cave. This was shown by three indications; (1) no bodies lay immediately under the entrance, as would have been the case had they fallen in; (2) stones were laid under, round, and sometimes above them; (3) a large quantity of charcoal found among the bones showed that a funeral-feast sacrifice or similar rite had taken place within the chamber." After further describing the position of the skeletons together with various bronze spearheads, etc., the writer continues; "Besides the bronze there was also found a cow's horn and a three-legged stone fire-dish for cooking. The latter was broken, and inverted over some sheep bones, no doubt the remains of a food deposit. It is not quite safe to assume that the fracturing of the fire-dish is in accordance with the well-known custom of fracturing objects deposited in graves, that their spirits may be released and minister to the needs of the spirits of the departed.[169] ...But the chief problem presented by the cave lies in the extraordinary circumstances attending the single female interment. The body had been cut in two just below the ribs, and the upper half alone was deposited in the cave. Obviously the explanation of the condition of this skeleton turns primarily on the question whether the mutilation was *ante* or *post mortem*. If *post mortem*, we have evidently to deal with a burial custom in some degree analogous to that illustrated by Dr. Petrie's discoveries at Naqada.... If the mutilation was *ante mortem*, two possible explanations are forthcoming; we have to deal with the victim of a murder, or of a sacrifice. The last seems to me the most satisfactory. Had the case been simply one of murder, of a peculiarly savage and clumsy character, most probably both halves of the body would have been got rid of by depositing them together. But in the case of sacrifice it is quite conceivable that the missing half might have been disposed of in some other manner. It might, for instance, have been burned, or even—so persistent are the survivals of savagery in natural religion, even when a comparatively civilized condition has been attained—ceremonially eaten."[170]

The *stratum* in which these skeletons were found belonged to pre-Israelite times; but this does not, of course, preclude the possibility of the episode having taken place in Israelite times; we have abundant evidence in the Old Testament that practically up to the end of the monarchy the old Canaanite rites and customs tended to crop up every now and again among the Israelites; indeed, the presumption is that they never wholly ceased until well after the exile. Whatever actually happened during the rather gruesome episode referred to, it may be regarded as certain that it had something to do with the Cult of the Dead; sacrificial meals and sacrifices in honour of a *deity* were celebrated in "high places" and other sanctuaries, not in underground burial caves; on the face of it, any ritual act which took place in such places had reference to the dead. The idea of the occurrence in question being a murder is fantastic; it was evidently a sacrifice to the dead, having regard to the *place* of offering, but of some very special kind. Human sacrifices to heathen deities by the Israelites are spoken of in the Old Testament; it is quite conceivable that it was in some sense an analogous rite that this fourteen year old girl was sacrificed—altogether abnormal as it would have been—to propitiate the dead for some special reason. But be that as it may, no doubt can exist that a sacrificial funeral feast of some sort took place on this occasion; the occurrence of such continued, according to the Old Testament, until comparatively late times, for in Isa. lxv. 3, 4, we read of "a people that provoketh Me to My face continually, sacrificing in gardens, and burning incense upon bricks; which abide among the graves and lodge in the vaults; which eat swine's flesh, and broth of abominable things is in their vessels."[171]

As to the object of these funeral feasts in general, this is well put forth by Hartland, who says that it is "not simply hospitality to the invited guests; they indeed very often contribute their full share in kind. Nor is the object merely the enjoyment of those who partake, or a natural reaction from sorrow, or ostentation on the part of those who provide them. Doubtless some or all of these impulses do enter into the motives for the frequently repeated and usually extravagant displays, and the gluttony and carousing inseparable from them. But there are deeper reasons for the observance. The above reasons would be insufficient of themselves to account for the practice, shared by civilized Europeans with savage Ainu, of holding the first formal meal in the presence of the corpse, or on the grave, if they would not indeed positively repel it. Moreover, the ceremonial of such a meal is not always that of abandonment to the pleasures of the table and of social intercourse; and, finally, the deceased is himself, even after cremation or burial, regarded as one of the *convives*. The belief that the dead man is present and joins in the feast is very widespread, and is evidenced in more ways than one...."[172]

III. The Cult of the Dead in the Old Testament; Isa. lxv. 3.

The quotation from Isaiah (lxv. 3) given above leads us to another piece of ritual in the Cult of the Dead. Reference is there made to "burning incense upon bricks," and the context shows that it was to the dead that this was offered; this is also spoken of in Jer. xli. 5. We referred in the previous chapter to the "burnings" for the dead kings and to Babylonian practice in this respect. Langdon quotes an inscription in which reference is made to the monthly sacrifices performed for the souls of the departed;

it is said there; "...As incense-offering, the choice incense as a regular offering I fixed for them and placed before them."[173] Wellhausen refers to the burning of sweet-smelling wood in honour of the dead among the Arabs.[174]

Here we may also touch upon another custom greatly in vogue in ancient Israel, though not referred to in the Old Testament, viz. that of placing little lamps in graves. These have been found in great quantities in the recent excavations in Palestine, and belong to pre-Israelite as well as Israelite times; they are frequently found together with little food-bowls (see further, Mourning and Burial Customs, Chap. XL) in tombs and under house-walls. Mr. Macalister suggests that these lamps may be reminiscent of the funeral sacrifice involving fire, which in the symbolized rite is typified by the lamp; in this case they would represent a sacrifice to the dead. But it is possible that these lamps were intended to give light to the departed on their journey to the underworld; in this case the subject would come under Mourning and Burial Customs. However this may be, the fact that they are found under house-walls as well as in tombs leads us to the further subject of bodies being buried in houses.[175] Whether this should come under the head of the Cult of the Dead is uncertain (we shall return to the custom when dealing with Mourning and Burial Customs), for the evidence is insufficient for reaching a definite conclusion. But we have seen, in speaking about the Teraphim, that the early Israelites had household gods; it is, therefore, conceivable that the burying of the dead in the walls of houses had something to do with this. Samuel, as we know, was spoken of as a "god," and we read of his having been buried in his house in Ramah (1 Sam. xxv. 1); the custom was evidently not uncommon, see 1 Kings ii. 34.

IV. CUTTINGS IN THE BODY AND HAIR-OFFERINGS

Finally, we must refer to a practice which, although it is to be reckoned among mourning customs, was, as we shall see intended to be an act of propitiation for the dead, and must therefore be considered here.

In Lev. xxi. 1–5 (cp. verses 10, 11) occurs the following prohibition addressed to priests; "There shall none defile himself for the dead among his people; except for his kin, that is near unto him, for his mother, and for his father, and for his son, and for his daughter, and for his brother; and for his sister a virgin, that is near unto him, which have had no husband, for her may he defile himself. He shall not defile himself, being a chief man among his people, to profane himself"; then follow the mourning customs which defile; "They shall not make baldness upon their head, neither shall they shave off the corner of their beard, nor make any cuttings in their flesh." The same prohibition, applied generally, is found in Lev. xix. 27, 28; "Ye shall not round the corners of your heads, neither shalt thou mar the corners of thy beard. Ye shall not make any cuttings in your flesh for the dead, nor print any marks upon you; I am Jahwe." That these prohibitions are found in the Levitical Code,[176] which at the earliest belongs to the exilic period, shows how tenaciously the people had clung to the customs referred to. Ezekiel refers to the same practices (vii. 18). Jeremiah mentions them several times; in foretelling the downfall of Judah he says there will be no mourners; "Both great and small shall die in this land; they shall not be buried, neither shall men lament for them, nor cut themselves, nor make themselves bald for them" (xvi. 6); in xii. 5 mourners are spoken of who shaved their beards, rent their clothes, and cut themselves for the dead, cp. xlvii. 5; and in speaking of the fall of Moab the prophet says; "...Every head is bald, and every beard clipped; upon all hands are cuttings, . . ." (xlviii. 37, cp. xxv. 23). In the same manner in much earlier times Micah takes up his lament, saying; "Make thee bald, and poll thee for the children of thy delight; enlarge thy baldness as the vulture; for they are gone into captivity from thee" (i. 16). So, too, Isaiah, in the "Oracle of Moab," says; "...On all their heads is baldness, every beard is cut off . . ." (cp. xxii. 12). Still earlier Amos says; "And I will turn your feasts into mourning, and all your songs into lamentation; and I will bring sackcloth upon all loins, and baldness upon every head; and I will make it as the mourning for an only son" (viii. 10). In all these passages, with the exception of Lev. xix. 27, 28 (in Lev. xxi. 1–5 the prohibition is qualified) there is no word of condemnation for these customs, and they are clearly looked upon as the regular thing. In only one other passage is there an unqualified prohibition, viz. Deut. xiv. 1: "Ye are the children of Jahwe your God; ye shall not cut yourselves, nor make any baldness between your eyes for the dead"; here, too, the prohibition is general, and not confined to priests.

It is thus only in two late codes that this prohibition is found; the prophets who mention the customs have nothing to say against them. The reason for this is conceivably owing to the fact that such "cuttings in the flesh" were common among the worshippers of Jahwe for other purposes, and were therefore not regarded as necessarily evil. It would take us too far afield to deal with this other category of markings and cuttings; we must content ourselves with the bare statement that the worshippers of Jahwe had marks upon their body as signs that they belonged to Him; for the proof of the statement the reader is referred to the following passages; Exod. iv. 24–26, xiii. 9, 16, 1 Kings xx. 35 ff., cp. Ezek. ix. 4, Isa. xliv. 5, Zech. xiii. 6; from the exile onwards circumcision was regarded as the sign *par excellence* of a worshipper of Jahwe; on the whole subject see Stade in the *Zeitschrift für die alt-testamentliche Wissenschaft*, xiv. pp. 308–318.

The customs, then, with which we are here concerned are (i) making bald the head and shaving the beard, besides tattooing, "for the dead," and (ii) making cuttings in the flesh "for the dead"; the two belong together and illustrate how difficult it is sometimes, in mourning customs, to say where a sign of affection merges into an act of worship. In the cases before us the fact that both offerings of hair and cuttings in the flesh constituted acts in the worship of a god shows that the cult-idea cannot have been altogether absent when these were offered to the departed. We have, first of all, the well-known case in 1 Kings xviii. 26 of the worshippers of Baal cutting themselves in order to propitiate their god; the same custom is referred to in Hosea vii. 14 (see R.V. marg., where the correct reading is given). "Among the Hebrews and Arabs," says Robertson Smith,[177] "and indeed among many other peoples both ancient and modern, the laceration of the flesh in mourning is associated with the practice of shaving

the head or cutting off part of the hair and depositing it in the tomb or
on the funeral pyre. Here also a comparison of the usage of more primitive races shows that the rite was originally two-sided, and had exactly the
same sense as the offering of the mourner's blood.… Now among the
Semites and other ancient peoples the hair-offering is common, not only
in mourning but in the worship of the gods, and the details of the ritual
in the two cases are so exactly similar that we cannot doubt that a single
principle is involved in both." Examples to any extent could be given; we
must content ourselves with the following references in addition to Robertson Smith; Hartland, *The Legend of Perseus*, ii. passim; Wilken, *Ueber
das Haaropfer und einige andre Trauergebrauche bei den Volkern Indonesiens*,
in the "*Revue colonial internationale*," iii. 225 ff., iv. 345 ff.; Wellhausen,
op. cit., 167 ff., 181 f.; Goldziher, *op. cit.*, i. 248 f.; Jevons, *op. cit.*, pp. 193
ff., 220; Frazer, "The Golden Bough," *The Dying God*, pp. 92 ff., *Adonis,
Attis, Osiris*, p. 268, *Taboo and the Perils of the Soul*, pp. 283 ff.; *Folklore in
the Old Testament*, iii. pp. 270 ff.

After his exhaustive examination of the evidence Frazer, in the last
work mentioned, p. 303, says; "So far as it goes, however, the preceding
inquiry tends to confirm the view that the widespread practices of cutting
the bodies and shearing the hair of the living after a death were originally
designed to gratify or benefit in some way the spirit of the departed; and
accordingly, wherever such customs have prevailed, they may be taken as
evidence that the people who observed them believed in the survival of
the human soul after death and desired to maintain friendly relations with
it. In other words, the observance of these usages implies a propitiation or
worship of the dead. Since the Hebrews appear to have long cut both their
bodies and their hair in honour of their departed relations, we may safely
include them among the many tribes and nations who have at one time
or another been addicted to that worship of ancestors which, of all forms
of primitive religion, has probably enjoyed the widest popularity and
exerted the deepest influence on mankind. The intimate connexion of
these mourning customs with the worship of the dead was probably well
remembered in Israel down to the close of the monarchy, and may have

furnished the religious reformers of that age with their principal motive for prohibiting extravagant displays of sorrow which they justly regarded as heathenish."

For other forms of offerings to the dead among the Bedouins of today, see Burckhardt, *Bedouinen und Wahaby*, pp. 84 f.; Doughty, *Travels in Arabia Deserta*, i. pp. 240, 293, 354, 442, 450 ff.

X

NECROMANCY

Necromancy is a department of the larger subject of Divination which has been practiced among men from very early ages, and which arose from the innate desire on their part to know the future. But those who are able, or who are supposed to be able, to give information regarding the future must clearly possess powers denied to men of ordinary nature; they must, that is to say, be supernatural beings. If the information which is required be sought from the signs given by animals, then those animals are believed to be supernatural themselves, or else they are thought to be indwelt, for the time being, by some supernatural spirit; "the universal Semitic belief in omens and guidance given by animals belongs to the same range of ideas; omens are not blind tokens, the animals know what they tell to men."[178] It is the same with those of other forms of Divination which are unconnected with animals; whatever form the indication takes, there is no idea of chance or "luck" about it; it is believed to be the result of the invisible action of some supernatural spirit *who knows*. Of the various kinds of Divination, whether Belomancy (divination by arrows, Ezek. xxi. 19 ff. [23 ff. in Hebr.]), Hepatoscopy (divination by looking into the liver of an animal), Lots (1 Sam. xiv. 41, 42), Oneiromancy (divination by dreams, Gen. xxxi. 10–13 and often in the Old Testament), Rabdomancy (divination by rods, Hosea iv. 12), etc., Necromancy, there can be little doubt, was the most awe-inspiring and most important, and was probably thought to be the most reliable, since the spirits of departed men might be expected to take a deeper interest in, and have a wider knowledge of the affairs of, those among whom they had once dwelt.

I. NECROMANCY AMONG THE BABYLONIANS

Before dealing with Necromancy in the Old Testament we will take a brief glance at Babylonian and Assyrian belief and practice. "Necromancy," says Margoliouth,[179] "which is an essential part of the cult of the dead, and which must also have been connected with the presentation of offerings to the shades consulted, undoubtedly held a prominent place among the magic arts of the Babylonians." There is in Babylonian literature, so far as is at present known, only one instance of calling up the dead from the underworld; it is that of the spirit of Eabani being consulted by Gilgamesh; the former tells his friend about "the law of the underworld," after having ascended thence "like a wind." But although there is only this one record in literature of actually calling up the dead, it is certain that Necromancy in general had the widest vogue among the Babylonians; this is proved, firstly, by the various categories of priests extant; for among these different classes are "conjurers of the dead," priests who "bring up the spirit of the dead," and the "questioner of the dead."[180] The ritual of calling up the spirits of the departed seems to be referred to in the closing lines of the *Descent of Ishtar*; it says there;" In the days of Tammuz, play to me upon the crystal flute, play to me upon the...[181] instrument, his dirge, ye mourning men and mourning women, in order that the dead may ascend and smell the incense."[182] It seems evident from this that the spirits of the departed were believed to be induced to rise up from their abode by the sound of the flute and the smell of the incense.[183] Possibly this throws some light on the origin of the mourning custom of flute playing; the departed spirit may have been supposed to be appeased by what was done in his honour.

Another thing that points to the practice of Necromancy among the

Babylonians is the fact of the spirits of the dead wandering about on the earth and not being willing to go back again to the underworld after having been, presumably, called up. The worst plague-demons, it is said, are those that come from the shades in the underworld. In one text a sick man complains that he has been delivered into the power of a wandering spirit from the realm of the dead. Another case is that of one dangerously ill who declares that his illness is due to an evil disposed spirit having come up from the realm of the dead. One tablet contains the prayer of a man who is convinced that he is "possessed" by a departed spirit.[184] There were various magical ways of counteracting these evils, but it was always by special priests and priestesses that the spirits of the dead could be forced back again to their abode.

We have not much detail regarding this subject; nor is this altogether surprising. In the immense majority of cases it would have been the private individual who went to consult the dead, and obviously no record would have been kept of these. This is not the kind of subject regarding which one could expect to find many records; its existence is taken for granted, and nothing could be more eloquent in this respect than the classes of priests and priestesses recorded, among which figure prominently such as include those who dealt in Necromancy. There is also the fact that where it was a case of banning some unwelcome spirit from below who had overstayed his time on earth, one fixed formula came to be used[185] so that a single record of this kind from a single temple might well imply thousands of cases dealt with. Furthermore, as many of the worst among the demons were believed to be the spirits of the departed, it is probable that many extant texts in which no direct reference to a departed spirit is made, were in reality protective formulas against such.

II. NECROMANCY IN THE OLD TESTAMENT

The classical case of Necromancy in the Old Testament is, of course, that of the witch of Endor, referred to already more than once. From that passage (1 Sam. xxviii. 3–25) we learn that those who had "familiar spirits," and "wizards"[186] had hitherto been tolerated in the land, since it is said that Saul had "put them away out of the land." That this latter statement is not to be taken *au pied de la lettre* is evident for several reasons; a practice which is known to have been universal among the early Semites, and which touched men in what may be regarded as one of the most sensitive parts of their nature, could not have been abolished at one stroke, earnestly though Samuel, the champion of Jahwe, must have striven. Again, Saul himself, who is supposed to have put these people out of the land is the first to realize that this had not been done; his words show that their continued presence in the land is to him a matter of course; "Seek me a woman that hath a familiar spirit," he says, "that I may go to her, and enquire of her" (verse 7). And his servants have no need to seek; they answer him at once; "Behold, there is a woman that hath a familiar spirit at Endor." If this was the case with Saul, how much more likely will it have been so among the bulk of the people, to whom "seeking unto the dead" was a sacred reality and a traditional custom handed down for untold generations! Furthermore, from what we read in later books of the Old Testament it is abundantly evident that throughout the period of the monarchy Necromancy was practiced among the Israelites. Thus, in Isa. viii. 19 it is said; "And when they shall say unto you, Seek unto them that have familiar spirits and unto the wizards; that chirp and that mutter; should not a people seek unto their God? on behalf of the living should they seek unto the dead? "It will be noticed how the prophet here takes for granted that the necromancers are flourishing in the land. It is the same thing in Isa. xxix. 4, where the prophet compares humbled "Ariel"[187] with one that has a familiar spirit; "And thou shalt be brought down, and shalt speak out of the ground, and thy speech shall be low out of the dust; and thy voice shall be as one that hath a familiar spirit, out of the ground, and thy speech shall whisper (marg. "chirp") out of the dust." Here, again, the prophet takes the existence of necromancers for granted. In Isa. xix. 3, although there is a note of contempt for such things, the prophet again recognizes that they are in vogue; he says in his prophecy against Egypt;" And the spirit of Egypt shall be made void in the midst of it; and I will swallow up the counsel thereof; and they shall seek unto the idols and to the charmers (marg. "whisperers"), and to them that have familiar spirits, and to the wizards." These passages show that the prophet, while implicitly, though not directly, condemning necromancers and their practices, knows quite well that such things appealed to the people and were resorted to by them. So that when we read of King Manasseh that he "practiced augury, and used enchantments and dealt with them that had familiar spirits, and with wizards" (2 Kings xxi. 6 = 2 Chron. xxxiii. 6), we must see in his action not so much the resuscitation of practices which had fallen into desuetude, but rather the official recognition of what had all along been done by the people. But the most instructive light is perhaps thrown on this subject by seeing the way in which it is dealt with in the different codes of laws preserved in the Old Testament. The oldest of these is the "Book of the Covenant" (Exod. xx. 22–xxiii. 33); this, "with which Exod. xxxiv. 14–26 constitutes the earliest stratum of legislation, presupposes a people settled in Canaan and practicing agriculture."[188] In this code there is no prohibition against Necromancy; in xxii. 18 (17 in Hebr.) it is said; "Thou shalt not suffer a sorceress to live," but sorcerers and sorceresses had nothing to do with Necromancy; they were concerned with magical practices. To suppose that because Necromancy is not prohibited in Israel's earliest Code of Laws therefore it did not exist at that time is out of the question. Necromancy was universal among ancient peoples, and we have no reason to believe—quite the contrary—that the Israelites formed an exception to the rule. But, apart from that, we have seen from 2 Sam. xxviii. that it was fully in vogue at the beginning of the monarchy; could anyone suppose that a thing so ingrained in man as Necromancy (until eradicated by something higher) came into existence among the Israelites within the period of the settlement in Canaan and some time before the beginning of the monarchy? One has only to mention such a thing to see its absolute absurdity. No, Necromancy was practiced by the early Israelites in common with all the Semites, and the reason why it was not prohibited, or even mentioned in Israel's earliest Code of Laws was because the thing as regarded as a natural and legitimate practice; it touched men in a low stage of culture too closely, and the religious leaders saw as yet no reason for prohibiting it. In the meantime the practice went on; the prophets, apparently, regarded it rather as a piece of folly than anything else. But, evidently, in course of time it was seen to constitute a menace to the worship of Jahwe; so that in the Deuteronomic legislation it is prohibited; "There shall not be found with thee…one that useth divination, one that practiseth augury, or an enchanter, or a sorcerer, or a charmer, or a consulter with a familiar spirit, or a wizard, or a necromancer. For whosoever doeth these things is an abomination unto Jahwe" (Deut. xviii. 10–12). In conformity with this, King Josiah, in order that "he might perform the words of the law which were written in the book that Hilkiah the priest found in the house of Jahwe," put away "them that had familiar spirits, and the wizards, and the teraphim, and the idols, and all the abominations that were spied in the land of Judah and in Jerusalem" (2 Kings xxiii. 2_4). It was all to no purpose; so much so that in the next Code of Laws ("the Law of Holiness," Lev. xvii.–xxvi.) put forth Necromancy is not merely prohibited, but condemned as one of the worst sins, and declared to be punishable with death; "Turn ye not unto them that have familiar spirits, nor unto the wizards; seek them not out, to be defiled by them; I am Jahwe your God" (Lev. xix. 31); "And the soul that turneth unto them that have familiar spirits, and unto the wizards, to go a whoring after them, I will even set My face against that soul, and will cut him off from among his people" (Lev. xx. 6); "A man also or a woman that hath a familiar spirit, or that is a wizard, shall surely be put to death; they shall stone them with stones; their blood shall be upon them" (Lev. xx. 27). Quite in accordance with this later view of things, the Chronicler accounts for the death of Saul by saying that it was because of "his trespass which he committed against Jahwe, because of the word of Jahwe, which he kept not; and also for that he asked counsel of one that had a familiar spirit, to enquire thereby, and enquired not of Jahwe; therefore he slew him…." But in spite of penal laws against Necromancy, we find that even long after the Exile it was practiced in Judaea; for a late writer complains of a "rebellious people,"

which walketh in a way that is not good, after their own thoughts; a people
that provoketh Me to My face continually…which sit among the graves,
and spend the night in vaults"[189] (Isa. lxv. 2–4). It needs no words to show
that the reference in this passage is to Necromancy.

These passages, then, are sufficient, it may be hoped, to establish the
fact that practically all through the history of Israel, as recorded in the Old
Testament, Necromancy was practiced in the land, in spite of vigorous
efforts to root it out. We may be sure that during and after the Exile the
practice became ever more discredited; it is also, we believe, probable that
from the prophetical period onwards it tended to be in the main confined
to the lower grades of society[190]; we have, indeed, nothing in the Old Testament to show that this was so, but all the world knows that superstition
is, generally speaking, more powerful where there is ignorance. At any
rate, the outstanding fact is that down to post-exilic times laws were put
forth to try to eradicate Necromancy, and that such laws witness to the
existence of that which they sought to rectify.

Our one object in referring to this subject is in order to point to it in
support of the belief in the continued life of men after death. This form
of the witness to that belief certainly illustrates also the superstition, cre-
dulity, and folly of men; but that is not our present concern. Necromancy
presupposes the continued life of men after they die, and as such it is a
subsidiary element in our inquiry.

III. SOME TECHNICAL TERMS IN THE OLD TESTAMENT

We have seen that among the Babylonians there were special categories
of priests, and, as the texts inform us, priestesses, whose function it was
to "bring up" the dead, and to "question" them. In the Old Testament
we find the mention of people of both sexes (they are not called priests
and priestesses) who exercised similar functions. Four words occur in this
connexion, always without explanation, since it is taken for granted that
everyone knows all about them; probably they refer to the same type of
person.

First we have what is called the *'Ob*, translated by "familiar spirit." The use of this word in the Old Testament is a little ambiguous; in 1 Sam. xxviii. 7 it is said; "Seek me a woman that doth possess (or "is mistress of") an *'Ob*"[191]; here it is clear that the woman and the *'Ob* are distinct; this is seen to be the case also in the next verse; "Divine unto me, I pray thee, by means of the *'Ob*." Still more distinct, if possible, is Deut. xviii. 11, where reference is made to "one that asketh an *'Ob*." In these three passages the distinction between the *'Ob* and the person who uses it for divining is as clear as can be; so much so that an *'Ob* could quite conceivably be regarded as some external object; and this is emphasized by the expression used in regard to it in 2 Kings xxi. 6 (= 2 Chron. xxxiii. 6), where it is said of Manasseh; "And he made his son to pass through the fire, and practiced augury, and used enchantments, and made an *'Ob*...." It is true the use of the root עשה is wide; it can mean "to do," "to Observe," "to acquire," etc., as well as "to make"; but the R.V. rendering "dealt with" is impossible, for the word is never used in this sense unless followed by a preposition; in 2 Kings xxi. 6 (but not in 2 Chron. xxxiii. 6) the R.V. gives a marginal alternative, "*appointed*, Heb. *made*"; the former is a possible rendering, though the usage is very rare (see 1 Kings xii. 31, xiii. 33); but in view of the other passages quoted above, there would be some justification in using the verb in question in its ordinary sense and regarding the *'Ob* as something that was "made." Gaster[192] believes that the *'Ob* was a mummified body, which could of course, in one sense, be spoken of as "made"; and when one remembers the belief about the soul hovering about the body,[193] Gaster's idea is not so fantastic as might at first appear to some. We believe the data are insufficient to accept Gaster's idea unreservedly, but it merits consideration.

However this may be, in the passages so far examined it is clear that there is a distinction between the *'Ob* and the person who uses it for divination. In Lev. xx. 27 it is said; "And a man or a woman in whom there is an *'Ob*...shall surely die..."; here, too, there is the same distinction, only the *'Ob* is not external to the man or woman using it, let alone anything material; it is the spirit of some departed person who speaks out of the diviner. In all the other passages in which *'Ob* occurs {Lev. xix. 31, xx. 6; 1 Sam. xxviii. 3, 9; 2 Kings xxiii. 24; Isa. viii. 19, xix. 3, xxix. 4) it is always used purely and simply of the person who divines. We have, thus, three stages of belief regarding the *'Ob*; first, it was a "something" believed to be the departed spirit of a man or woman who could be called up from the abode of the dead; then, something representing the *'Ob* was constructed, and the *'Ob* was believed to enter it, compelled to do so by one who understood the ritual; then a stage was reached in which it was believed that the *'Ob* entered into the "diviner" and spoke through him or her, so that the word *'Ob* came to be applied to the diviner. Or, to put it in another way; first it was believed that a ghost, or *'Ob*, actually appeared to the diviner; then an image of an *'Ob* was made, and the diviner who understood his business compelled the ghost to enter the image; and finally the diviner believed himself or herself to be "possessed" by the ghost, and thus came to be called by the same name.[194]

The derivation of the word *'Ob* is differently explained, but that given by Delitzsch and Baudissin seems to be the right one; according to them it comes from the root meaning "to swell up," i.e. something convex, round from the outside, but hollow inside; and thus it came to be applied to a spirit or a ghost which was believed to appear in bodily form but was hollow inside. The same word, *'Ob*, is used of a "wineskin" in Job xxxii. 19, which points to the probable correctness of this view.

The word *'Ob* often stands by itself; but another word, *Yidde'oni*, is also found; this latter, however, never stands by itself, but is always used in conjunction with *'Ob*; the R.V. translates it by "wizard"; it comes from the root meaning "to know," and is probably descriptive of the *'Ob* (in the earliest stage of its use), who "knows," and is therefore consulted. Other expressions, which do not often occur, are "he who inquires of the dead," *Doresh el ha-methim*, and "he who asks an *'Ob*," *Sho'el 'Ob*. The former of these describes the function of the *'Ob*, in the later stage of its use; the latter refers to the person who comes to consult the *'Ob*, also in the later stage of its use. Finally, there are the *'Iltim*, meaning "whisperers"; this refers to the method of procedure of the *'Ob* (in the later stage of its use) when going through his ritual (*see* section V). All these expressions, then, though translated in the Revised Version as though they were different categories of diviners—"one that hath a familiar spirit," "wizard," "necromancer," "whisperer"—refer, we believe, to the same class of people, and merely describe characteristic function, and action. The probability of this lies in the fact that in Necromancy there is and can be only one type of "diviner," viz. the type that consults the dead (or thinks he does). One can understand that there should be various categories of "diviners," one class dealing with Lots, another with Belomancy, another with Hepatoscopy, and so on; but there is no scope for variety of categories in any one of these; and so, too, of Necromancy. Hence all four words mentioned probably refer to one and the same class.

IV. THE 'OB AND THE TERAPHIM

In Ch. VIII, § VI we spoke of the Teraphim, the household gods whose worship was a remnant of Ancestor-worship. In several passages in the Old Testament their mention in close connexion with the *'Ob* demands a brief reference to the subject again. In 1 Sam. xv. 23 the prophet condemns Teraphim as iniquitous and makes the use of it parallel to divination; that they were used for purposes of divination is evident from 2 Kings xxiii. 24, for they are there mentioned in the same category as the *'Ob*; and in both Judges xvii. 5 and Hosea iii. 4 it is clearly implied that the Teraphim stood in the sanctuary,[195] which would have been an obvious place to come to if an oracle were sought. But the clearest evidence is seen in Zech. x. 2; "For the Teraphim have spoken vanity, and the diviners have seen a lie." That the practice was a Babylonian one is seen from Ezek. xxi. 21 (26 in Hebr.); "And the king of Babylon stood at the parting of the way, at the head of the two ways, to use divination; he shook the arrows to and fro, he consulted the teraphim, he looked in the liver." These passages lead to the belief that the Teraphim were images of some ancestor in which the spirit of the ancestor was supposed to come when conjured up by the *'Ob*, and before which the latter stood and received the answer to the question which an inquirer sought. J Schwally's suggestion[196] that the Teraphim are to be identified with the Rephaim is very attractive; the two words may well come from the same root.

The Ephod is sometimes mentioned together with the Teraphim; but this subject does not concern us here; sufficient to say that this kind of Ephod was a different thing from the priest's garment of the same name (cp. 1 Sam. ii. 18, xxii. 18, 2 Sam. vi. 14 together); it, too, was an image, see Judges viii. 22–27, xvii. 1–5, 1 Sam. xxi. 10, and was presumably used for divination; but we have no evidence to show that it had anything to do with Necromancy.

V. The Modus Operandi of the Necromancer

Necromancy assumes the belief in the "external soul." If there was a certain freedom accorded to the soul while still more or less bound to the body, how much more would this be the case when the soul was permanently released from the body. For just as it was believed that during a man's lifetime his soul could make distant excursions and return, so it was also believed that after death the soul, though detained in Sheol, could come out of there and roam about provided that the requisite means were employed to bring it up. How certain men originally brought themselves to believe that they had the power to bring up the dead and to consult them, it would be difficult to say; but it would be a great mistake to suppose that the whole thing was chicanery. No doubt in course of time cases of conscious deception would have occurred; but knowing what we do about the mentality of man in a not very advanced stage of culture, we may confidently believe that in the vast majority of cases there was a firm conviction on the part of the diviner that he was really able to accomplish what he professed he could. It is worth noting that throughout the Old Testament, although divination of all kinds is often (though not always) strongly condemned, there is rarely a hint that it was not a real thing. Indeed, the reason of its condemnation, viz. that it formed a rival to Jahwe-worship, suggests belief in its reality, otherwise it might have been treated with contempt, and have been left to languish and die out of its own inanity.

Now it will be interesting to gather, if we can, from the Old Testament, any hints as to what lay at the back of the mind of these necromancers and their clients regarding this matter, and to see if any points are forthcoming which will give indications as to the *modus operandi* of the necromancer. We must confess at the outset that there is not much material of the kind desired; but some little there is.

In the narrative of the witch of Endor (1 Sam. xxviii) the witch must be thought of as looking downwards and peering into space—for she says she sees a god coming up out of the earth. Saul sees nothing, since he asks the witch what she sees. The narrator evidently believes that Samuel actually speaks, for he makes a clear distinction between what the woman says and what Samuel says. It would seem, therefore, that when Saul carries on a conversation with Samuel, we are intended to understand that this was done directly, and not through the medium of the witch. From other passages, however, we are enabled to see that it was the "medium" who actually spoke on such occasions, whatever the credulous believed. For in Lev. xx. 27 we learn that it was believed that the spirit of the dead came into the diviner; the spirit therefore used the voice of the diviner as his instrument. It is not necessary, however, to think that the witch, as "medium," was conscious of deceiving Saul; even in these days it is well known that people of this kind are capable of working themselves up into a state in which they really believe that an inner voice is speaking to them, and this they repeat. There are also cases on record in which a "medium" falls into a state of trance during which he or she utters what is purported to be a message from the other world. The possibility must be allowed of something of this kind having taken place in the case of the witch of Endor. The narrative all through, and especially what is said in verses 21–25, has a ring of *bona fides* about it. Self-deception is very easy when a person really believes that he or she has the power to communicate with spirits; and in those days everybody believed that this power was possessed by some. From Isa. viii. 19 we learn the way in which a diviner spoke; two expressions are there used; the first, which is translated by "chirp," comes from the onomatopoetic root *zaphaph* (used only in the *pilpel* form, *mezaphzaph* (the *z* should be pronounced as *ts*); this is used primarily of the twittering of birds (e.g. Isa. xxxviii. 14). The other, translated by "mutter," comes from the root *hagah*, used of the "cooing" of a dove (also occurring in Isa. xxxviii. 14). The former word is used also in Isa. xxix. 4, where further information is given by the words, "thou shalt be brought down and shalt speak out of the ground, and thy speech shall be low out of the dust; and thy voice shall be like that of the '*Ob*, out of the ground, and thy speech shall chirp out of the dust." One other word occurs (once only, in Isa. xix. 3) which is translated "charmers," but in the margin "whisperers"; it is used of Egyptian diviners, and occurs together with the '*Ob* and the *Yiddeoni*. Incomes from a root *attat*, which, on Arabic analogy, probably means much the same as *hagah*, mentioned just now, i.e. to speak in a low muttering voice. It would thus appear that the diviner lay on the ground, from which the spirit would be supposed to arise, and spoke in a peculiar tone of voice; or else it was by means of ventriloquism (the Septuagint usually translates "them that have familiar spirits," i.e. the '*Ob*, by ἐγγαστρίμυθοι). Ventriloquism is an easy explanation, and may have been adopted in some cases; but there was no need for it, and the words used, "chirp," "mutter," "whisper," do not necessarily suggest it. There may have been a special reason for imitating the sounds made by birds; for there was a very widespread belief that after death the soul assumed the form of a bird; this is nowhere definitely stated in the Old Testament to have been the belief of the Israelites, but the thought may well have been implicit in such a passage as Ps. lv. 6 (7 in Hebr.); Jahwe, and supernatural beings generally, are conceived of as having wings (Ps. xvii. 8, xviii. 10, xxxvi. 7, lvii. 1, lxiii. 7, Exod. xxv. 20, xxxvii. 9, etc.). But even though we have no direct evidence of the Israelites believing that the soul took the form of a bird, the widespread character of this belief makes it pretty certain that they did believe this. It was believed by the ancient Babylonians that the departed soul became a bird in form[197]; the Arabs believed the same, they held that the soul took the form of an owl[198];

the Egyptians had conflicting views on the subject, but one view was that the departed soul took the form of a half-human bird (*bai*) which lived in or near the grave[199]; in Greek art the human soul is generally represented with wings,[200] sometimes as a butterfly. "Often the soul is conceived as a bird ready to take flight. This conception has probably left traces in most languages,[201] and it lingers as a metaphor in poetry. But what is metaphor to a modern European poet was sober earnest to his savage ancestor, and is still so to many people."[202] Frazer gives a number of examples. If, then, as may well have been the case, the Israelites had a similar belief regarding the soul, the object of the necromancer in articulating in a bird-like fashion may quite well have been that by this means he would presumably be more likely to attract the attention of the bird-shaped soul. In this event there would have been no question of duping an inquirer, it would rather come under the head of imitative magic.

Regarding the passage Isa. lxv. 4, already referred to, it would appear that here we have a case of what is called "incubation"; by resorting to a grave and spending the night there, it was thought that the departed spirit would appear to the sleeper in a dream and that the desired information or guidance would be imparted in this way. That God spoke in this way was firmly believed (see Gen. xx. 3, xxxi. 11; Num. xii. 6; 1 Sam. xxviii. 6, 15, etc.). For other examples of the belief that departed spirits appear to men in dreams, see Frazer's volume just quoted, pp. 368 ff., and *Adonis, Attis, Osiris*, ii. pp. 162, 190.

Necromancy, then, however *naive* and crass, witnesses to the belief among the Israelites in Immortality.

Mourning
and
Burial Customs

XI

MOURNING AND BURIAL CUSTOMS

I. INTRODUCTORY

A consideration of the mourning and burial customs, as well as the funeral rites, among the Israelites offers perhaps the most instructive illustration of their belief in Immortality. How entirely incompatible with the "official" Sheol belief these customs were is one of the strongest arguments in favour of the contention that throughout the Old Testament history of Israel from the foundation of the monarchy there was a "popular" as well as an "official" doctrine of Immortality.

For the most part these customs go back in their origin to a remote past; and they were kept up when the original meaning was forgotten; then new meanings were offered; one must, therefore, allow for a variety of reasons in some cases for the rites and customs, and it is likely enough that modifications in regard to them arose owing to these reasons being given. They involved what at times proved to be contrary conceptions regarding the dead, but such contradictions do not trouble men in a comparatively early stage of culture.

There can be no doubt that Hartland is right when he says that "throughout the rites and observances attendant on death, two motives— two principles—are found struggling for the mastery. On the one hand, there is the fear of death and of the dead, which produces the horror of the corpse, the fear of defilement, and the overwhelming desire to ban the ghost. On the other hand, there is the affection, real or simulated, for the deceased, which bewails his departure and is unwilling to let him go."[203] This applies, in greater or less degree, to all peoples of all ages, in so far as these are known to us; other elements came in, in course of time, especially among the more cultured nations; with these we are only incidentally concerned.

In the following investigation our attention will be centered primarily on the Hebrews; the mourning customs of other Semitic peoples will be mentioned for purposes of illustration, and in some cases the customs of peoples other than Semitic will be incidentally referred to. We have not dealt in any detail with Egyptian or Greek customs, as so much has been written on these that they are probably well known.[204]

In seeking for the original meanings and objects of mourning customs and funeral rites, much diversity of opinion among scholars is to be expected, for the material is very large, and the same rite or custom is often susceptible of several explanations; conclusions must be largely based upon analogous things, not only among the Semites in general, but also among other races, as well as among savage tribes. But it is supremely necessary to guard oneself against attempting to explain any of these customs from the point of view of modern ideas; this has not infrequently been done; but it is pretty nearly certain to obscure the original meaning.

When one contemplates the nature of some of the early conceptions among the Israelites regarding the dead referred to in the previous chapters, it must be granted that in seeking the original meaning and object of a mourning custom analogies may in some cases be drawn from men's actions when they believe themselves to be in the presence of a deity. It is in all probability not a mere coincidence that the regular period for mourning lasted, seven days (see Gen. l. 10, 1 Sam. xxxi. 13, *Judith* xvi. 24, *Wisdom of Ben Sira* xxii. 12, etc.), and that this was also the length of feasts in honour of the deity. There can be no sort of doubt that the souls of the departed were believed, like the deity, only of course in a less degree, to be able to benefit and to harm men on earth. A striking example of the interest which the dead were believed to take in the affairs of the living is to be found in Jer. xxxi. 15, where Rachel is conceived of as weeping for her children. In the following discussion on mourning customs this subject will be touched upon more than once.

The classification of these customs and rites is difficult, mainly because of the different meanings and objects that a particular custom may have; some are done in relation to the dead, others in relation to the survivors; yet others may have a twofold object. The classification in the following pages may not be scientific, but it will be found convenient; we shall first deal with rites and customs carried out by the mourners *for* or *to* themselves; then those done by the mourners *for* or *to* the dead. This will not mean that the rite or custom in question is necessarily done *exclusively* for the benefit of either the living or the departed, but it will divide those things which the living do to or for *themselves*, primarily, from those which they do to or for the *dead*, primarily.

II. THE RENDING OF GARMENTS

Gen. xxx. vii. 33, 34; "…It is my son's coat; an evil beast hath devoured him; Joseph is without doubt torn in pieces. And Jacob rent his garments…" (2 Sam. i. 11); "Then David took hold of his clothes, and rent them; and likewise all the men that were with him…" (see also 2 Sam. iii. 31, etc. etc.).

A similar custom was in vogue among the Babylonians and Assyrians; when Asshurbanipal poured out his libation to his dead predecessors he appeared in rent garments.[205] The ideogram for "the rending of garments" is explained in Assyrian by "overwhelming grief" and "uncontrollable wrath."[206] In like manner, the Arabs rent their garments as a sign of mourning, and the women went half naked[207] (cp. Isa. xxxii. 11). Among the ancient Greeks the women followed the dead to burial practically naked,[208] though it does not necessarily follow from this that they rent their garments. This was, however, the custom among other peoples.[209]

Various theories have been put forward in explanation of this rite. In the Old Testament, Joel ii. 12, 13, the idea of its being a symbolic action seems to underlie the prophet's words; "Turn ye unto Me with all your heart, and with fasting, and with weeping, and with mourning; and rend your heart and not your garments"; but this would, in any case, be a developed idea, in no sense answering to its original meaning. If we are to be guided by the Assyrian explanation, and there is certainly much to commend it, we must look upon it as an oriental way of expressing unbounded grief combined, it may be, with an undefined feeling of fear. We all know the tendency of the oriental to give way to what to the Western appears exaggerated emotional expression; since the death of a near relative must often be regarded as a crisis in the lives of the survivors, one can understand the naturalness of unrestrained grief finding vent in what to modern ideas may appear unexpected forms.

A third explanation connects it with the putting on of sackcloth. It is true that we often find the two rites mentioned together; for example, in the passages just cited and in Isa. xxxii. 11 stripping oneself of clothes seems to be for the purpose of girding on sackcloth[210] (the reference is to women). It has, therefore, been explained that the rending of the garments took place as the quickest mode of getting them off in order to put the sackcloth on; this would again be a case of oriental exaggerative action and impulsiveness. Lagrange, who also sees a direct connexion between the two rites, believes, however, that the rending of the garments was not so much with the idea of putting on the sackcloth quickly, as to make an immediate profession of the desire not to wear anything but the coarsest material[211] (see further on this the next section III). He believes that the rent garment was meant to be a visible proof of the renunciation of pleasant intercourse among one's fellows.

While it is realized that there is something to be said for each of these four explanations, they do not seem to go sufficiently to the root of the matter to be wholly satisfactory. The symbolism theory is confessedly a development, which is altogether edifying, but which does not profess to explain the origin of the rite. This, too, is the objection to the Assyrian explanation; doubtless to Asshurbanipal and his contemporaries the rite expressed grief; but there must originally have been some reason for this *form* of the expression of grief. And in regard to the other two explanations, these take for granted that there was always a connexion between the rending of the garments and the putting on of sackcloth; but what proof have we of this? Indeed, we know that this was by no means always the case,[212] as, for example, among the Arabs and Greeks, who went half naked, if not wholly so. It is acknowledged on all hands that the rite of rending the garments as a sign of mourning goes back to a remote antiquity; but even during the nomadic stage it may well be doubted whether this change of garments ever took place; after all, the "sackcloth," roughly woven of the hair of goats or camels, was only the normal dress of early nomads. The explanations given above may well all have had their place at different periods; but none of them fits in satisfactorily with the ideas of man in an early stage of culture during which, there is every reason to believe, this rite originally arose.

Other explanations have been given which take into fuller consideration the ideas of man in a low stage of culture. That at one time the spirits of the departed were regarded with fear is too well known to need illustration; the powers, superior to those of men, which they were believed to possess, would be quite sufficient to account for this fear; nor would the fact that in some respects they were thought to be dependent on the living necessarily detract from this fear; nor would affection for the departed be inconsistent with a feeling of fear. The fact of their invisibility combined with the firm belief in their presence would also have inspired dread. In short, whatever the causes, fear of the dead existed. It is held, then, by many authorities[213] that the original object of rending the garments was a quick way whereby to disguise oneself from the dead and thus escape detection in the case of any harm which the departed spirit might intend. Another theory, based upon the well-known belief among men in a low stage of civilization that demons gather in the vicinity of a corpse, is that the garment is rent in order to prevent some evil-disposed demon, or the spirit of the departed himself,[214] from hiding in the mourner's clothes, a rent in the garment being considered a sure means of driving him away again. Robertson Smith is inclined to see in the rite the relic of what was originally intended to be an offering to the dead; he says; "Closely allied to the practice of leaving part of oneself— whether blood or hair—in contact with the god at the sanctuary, are offerings of part of one's clothes or other things that one has worn, such as ornaments and weapons. In the *Iliad*, Glaucus and Diomede exchange armour in token of their ancestral friendship; and when Jonathan makes a covenant of love and brotherhood with David, he invests him with his garments, even to his sword, his bow, and his girdle (1 Sam. xviii. 3 ff.). Among the Arabs, he who seeks protection lays hold of the garments of the man to whom he appeals, or more formally ties a knot in the head-shawl of his protector. In the old literature, 'pluck away my garments from thine' means 'put an end to our attachment.' The clothes are so far a part of a man that they can serve as a vehicle of personal connexion. Hence the religious significance of suspending on an idol or *Dhiit Anwiit*, not only weapons, ornaments, and complete garments, but mere shreds from one's raiment. The rag-offerings are still to be seen hanging on the sacred trees[215] of Syria and on the tombs of Mohammedan saints; they art not gifts in the ordinary sense, but pledges of attachment. It is pos-sible that the rending of garments in mourning was originally designed to procure such an offering to the dead..."[216] This is very suggestive; the rite, according to this theory, would denote a mark of affection on the part of the survivor for the departed. There is, however, an alternative; the old Semitic idea of the garment being part and parcel of a man would be some justification for regarding this rite as a palliative of lacerations of the body on behalf of the dead. This, too, would be a relic of an offering to the dead; but it would be in the nature of a propitiatory offering rather than a mark of affection. The fact that laceration of the body as well as rending the garment are both referred to in the Old Testament[217] would, of course, not militate against this view; we have other cases of ancient practices together with modifications of them existing side by side. Still less would this view be invalidated by the further fact that the rending of the garment was not exclusively a mourning custom, but was also practiced at the time of calamity;[218] for there were a variety of these mourning customs of which the same can be said; in each case it was an adoption of the much earlier mourning custom.

The tenacity of suchlike customs is well illustrated by the fact that even at the present day orthodox Jews make a rent in their outer garment as a sign of mourning, it must be not less than four inches, i.e. a handbreadth, in length. It is the custom among the Persians today to make a rent in the outer garment from the neck to the girdle.[219] The Jews are now permitted to sew up the rent again after thirty days, but this was not allowed for centuries after the beginning of the Christian era.[220]

III. LACERATION OF THE BODY AND CUTTING OFF THE HAIR

These practices have already been referred to; but as mourning customs a few remarks upon them are called for here. The Old Testament references have been given above. The more important views in explanation of the rite are as follows:

The opinion that these practices were originally offerings to the dead and that they witness to the existence of the cult of the dead at some early period is denied by some scholars. We believe that, in face of all the facts, the view of these scholars cannot be sustained. But these practices may very likely have had other purposes in addition to their original one; for, as already remarked, some mourning customs did undoubtedly serve more than one purpose; the same rite sometimes expresses more than one intention. There are good reasons for believing that in its original form laceration of the body was practiced over the dead so that the blood dropped upon the corpse; this may have signified either that a blood covenant with the dead was effected, or, bearing in mind the ancient belief of life residing in the blood, it may have had the purpose of assisting the departed in his new life.

The view that the laceration was intended as a disguise in order that the mourners might be unrecognizable to the departed spirit in case he should return and harm them[221] has much in its favour and can be supported by the existence of practices which had a similar object.

The idea that laceration, by letting blood flow, i.e. by letting out life, had the effect of bringing the survivor to the same state as the dead, seems fantastic to moderns; but that this was one of the beliefs is proved by an ancient Arabic poem in which it is said;

"Of a truth, the mourner who sea.rs his face [as a sign of mourning].
 Is no more living than he that is buried,
 For whom a memorial stone is erected."[222]

This is certainly a modification of earlier belief. Further, it is probable that we have a modification of the rite itself in the custom of beating the breast or thigh, referred to in Isa. xxxii. 12; "They shall smite upon the breasts for the pleasant fields, for the fruitful vine"; Jer. xxxi. 19; "Surely after that I was turned, I repented; and after that I was instructed, I smote upon my thigh . . .," cp. Ezek. xxi. 12. Such modifications, taking some palliative form of the original rite, can be paralleled by other Semitic religious customs, e.g. the redemption of the first-born.

The mourning custom of cutting off the hair also comes under the category of those which may be regarded as expressing more than one intention. The chief Old Testament passages which deal with the subject have already been given,[223] but they may be supplemented here by one or two others. In Isa. xv. 2 it is said in reference to mourning; "...on all heads is baldness, every beard is cut off." Jeremiah bids Jerusalem cut off her crown (hair is probably implied) "and cast it away, and take up a lamentation on the bare heights" (vii. 29); this is not in reference to mourning for the dead, but it has already been pointed out that some of the customs for general mourning for calamity have been adopted from those of mourning for the dead, cp. Jer. xli. 5[224]; in Ezek. xxvii. 31, in the lamentations on Tyre, the prophet says; "And they shall make themselves bald for thee, and gird them with sackcloth, and they shall weep for thee in bitterness of soul with bitter mourning," cp. v. 1–4. This custom was in vogue among the Assyrians,[225] the Arabs[226] the Greeks,[227] and many other peoples.[228] The purpose of the practice, apart from what has been said previously as to its being an offering to the dead, is well expressed by Hartland: "One object, at all events, of the dedication of the hair is, like that of the blood, to form a bond of union with the dead. The converse rite of taking a lock of hair of the dead may be said to be worldwide. Nor is it confined to a lock of hair; it extends in some cases to the nails and pieces of the garments.... It must be borne in mind that, according to the theory of sympathetic magic, any portion of a human being, such as hair, nails, skin, bones, and so forth, which has become detached, is still, in spite of separation, in effective sympathetic union with the body of which it once formed part; for the personality inheres in every part of the body.... Not only, therefore, if I take a lock of a dead man's hair do I establish effective union with him so as to prevent him from inflicting any harm upon me; but, conversely, if I give him a lock of mine or a drop of my blood we are bound together by a similar bond."[229] This is also evidently the view of Robertson Smith.[230]

It is conceivable that the custom of covering the head was a modification of this rite, but other and more cogent reasons for it have been put forward.

IV. Putting on Sackcloth

2 Sam. iii. 31; "And David said to Joab, and to all the people that were with him, Rend your clothes, and gird you with sackcloth, and mourn before Abner." Amos viii. 10; "...and I will bring sackcloth upon all loins...and I will make it as the mourning for an only son...." etc. etc.[231]

That this custom was in vogue among the Babylonians,[232] Assyrians[233] (who called sackcloth *sakku*), and other peoples,[234] is what we should expect; it does not, however, appear to have been in use among the ancient Arabs; the women went half-naked, and the men shortened their garments, but the putting on of sackcloth is not mentioned, apparently.[235]

The Hebrew expression is "to gird on" sackcloth, which suggests that it was originally only worn round the loins; it has, therefore, been conjectured that the custom arose in the first instance by rending a piece from one's garment and girding it round the loins; this implied that one was reducing oneself to a primitive state of dress, which meant putting on a sacred dress,[236] the ancient way was always regarded as holy by early man (cp. 1 Kings xx. 31).[237] It is, therefore, quite conceivable that among the Israelites of historical times to put on sackcloth meant that a holy garment was worn in honour of the dead; whether this originally implied an act of worship or not cannot be stated with certainty; but presumably this would have been the case, provided this explanation of the custom be the correct one.

Others hold that the custom arose from the same cause as that for which (as they maintain) the garment was rent, namely to disguise oneself from the dead, lest, being annoyed at his forcible separation from his accustomed mode of life, he should be inclined to vent his displeasure on the survivors.

Hartland thinks it was intended to mark those who were under the tabu; in speaking of the mourning garb generally, which is everywhere an essential part of mourning observances, he says; "Primarily it seems intended to distinguish those who are under the tabu. For this reason it is usually the reverse of the garb of ordinary life…those who wear clothing go naked, or wear scanty, coarse, or old worn-out clothes.…" He then goes on to show what is a very important point, namely that a mourning custom may have more than one use, and may therefore sometimes have more than one meaning; the mourning garb, he says, "is more than merely distinctive; it is, like other mourning rites, intended to express sympathy for the deceased and grief at his loss; it is intended to call forth pity, to avert the suspicion of foul play on the part of the mourner, and to deprecate the anger or ill-humour of the deceased at his separation." Then, in opposition to the view that it is put on for the sake of disguise, he says; "It has sometimes been suggested that there is a further motive, namely the desire to escape by means of disguise the persecution of the deceased. A careful examination fails, however, to disclose sufficient evidence in favour of this interpretation. Protection is often held to be needed; but it usually takes a different form.... In short, open war rather than guile is the favorite defense. But so protean are human motives that it is impossible to aver that in no case is disguise the intention."[238]

Arising out of a very different train of thought is the explanation given of the rite by those who see in it a symbolic act of renunciation, i.e. reducing oneself to a simulated state of poverty (sackcloth was the dress of the very poor), and thus bringing oneself to the same condition as the departed who now possessed nothing. This view of the rite being a symbolic act of sympathy with the deceased is well expressed by Torge[239]; "One ought to become like the departed, to renounce everything and to possess no advantage over him, i.e. one ought also to die. But as this was not feasible, all the necessaries of life were reduced to a minimum. The usual mode of life was set aside, its direct antithesis was adopted instead; everything was neglected which at other times constituted the joy and delight of life. This would be the less distasteful to the mourners inasmuch as they believed that the spirit of the departed witnessed what was being done, and experienced satisfaction at the affection thus evinced."

All these views, again, have much to commend them; and against each there are some fairly obvious objections which could be raised. It is very difficult to form a definite conclusion as to what the rite originally meant to those who practiced it. Schwally's view (see above, the first view mentioned) seems, on the whole, to be the most satisfactory, especially as it implies (so it seems to the present writer) that the putting on of sackcloth was not one of the earliest among the mourning rites.

The modern usage among Jews is the same as that of the rest of the world, black clothes having taken the place of sackcloth.

V. Sprinkling Ashes or Earth on the Head

It is important to notice how rarely this custom is mentioned in the Old Testament in *reference to mourning for the dead*. It *does* occur in this connexion, but only in quite a few passages. In the great majority of cases in which the custom is spoken of it is in reference to calamity, humiliation, contrition, or grief owing to causes other than that of the loss of friends. Three words are used; *'Epher* (אֵפֶר), "ashes" in the ordinary sense of the word, e.g. the ashes of a red heifer, Num. xix. 9, 10, where the reference is to purification by putting the burnt remains of the sacrifice "without the camp," and using them "for a water of separation (or "impurity "), it is a sin offering"; this "water of separation" is sprinkled on a man, and he is cleansed thereby (see verse 13). It is used in reference to mourning in Jer. vi. 26; "O daughter of my people, gird thee with sackcloth, and wallow thyself in ashes; make thee mourning, as for an only son, most bitter lamentation." In Ezek. xxvii. 27 ff., it is said of Tyre; "Thy riches and thy wares...with all thy company which is in the midst of thee, shall fall into the heart of the seas in the day of thy ruin.... And all that handle the oar, the mariners...shall cause their voice to be heard over thee, and shall cry bitterly, and shall cast up dust upon their heads, they shall wallow themselves in ashes...in bitterness of soul with bitter mourning." But even in this passage, although there is a reference to death, the mourning is evidently more on account of the ruin of Tyre than because of those who have died by falling "into the heart of the seas." Otherwise the sprinkling of ashes on the head and sitting in ashes is a sign of grief brought about through other causes, such as contrition (Job xlii. 6, Isa. lviii. 5, Jon. iii. 6, Dan. ix. 3), or sickness (Job. ii. 8), or shame (2 Sam. xiii. 19), or national calamity (Esther iv. 1, 3). It is also used in a figurative sense to denote something that is insignificant (Gen. xviii. 27), or worthless (Job xiii. 12, Isa. xliv. 20), cp. Ps. cxlvii. 16, "He scattereth the hoar frost like ashes."

The next word is *'aphar* (עָפָר), "dust," i.e. dry earth; and here again the word is rarely used in connexion with mourning for the dead; in Josh. vii. 6 we read that "Joshua rent his clothes and fell to the earth before the ark of Jahwe until the evening, he and the elders of Israel; and they put dust upon their heads"; but although the context speaks of the death of thirty-six men, the mourning is probably due rather to the calamity of defeat. The same remark applies to Ezek. xvii. 27 ff., already quoted, where this word also occurs; otherwise it is used, though less frequently, like 'epher (e.g. Gen. iii. 14, Lam. ii. 10, Job ii. 12, Isa. xlvii. 1). In its sense of "soil" used for ordinary purposes it is, of course, common. But there is one specific way in which it is used which requires emphasis, viz. as earth from a grave; thus in Job vii. 21 it is said; "For now shall I lie down in the dust ('aphar); and thou shalt seek me diligently, but I shall not be"; Job xx. 11; "His bones are full of his youth, but it shall lie down with him in the dust ('aphar)"; Job xxi. 26; "They lie down alike in the dust ('aphar), and the worm covereth them"; Ps. xxii. 29 (30 in Hebr.); "All they that go down to the dust ('aphar) shall bow before him, even he that cannot keep his soul alive," cp. Isa. xxvi. 19. Then we have the common words for "earth," viz. 'adamah (אֲרְמָה), e.g. 2 Sam. i. 2; "…behold, a man came out of the camp from Saul, with his clothes rent, and earth ('adamah) upon his head"; though this is not used where it is a question of mourning for the dead, but only in cases of humiliation or calamity.

There are thus comparatively few references in the Old Testament to this custom in connexion with mourning; the passages quoted or referred to above are fairly exhaustive. Nevertheless, there can be no doubt that as a mourning custom it was very common in Israel; this is clear from the way in which it is spoken of, e.g. in Jer. vi. 26, namely as a well-known thing which needs no explanation. Moreover, it's very wide prevalence among Semitic and other peoples of itself suggests that the Israelites would have been like the rest of men in this. Thus, the Arabs sprinkled dust on their heads and on their naked backs[240]; the Greeks "showed their sorrow at bereavement by strewing themselves with ashes (Homer, *Iliad*, xviii. 22; *Odyssey*, xxiv. 315; Plutarch, *de Superstit*. Iii. …); and the practice of sprinkling ashes over the head as a sign of affliction is widespread."[241]

Connected with this rite was the sitting in ashes, or on the ground, see, e.g., Isa. iii. 26, xlvii. 1, Lam. ii. 10, Job i. 20, ii. 13, Jon. iii. 6, which was also common among the Babylonians.[242]

In seeking the origin and meaning of this custom it is important to consider where the dust and ashes were sought. Lagrange, in commenting on passages like Job ii. 8, 12, xlii. 6, says;

"Il s'agit de ces tertres places a l'entree des villages et qui sc composent de debris. Le fond du tumulus c'est le cendre qu'on enleve des fours a cuire le pain; puis avec le temps, c'est une masse de fine poussiere. Lorsqu' une ville est prise, detruite, brulee, c'est le refuge naturel des habitants. La on peut s'asseoir sur la poussiere, ou sur la cendre, se rouler dans la cendre, se mettre de la poussiere sur la tete ou faire les deux a la fois. Avec le temps, l'usage de se placer de la cendre sur la tete devint le symbole d'une violente douleur. Lorsqu'on venait annoncer une mauvaise nouvelle, le rite etait de rigueur; mais il est du moins assez a noter que dans ce cas c'est de la terre que le messager ramasse sur son chemin, et cela parut ensuite suffisant comme expression de la douleur. Dans aucun de ces textes il n'est question de la mort et du deuil qu'elle cree dans une famille par le depart d'un de ses membres. Sans doute la mort est fa cause principale de toutes les actions qui marquent de la douleur; mais ne peut-on pas supposer aussi que les calamites nationales ont open dans les ames une emotion specialc, occasionne des rites speciaux? Des lors, ce n'cst pas dans ces rites qu'il faut chercher a entrevoir l'opinion qu'on avait de la survivance, puisque le temoignage de la douleur etait rendu plus directement aux vivants qu'aux morts."[243]

We have quoted this passage in full in order to give the writer's argument in his own words; the theory is interesting and ingenious, and if the statement contained in the last sentence always held good, the argument would be very strong; but when one has such a passage as Jer. vi. 26, "gird thee with sackcloth, and wallow thyself in ashes; make thee mourning, as for an only son," it seems pretty clear that the rite was originally transferred from one which had the purpose of evincing grief for the sake of, and probably (as was believed) in the sight of, the dead, rather than with any thought of consideration for the living. According to Lagrange's view this custom must be a very late one if it originated, as he seems to imply, as a result of national calamities, i.e. after settled city life had taken the place of the nomadic life; but there is every reason to suppose that it goes back to a time long before settled life in cities had arisen; the fact of its existence, or something equivalent to it, among savage communities (see the references given above) points to this. We believe that the rite in its origin was a mourning custom pure and simple, and that in course of time it was adopted as a sign of mourning on the occasion of any calamity, national as well as individual. The rare reference to the custom in the Old Testament in connexion with mourning for the dead, together with the clear indication here and there that it was practiced on such occasions—this, taken together with the further fact that it is often spoken of in connexion with other forms of calamity, simply means that in the Old Testament we see the process going on of the old custom being kept up in a new connexion and its original meaning and significance dying out, or, more probably, entirely forgotten. As to that original meaning and significance, it is probable that a hint of this is to be discerned in those passages in which the word 'aphar ("dust") is used of earth from a grave; they are cited above; if that was the place whence the "dust" was gathered originally, then the significance will be seen to be very striking. The ancient Arabs had a magic way of assuaging their grief for the loss of some dear one; they took some dust from his grave, mixed it with water, and drank it![244] If this meant anything at all (and all these things did mean something very real to the people of old), it meant that contact with what was connected with the dead, such as the soil on the grave (whether from the dug grave or from a rock-hewn tomb), had an effect upon the living which was to them as real as anything could be. If this interpretation of the origin of the rite should be correct, it would give an explanation which would be more satisfactory than those usually given, for it touches upon something which was of real importance to the mourner of old; to him it was an act of profound significance; it gave him what was and is, after all, the prime *desideratum* of the mourner— comfort in his sorrow.

When we read of ashes (i.e. cinders) as well as dust (i.e. powdered earth) being sprinkled on the head, this may well be an echo of an original custom of taking the ashes remaining from sacred offerings to the dead (cp. 2 Chron. xvi. 14, xxi. 19).[245]

The modern custom among the Jews of mourners sitting on the ground is doubtless a remnant of this ancient rite.

VI. Fasting

1 Sam. xxxi. 13; "And they took their bones [i.e. those of Saul and his sons], and buried them under the tamarisk tree in Jabesh, and fasted seven days," cp. the parallel passage 1Chron. x. 12, where it is the "oak" or "terebinth" in Jabesh. 2 Sam. i. 12; "And they mourned, and wept and fasted until even, for Saul, and for Jonathan his son, and for the people of Jahwe, and for the house of Israel; because they were fallen by the sword" (see also 2 Sam. iii. 15, xii. 16, 17, Gen. i. 10, etc.).

This custom was also in vogue among the ancient Arabs, and was practiced more especially by the women.[246] It does not seem to have played an important part among the Babylonians, for there are not many references to it; but it is impossible to believe that it was not generally practiced. It is also known to have existed among the Greeks,[247] and also among savage peoples.[248]

It is difficult to discover the origin and to find a really satisfactory explanation of this rite. To say that it is merely the adaptation to mourning of a custom practiced generally for other purposes[249] is simply to ignore the difficulty. It has been explained as "propitiatory of the ghost, as a practice contrary to ordinary actions and so resembling the actions of the land of ghosts which differ from those of this earth"[250]; or, according to Frazer, it was supposed to have the effect of preventing the spirit of the deceased from entering into the body of the living and harming him; the hungry ghost might be tempted to do this if he perceived food in the body; hence the efficacy of fasting. This idea may strike us as absurd, but it is entirely in accordance with the ways of thought of uncultured man. The explanation seems inadequate, but for the reason that it postulates enmity on the part of the ghost; it is certain, however, that it was not always believed that the ghost was inimically inclined to the living. Further, the idea that food was abstained from lest it should be polluted by the presence of the dead, and thus affect the living, seems unsatisfactory in view of the very fact of that presence; the danger of pollution from the dead *directly* was at least as dangerous as that of its acting *indirectly* by means of food. Another explanation is that "actual grief, making mourners indifferent to the pangs of hunger, may have given rise to fasting as a conventional sign of mourning"[251]; this assumes a very widespread effect due to grief, the existence of which is not borne out by the facts of experience; men usually get hungry, grief or no grief, it is the exception when the poignancy of grief is such as to drive hunger away excepting for quite short periods.

Taking into consideration the mode of envisaging things among uncultured men, there is much to be said in favour of Schwally's interpretation; he regards the rite as analogous to that of fasting in order to propitiate a god and avert his wrath.[252] There is here, however, the objection to be raised again that this theory assumes fear of the deceased on the part of the living, and this cannot always be postulated. It is, once more, Robertson Smith who seems to us to have hinted at the true explanation; the fast was a sacred preparation for the funeral feast; "The usage of religious fasting is commonly taken as a sign of sorrow, the worshippers being so distressed at the alienation of their god that they cannot eat; but there are very strong reasons for believing that, in the strict Oriental form in which total abstinence from meat and drink is prescribed, fasting is primarily nothing more than a preparation for the sacramental eating of holy flesh."[253] It was this idea which lay at the back of fasting as a mourning custom; the funeral feast which followed was also a partaking of holy food. That there are cases on record in which the fasting *follows* the funeral feast does not vitiate this theory, since we are dealing with what was the *original* object of the custom; when that had been forgotten all kinds of varieties could arise. Among modern Jews this custom has been greatly modified; only meat and wine are prohibited, and the mourner must eat in solitude; but if the Sabbath, or a holy day, supervenes, these rules are suspended. During the period of death and the carrying out of the corpse for burial all eating in the house of the dead is forbidden.

VII. Lamentation and Wailing

Gen. xxxvii. 34; "And Jacob rent his garments, and girded sackcloth upon his loins, and mourned for his son many days."

2 Sam. iii. 31–34; "And David said to Joab, and to all the people that were with him, Rend your clothes, and gird you with sackcloth, and mourn before Abner. And King David followed the bier. And they buried Abner in Hebron; and the king lifted up his voice, and wept at the grave of Abner; and all the people wept. And the king lamented for Abner, and said…" (cp. 2 Sam. ii. 12, Ezek. xxvii. 32, etc.). The wailing expressed itself also by cries of "Ho, ho" (1 Kings xiii. 30, Jer. xxii. 18, xxxiv. 5). It was accompanied or introduced by the sound of pipes or flutes (Jer. xlviii. 36, cp. Matt. ix. 23, xi. 17[254]; there were professional mourners, "such as are skillful of lamentation" (Amos v. 16); especially women; "call for the mourning women that they may come; and send for the cunning women, that they may come; and let them make haste, and take up a wailing for us.…" (Jer. ix. 17, 18). The lamentation also developed into poetry with a special rhythm called the *Kinah*-strophe, used on special occasions[255] (cp. 2 Chron. xxxv. 25).

At first sight we should imagine that lamentation for the dead is such an obvious and natural thing that no explanation could be needed; indeed, some might feel inclined to say that it is quite inappropriate to reckon it among mourning "customs;" As Lagrange puts it, this must be regarded as an outburst of affectionate feeling (*effusion de tendresse*) which is sufficiently explained by its nature.[256] And, undoubtedly, this is true so far as it goes. But there are reasons for believing that, in *addition*, something else originally played a part in wailing for the dead. If this was, and always had been, only the natural outburst of affection, why did one need professional mourners and professional flute players? Further, let the passage Zech. xii. 10–14 be studied, and it will be seen that the formal way in which the mourning ("as for an only son ") is spoken of shows that something else besides personal grief for the departed is in question; it points to a fixed, traditional ceremonial in mourning. As one writer on the subject says, this passage "makes for the view that the lament for the dead was a religious ceremony conducted under rules handed down by tradition."[257]

It will be instructive to glance at the usage among some other peoples. Although, according to Langdon, the sources offer but meagre material on the subject of wailing for the dead, there is, nevertheless, sufficient to show that it was customary among the Babylonians and Assyrians. The official wailer is referred to on an ancient Sumerian inscription, together with his pay. In the Gilgamesh Epic it is said that the hero mourned for his friend six days and six nights. In the reign of Asshurbanipal one of his officials who died was mourned for; his burial, and the accompanying ceremonies, are thus described; "The tomb we made; he and the women of his palace rest in peace; the psalms are ended; they have wept at the grave; a burnt-offering has been burned; the anointings are all performed... ceremonies of incantation, penitential psalms...they have finished." Elsewhere it is said that three days mourning and wailing took place on the death of the mother of King Naponidus, and the official mourning went on for a month.[258] Pinches gives the translation of a long inscription on which wailing for the dead is mentioned several times.[259] We are told, further, of how at the burial of an Assyrian king the leader of the music with his mourning women began their music when the mourners had all assembled. On another inscription it is said; "The wives wailed, and their friends responded."[260] On another text mention is made of "the stool of mourning," or else, as Jastrow says in his note on the passage, "the place of wailing."[261] Again, concerning the ancient Arabs we are told that the period of wailing lasted seven days; it was the duty of the female relatives to do the wailing[262]; they were called *reddddat*, i.e. the responders.[263]

Among the Greeks wailing and lamentation took place during the different stages of a funeral not only by the relatives and friends of the deceased, but also by professional mourners (θρηνῳδοί); these were of both sexes; the women, especially, sang dirges over the dead; flute playing was also a customary element in the wailing.[264]

For similar rites, on a more exaggerated scale, among savage peoples, see Frazer, *The Belief in Immortality*, i. pp. 271 ff., 280 ff., where it is clearly shown that wailing as an expression of grief is only a subordinate element in mourning for the departed; see also Hastings, *op. cit.*, iv. 415 f.

There is a striking uniformity of custom among different peoples in this matter; and there is no getting away from the fact that we must look for some additional reason, beyond the expression of sorrow at the loss of a friend or a relative, to account for the form of this mourning custom. A number of explanations have been offered to account for the origin of this custom; one thing seems quite certain, and that is that although some one dominant reason (apart from natural sorrow) may underlie the rite, it is not that one alone which sufficiently explains it. As in a number of other mourning customs, there were probably several reasons why the thing was done. Ancient and modern men are alike in this, if in nothing else, that they are always willing to hit two birds (at. least) with one stone. It appears to us that this is illustrated, so far as early man is concerned, by this mourning custom. Rohde[265] shows good grounds for the view that the exaggerated forms of lamentation both among the ancient Greeks and among savage peoples were, in the main, due not to natural affection (he would not, of course, deny that this was one element), but to the belief that the spirit of the deceased was present and witnessed with delight the tokens of affection for him.[266] If, on the other hand, these indications of regard should have been omitted, it was believed that the chagrin of the departed spirit might vent itself upon the survivors, and make things very disagreeable for them.

Other authorities hold that the wailing, and especially the shrill screaming and other hideous noises, had the effect of driving away the demons who were supposed to gather in the vicinity of a dead body. This is undoubtedly the reason in some cases.[267]

It is possible that there was yet another element in this custom of wailing; it may have had the purpose of recalling the dead, either in the hope that he might come back, or to make quite sure that the soul had permanently departed this time (we have referred to the belief in the external soul above, pp. 15 ff.), and was not merely in a deep sleep; we recall the cry of the ancient Arabs which they uttered on the grave of the departed, "Be not far."

In Talmudic times among the Jews the funeral procession was accompanied by professional mourning women; the *minimum* allowed was two flute players[268] and one mourning woman. They struck up their lamentation as soon as the procession started; sometimes they leapt on to the bier and continued their cries there. At times the lamentation took an antiphonal form, at others it was a general chorus. This custom continued as long as the Jews lived in Palestine and Babylonia, or in the midst of a Jewish colony in the Dispersion. It has now long ceased among the Jews of the West.[269]

VIII. SOME MISCELLANEOUS CUSTOMS

There are a few minor customs which may conveniently be grouped together. The *taking off of the sandals* in presence of the dead is referred to as a sign of mourning in Ezek. xxiv. 15–18; cp. 2 Sam. xv. 30, Isa. xx. 2–4. In these last two passages there is no reference to the dead; it is another example of a custom originally practiced in mourning for the dead being adopted by mourners in face of a public calamity. Lagrange regards this merely as complementary to the taking off of one's clothes in order to put on sackcloth ("*c'est un complement necessaire de toilette*").[270] The original meaning is probably deeper than this; to get at the significance of mourning customs which touched the most deeply-seated of human emotions, one must try to envisage things from the point of view of uncultured man, not from that of the modern. We have already more than once seen reason to believe that just as modes of expressing sorrow and distress were derived from the customs in vogue in primitive times of mourning for the dead, so also some of the conceptions regarding the relationship between men and the dcity, and the means of keeping this up, were also held when it was a question of the relationship between the living and the dead. Both sprang from similar emotional instincts;

the elements of fear and reverence, the sense of mystery due to the belief in the reality of the presence of one who was invisible, were common to both. We are justified, therefore, in explaining some mourning customs at any rate, on the analogy of religious rites, performed in the presence of the deity. In the story of the burning bush the command comes to Moses; "Put off thy shoes (sandals) from off thy feet, for the place whereon thou standest is holy ground" (Exod. iii. 5, cp. Josh. v. 15); the holy presence demands definite signs of reverence; cp. Eccles. v. 1 (iv. 17 in Hebr.); we are reminded of the practice at the present day of the Muhammadans, who always remove their sandals when they enter a mosque. The removal of the sandals in the presence of the dead, then, was in its origin due to reverential awe. It was thus not strictly speaking a *mourning* custom, though practiced by mourners.

It is possible that the *covering of the head had* a similar origin.[271] In a passage just referred to, 2 Sam. xv. 30, it is said of David and of those who went with him that "he had his head covered…and all the people that were with him covered every man his head, and they went up, weeping as they went up" (cp. Jer. xiv. 3, 4). The idea that this was done in order to hide one's grief betrays ignorance of the oriental character; all we know of the ancient as well as of the modern oriental shows that he prefers to share his grief. It is far more likely that, on the principle of what has been said above, it was due to the feeling of awe in the presence of the supernatural, just as Elijah covered his head with his mantle when Jahwe was passing by (1Kings xix. 19).

Covering the lips (Mic. iii. 7, Ezek. xxiv. 17, 22), and *Laying the hand on the head* (2 Sam. xiii. 19) may have been due to the same cause. Some would see in the covering of the head a means of averting the evil eye; among the Arabs a fine looking man will often cover his face when in a crowd lest the evil eye should be cast upon him.[272]

The Mourning Customs so far dealt with have all been acts done by mourners to or for themselves, primarily; in some cases the act is certainly intended to affect the departed as well; but in all of them it is first and foremost something that the mourners do to or for themselves. Now we come to consider some customs and rites which are accomplished by the mourners first and foremost to or for the dead, whether for the corpse or the released soul. And here again there are some cases in which, in all probability, the mourners have an eye to themselves; but it is to or for the dead that the initial act is undertaken.

IX. CLOSING THE EYES OF THE DEAD

In Gen. xlvi. 4 the following words to Jacob are put into the mouth of God; "I will go down with thee into Egypt; and I will also surely bring thee up again; and Joseph shall put his hand upon thine eyes."

Looked at from the modern point of view this act suggests nothing more than the outward expression of dutiful affection; and in the passage quoted (the only one in the Old Testament in which the custom is alluded to) we are evidently intended to understand nothing more by it than this; it was a comfort to Jacob to know that this final act of filial affection would be accorded him. But when we come to observe the similar custom among other peoples the conviction is forced upon one that although the sign of affection may always have been an element, there was originally some other purpose in it as well.

That it was done among the Arabs and Babylonians may be taken for granted, since so many mourning customs were identical among the Semites. So, too, among the Greeks[273] and various other peoples in all parts of the world.[274] The object of the rite has been variously explained; Nowack thinks that the purpose was simply to make the departed appear as sleeping[275]; but there is reason to believe that the custom originally meant more than this. In the Mishnah it is said that "one may not close the eyes of the dead on the Sabbath, and not on weekdays at the going-forth of the soul (נפש יצאא). He who closes the eyes at the going forth of the soul, behold, he sheddeth blood "(*Shabbath*, xxiii. 5). The curious expression "the going forth of the soul "may simply mean the moment of death, and to close the eyes before this takes place is, as it were, to curtail life for a few moments and thus a "shedding of blood." But in view of the fact of the widely spread belief that the soul resides in the pupil of the eye, it may mean that to close the eyes prematurely is to prevent the free flight of the soul, which is compared with "shedding of blood." Another, directly contradictory, explanation is that by closing the eyes, wherein the soul resides, one is able to retain it a little longer among the living. The latter explanation is not very convincing, because in any case it was believed that the soul continued near the body for some time after death. Yet another explanation, based upon the widespread belief in the gathering together of demons where a corpse is, is that both the closing of the eyes and every other opening of the body[276] was effected in order to prevent demons from entering it. Finally, there is the explanation that this was done in order to avert the evil eye; this assumes an entirely different belief as to the feelings of the departed towards the survivors (unless it be held that a demon utilizes a dead man's eye); but it is evident that among some peoples this was the cause of the rite, for it was done from behind the corpse, never from the front, lest a look from the not yet closed eye should be cast upon the person performing the rite, to his very great detriment.[277]

X. Kissing the Dead

Gen. 1. 1; "And Joseph fell upon his father's face, and wept upon him, and kissed him." This occurs after the than an outward expression of affection is in question. But there are cases on record in which this widespread custom among various races had a different object and meaning, and in which it was evidently parallel with a ceremonial touching of the corpse.[278] Further, if there is any justification at all in the contention that in seeking the original meaning and object of a custom analogies may in some cases be drawn from men's actions when they believed themselves to be in the presence of the deity—and the majority of authorities seem to hold this view—then it may be that one element, at all events, in this custom in its origin was analogous to that of kissing or stroking an object in which a deity was supposed for the time being to be present.[279] In Hosea xiii. 2 it is said; "And now they sin more and more...they say of them, Let the men that sacrifice kiss the calves"; cp. 1 Kings xix. 18, "Yet will I leave me seven thousand in Israel, all the knees which have not bowed unto Baal, and every mouth which hath not kissed him"; a similar rite is referred to in Job xxxi. 26, 27. Of the same nature was the custom among the Arabs, still practiced by Muhammadans, who kissed the black stone (*Ka'aba*) at Mecca, or else touched it with the hand; the object was to effect close contact with the divinity supposed to reside in the stone.[280] Others believe that so far as the kiss is concerned, the idea was that "in some way the breath was the life of man, and that giving a part of the breath of the object adored was in the nature of a sacrifice."[281] Among the ancient Greeks the nearest relative received the last breath of the dying man in a kiss; this was the act of the departing person to the living; presumably the object here was that of transferring the life of him who was departing to his posterity.

There are thus several ways of explaining the origin of the custom; we are inclined to believe that the first explanation comes nearest to the original meaning of the rite; reverential awe and affection would easily run into one another on such occasion. To the ancient Israelite there was the belief of being in presence of the supernatural when he stood by the dead body of his father, yet affection for the departed must have been one of the predominant elements.

That superstitions of some sort were connected, in much later times, with the kissing of the dead seems to be the natural inference from the fact that it was forbidden by a Church council, namely that of Auxerre, in 578.[282]

Whether the custom of circumambulation around the corpse[283] — either an act of reverence for the departed, or a magical rite to prevent the return of the soul was ever in vogue among the ancient Hebrews cannot be said; but it is a widespread custom; among the Sephardic Jews it has been practiced apparently from time immemorial, and at the present day it is always done; seven circuits are made round the bier, during which prayers for the departed are chanted to a plaintive melody.[284] In substance some of these are believed to date back to the time of Hillel, *circa* 30 B.C.—10 A.D.

XI. Treatment of the Corpse

That we have but scanty references in the Old Testament to the treatment of the corpse immediately after death does not, of course, mean to say that there was any neglect in this respect; it simply means that only rarely did occasion arise for mentioning any details. We have ample information on the subject so far as the Jews of later periods are concerned; and, knowing the rigid conservatism in all that has to do with mourning customs, we are justified in believing that the customs of later times hold good for earlier periods as well. True, there are exceptions here; whatever the reasons may have been, ancient customs were sometimes modified, and in some cases fell out of use altogether; and later customs have come into vogue which were unknown in earlier ages. But unless there are good grounds for believing the contrary, one may say that, in general, customs practiced among the Jews, say, at the beginning of the Christian era had been in use centuries before.

So far as the *washing of the corpse* is concerned the Old Testament is silent, but in Acts ix. 37 this is mentioned as the ordinary thing. In the Mishnah it is said that it must be done, even on the Sabbath (*Shabbath*, xxiii. 5). Among the Arabs the corpse was washed by the nearest relations and friends of the deceased; sometimes the water was mixed, with salt, or with camphor; but those who fell in battle, and martyrs, were not washed, but were buried in their blood.[285] Concerning the Babylonians and Assyrians we have no information on the subject, but it may be taken for granted that it was done; that it was certainly practiced among the Greeks we know from various sources,

The *anointing of the corpse* is not mentioned in the Old Testament, but it was probably done, at any rate among the wealthier classes, cp. in the New Testament Mark xvi. 1, Luke xxiv. 1, John xii. 7, xix. 40. In Talmudic times it was customary to place metal vessels on the body, and to lay it on sand or salt; this was done to postpone corruption, which supervenes so soon in Eastern climates.[286] Among the Babylonians the corpse was rubbed with milk, honey, oil, and salt; spices were also laid upon it.[287] The Arabs, too, frequently used spices for this purpose.[288] The Greeks poured oil over the body. The purpose of these two customs was, no doubt, the temporary prevention of corruption; they were probably not very ancient among the Hebrews, as they imply, especially the second, some degree of settled life.

As to the *embalming of the corpse*, although this is mentioned in Gen. I. 2, 3, of Jacob, and in verse 26 of Joseph, we have no reason to believe that it was customary among the Hebrews; these passages reflect Egyptian usage. The Babylonians embalmed the corpse in honey, according to Herodotus, i. 198; the Jews and Arabs placed spices within the grave-clothes. For a full account of the method of embalming among the Egyptians, see Herodotus, ii. 85–90. The Greeks did not embalm the bodies of the dead.

Regarding the *clothing of the corpse*, in the Old Testament it is implied that a man was buried in his ordinary clothes; in 1 Sam. xxviii. 14 the witch of Endor describes the appearance of Samuel, on his coming up from the abode of the dead, as being "covered with a robe," a description sufficient to enable Saul to declare that it is Samuel. The same is implied in Isa. xiv. 9 and Ezek. xxxii. 27.[289] But in the New Testament special grave-clothes of linen seem to be the custom, see Matt. xxvii. 59, Mark xv. 46, Luke xxiii., John xi. 44, xx. 6, 7; this was also done in Talmudic times, it being considered a shameful thing to be buried naked; this, however, often occurred, especially among the wealthy, who could afford to be buried in stone *sarcophagi* and in built vaults; but among the poor it was always the custom to be buried in grave-clothes.[290] The Babylonians, too, were usually buried in the same way,[291] as well as the Greeks; but the Arabs were accustomed to be buried in the clothes they usually wore in lifetime.[292]

Cremation among the Hebrews was abhorred; we may well believe that the reason of this was the conviction that the soul was in some undefined way connected with the body after death (see next section). Among the Hebrews the burning of a dead body was reserved only for some of the worst criminals (Lev. xx. 14, xxi. 9,[293] Josh. vii. 25); but that the very idea of it was hateful is clear from Amos ii. 1; "For three transgressions of Moab, yea, for four, I will not turn away the punishment thereof; because he burned the bones of the king of Edom into lime," op. 2 Kings iii. 27.[294] Among the Arabs, too, burning of dead bodies was unknown. The Babylonians did not burn their dead[295]; it is true, two vast finds of burnt bodies in regular "cities of the dead" in Babylonia have been unearthed by Koldewey (in 1887), but, as Jeremias says, these are not Babylonian.[296] The early Greeks burned their dead, but with the rise of higher culture burying also became customary.

Recent excavations in Palestine have shown that the pre-Canaanite dwellers in the land were in the habit of burning their dead; for full details, see the *Quarterly Statement of the Palestine Exploration Fund*, 1902, pp. 347 ff., 1904, pp. 324 ff., 1905, p. 318; Sellin's sumptuous work on the excavations at *Tell Ta'annek*; Bericht…, pp. 88 ff., 98; Vincent, *Canaan d'apres l'exploration recente*, pp. 207 ff., 262 ff.; and see also the very interesting remarks on the general subject by Rohde, *Psyche*…, i. pp. 27 ff., 225 ff.

XII. DISPOSAL OF THE DEAD

It is necessary here to emphasize once more the parallel views held regarding the belief in Immortality among the Israelites, viz. the popular and the "official." A Sheol belief of some kind was undoubtedly ancient; all the evidence points to this; but it became greatly modified with the rise of the religion of Jahwe. The normal teaching in the Old Testament represents Sheol as a closed city from which there was no exit; such a view was quite compatible with Jahwe-worship because it excluded any idea of relationship between the living and the dead. The ancient belief was wry different; here Sheol was, indeed, the abode of the dead, but it was not the closed city which it became in later days; the souls, not mere shades, of men who went there could and did hover around and in the neighborhood of the body, with which it was in some undefined way attached even after death. The care of the body, of its supposed wants, and of the place where it lay

were, therefore, matters of paramount importance. In view of the later
"official" teaching these things ought to have been altogether unnecessary.
Very likely this was the opinion of the official teachers, but it is certain that
they found it quite impossible to do away with the immemorial usages
of the people regarding their dead; the tenacity with which these were
clung to shows the deep-seated belief that the dead had consciousness and
power.

The matters to be considered in this section and in the next, which
will show the immense solicitude the Israelites had for the corpse's place of
rest and for its supposed requirements, would be incomprehensible except
on the supposition that there was believed to exist a relationship of some
kind between the soul and the body after death.

A word must first be said about the horror among the Israelites at the
idea of an unburied corpse. The most terrible judgement upon the kingdom for its wickedness which the prophet can conceive of is uttered in
this way; "At that time, saith Jahwe, they shall bring out the bones of the
kings of Judah, and the bones of his princes, and the bones of the priests,
and the bones of the prophets, and the bones of the inhabitants of Jerusalem, out of their graves; and they shall spread them before the sun, and
the moon, and all the host of heaven, whom they have loved, and whom
they have served, and after whom they have walked, and whom they have
sought, and whom they have worshipped; they shall not be gathered, nor
be buried; they shall be for dung upon the face of the earth" (Jer. viii. 1,
2).[297] Again, it is said of the wicked that this shall be their punishment;
"...they shall have none to bury them, them, their wives, nor their sons,
nor their daughters; for I will pour their wickedness upon them" (Jer. xiv.
16, cp. vii. 33, ix. 22, xvi. 4; see also 1 Kings xiii. 22, xiv. 11, xvi. 4, xxi. 24,
2 Kings ix. 10, Ezek. xxix. 5, Ps. lxxix. 2–4). If anyone came across a dead
body anywhere it was his duty to bury it (cp. the passages just referred to
and *Tobit* i. 17, ii. 3–8). According to the Deuteronomic Code, burial
was to be accorded even to criminals who had suffered the death penalty
by hanging (Deut. xxi. 22, 23). An interesting notice in Josh. vii. 24–26
shows that when a man suffered the death penalty of being stoned his

body was covered over with a heap of stones.[298] The horror of a dead body lying unburied was due to the same cause which impelled men to cover over blood which had been shed, whether of man or beast (see Lev. xvii. 23, Gen. xxxvii. 26); such uncovered blood cries out for vengeance (see Ezek. xxiv. 7–8, cp. Gen. iv. 10, Isa. xxvi. 21, etc.). The reason was that the life or soul resided in the blood, according to the old belief (see Lev. xvii. 11, 14), so that if it, or the body wherein it resided, was not covered the soul would not be laid to rest, but would wander about harming men. How ingrained was the belief in the possibility of souls wandering about the earth may be gathered from the tenacity with which it was held by the Jews in later times; in a Midrash belonging, in its present form, to the fifth century A.D. this belief (though it is not a question of *unburied* bodies) is thus expressed; "the souls of the godless wander about over the whole world, and shall find no place of rest for their feet. His soul [i.e. that of the godless] does not enter into the place it is destined for until twelve months have passed, that is until the body has decayed. What does it do? It goes and comes again, always hovering around the grave; and it is painful for it to behold the body which is buried and which worms cover" (*Tanchitma, Wayyikra*, viii.).[299] This echoes ancient belief regarding the soul after death and the relation between the two. It was this wandering about of souls which was believed to take place if the body was unburied; if it was buried the soul to which it belonged would be content, and the living would be safe from molestation. It was, therefore, for the benefit of the living that the dead body should have proper burial. But that is not all. The question naturally suggests itself as to *why* the unburied body should have the effect of making the spirit unquiet; and why should the spirit in this case wander about the earth and molest men? We have seen that the relationship between the body and the soul (spirit) which there is in the living man was believed to continue to exist in some manner after death—and the reason for this belief is not difficult to understand; it might, therefore, be argued that the want of respect shown to the departed by not burying his body was a source of annoyance to the spirit, which for this reason punished those who were responsible for this duty. But this answer is not wholly satisfactory, for one can conceive of the greatest care and reverence being shown to the body without according it burial; what the spirit wanted, according to ancient Hebrew belief, was the consignment of its body to the earth; and why? Lagrange has dealt with this in a very convincing way; he says; "The *tabellae devotionis* show that by means of the tomb not only are the living able to have communication with the dead man, but they are also able to send their messenger to the nether regions. There is thus a free passage from the tomb to the realm of the dead. It is frequently said that the idea of this realm is an amplification of the family tomb. It is in any case a very ancient idea and may throw light upon our subject. The world, so far as our texts teach us, was divided into three realms; that of the gods, that of the living, and that of the dead. That of the dead was under the earth. The spirit of the dead belonged to it naturally. Moreover, between the corpse and the soul all relationship did not cease. If the corpse remained exposed to the air, the soul was prevented from descending to the lower regions, and found itself condemned to wander about on the earth, a domain to which it no more belonged. But if the corpse was buried, the soul could, according to will, either keep it company or rejoin the other souls...."[300] It was, therefore, at least as much for the benefit of the deceased as for that of the living that every care was taken to have the body properly buried; indeed, one must say that this was *primarily* the object; the benefit to the living, which no doubt was believed to be very real, was only secondary. From what has been said, and especially from what is implied in the Old Testament passages mentioned, one sees how incompatible the "official" Sheol belief was with the current beliefs.

The same fear of an unburied body is found among the Babylonians and Assyrians. Jastrow says on the subject; "An unburied corpse was not only regarded as a curse upon the deceased, but also as a danger to the living. The wandering shadow of the unburied sought to be revenged on the living by causing all manner of mischief...certain demons which were believed to lurk in the neighborhood of graves were doubtless really identical with wandering spirits. In any case it was necessary to protect oneself against the dead, who were able, under certain circumstances, to return to the earth and to plague those who were sick. It is on the basis of this conception that the many precautions which were taken among the Babylonians and Assyrians, as well as among all other peoples, to keep the dead within their graves are to be explained."[301] The Assyrians called the grave "the abode of eternity,"[302] a name which implies that the body required a permanent dwelling-place.

It is, therefore, precisely what we should expect when we find in the Old Testament many references to the careful burying of the dead; and there is something peculiarly significant in the phrase "to be gathered to the people" (Gen. xxv. 8, 17, xxxv. 29, cp. xv. 15), or "to sleep with one's fathers" (Gen. xlvii. 30), or "to be buried with one's fathers" (Gen. xlix. 29), that is, to lie in the same sepulcher with them (2 Sam. xvii. 23, xxi. 14; see also Num. xxvii. 13, xxxi. 2, xxxii. 50, 1 Kings xiii. 22, xiv. 31, xv. 8, 24, etc. etc.); for this meant a gathering together again which was believed to take place in the sepulcher, a belief none the less real for being vague and undefined. Interesting in this connexion was the old custom of *burying in houses*; a reference to this has been made above (p. 119), but a few more details are well worth giving here. This custom is only rarely spoken of in the Old Testament; in 1 Sam. xxv. 1, e.g., it is said that they buried Samuel "in his house at Ramah" (cp. 1 Kings ii. 10, 34, xi. 43, xiv. 31, Ezek. xliii. 7–9, but these all refer to kings); but recent excavations in Palestine have proved that in the earliest period of the Israelite monarchy this was not a rare occurrence.[303] In one of his reports on the excavation of ancient Gezer Mr. Macalister says; "That in early times the dead were buried within the city walls is shown not only by the burial cave of the most ancient inhabitants, but also by the occurrence of skeletons among the house-walls of the upper strata. These seem to show that in late pre-Israelite (and early Jewish?) times the dead were buried, not only within the city, but even within the houses."[304] There is a good deal of evidence showing that the Babylonians buried their kings in palaces,[305] as did the Israelites; Langdon says that the earliest graves are found in the temple courts. Whether or not the Babylonians and Assyrians ever buried their dead in houses does not seem to be known for certain; though in view of the widespread character of the custom it is probable that they did. Koldewey writes on the subject as follows: "In Babylon the dead were buried by the fortification walls, in the streets, and in such parts of the inhabited town as were unappropriated for dwelling-houses at the time of the burial....The house ruins of an earlier period were often encroached upon, and where the ancient walls were recognizable the pit was dug parallel with them; where they were not recognizable the walls of the ancient house were often cut through by the grave, while the wall of a later building period once more turned off from the burial site. If an ancient brick pavement was reached this also was frequently cut through, and the sarcophagus lay partly above and partly below it. From such clear cases, against which situations that cannot be made out can adduce no conclusive evidence, it can be distinctly seen that in Babylon, at any rate, no interments took place inside inhabited houses."[306] Evidently it is not easy to say for certain whether there were house-burials or not; moreover this evidence only refers to the city of Babylon.

On the other hand, there is plenty of evidence for this among the ancient Arabs; those who lived a settled life buried their dead either in the houses or nearby; an interesting illustration of this occurs in an ancient Arabic poem, part of which runs thus;

"The people have a burying-place around the court-yard square;
The graves increase in number, but the living get more rare;
The dwelling-place may ancient grow, in ruins it may fall,
Still grows the number of the dead beside the court-yard wall.
The living as their neighbors have the spirits of the dead,
Though intercourse with them is rare, since far away they've sped."[307]

Among the nomadic Bedouins it was, of course, different. With the rise of Islam the custom was forbidden, though Muhammad himself was buried in his house, and by his side his first successors.[308]

Among the Israelites the custom must soon have ceased with the growth of the population following upon settled life, though the evidence shows that kings continued to be buried in their palaces. There are very many natural caves in Palestine, and these were utilized as burial places (see, e.g., Gen. xxiii. 1 ff., 2 Kings xxiii. 16, etc.); from the importance attached to the possession of such it is easy to see the need felt for a fitting abode for the dead. Artificially hewn-out sepulchers in the rock are also referred to; "What doest thou here? And whom hast thou here, that thou hast hewed thee out here a sepulcher? hewing him out a sepulcher on high, graving an habitation for himself in the rock!" (Isa. xxiii. 16, cp. 2 Chron. xvi. 14, Matt. xxvii. 60). These are the only types of burial places mentioned in the Old Testament so far as family sepulchers and tombs for individuals are concerned; but other types existed, such as those sunk in the rock, like the ordinary modern grave, or cut out of the face of the rock, or chambers with vaulted roofs in which the body lay upon a small raised platform; these have all been found in abundance by travelers and excavators in Palestine.[309] Then there were, of course, the ordinary public cemeteries; these, too, have been discovered by modern explorers, but they are only incidentally mentioned once or twice in the Old Testament, e.g. Jer. xxvi. 23, "…and they fetched forth Uriah out of Egypt…who slew him with the sword, and cast his dead body into the graves of the common people," cp. Isa. liii. 9, 2 Macc. ix. 4.

XIII. PROVISION FOR THE DEPARTED

It is very doubtful whether the Old Testament really contains more than one reference to the practically universal custom of antiquity of providing food and other requirements for the departed; in Deut. xxvi. 14 it is certainly implied that this was done by some; but in Hosea ix. 3, 4, Jer. xvi. 7, Lev. xxi. 6, Ezek. xxiv. 17, the reference is to the funeral feast and offerings to the dead. In the Apocrypha there are also one or two references; thus, in *Tobit* iv. 17 it is said; "Pour out thy bread and thy wine on the tomb of the just"; in the *Wisdom of Ben-Sira* vii. 33 the precept is given: "Acceptable is a gift to every living man, and also from the dead withhold not kindness."[310] One must distinguish between an offering to the dead, which comes under the head of the cult of the dead, and gifts of food, etc., which the dead were believed to require. The distinction is a real one, though the two things may seem at first to belong to the same category; the last two passages cited, however, show clearly that there was no thought of worship in the act, but merely the giving of a gift to the dead just in the same way as a gif t was given to a living man. The two things continued side by side for many ages, but among the Jews the giving of gifts evidently continued when there was no thought of the worship of the dead.

There is no rite in connexion with the dead in ancient times which has been more profusely illustrated through the work of excavators than this one. It will be worthwhile to give a few examples of this. We shall restrict ourselves here to excavations in Palestine, as the material is so immense if the subject is treated more widely that the space at our disposal would not suffice.

The important excavations on the site of ancient Gezer, carried out by the Palestine Exploration Fund (1902 onwards), have brought to light some "finds" which offer interesting illustrations of the subject in hand. Among the seven *strata* excavated the two lowest do not concern us as they are pre-Semitic; but the third and fourth, though in the main pre-Israelite, are "Amorite," i.e. Semitic, and belong to about 2000 B.C., more or less. In the fourth *stratum* a Burial Cave was discovered; the extremely interesting questions raised by what was found in this cave (mention of it has been made above, pp. 115 ff.) must not detain us[311] as we are here only concerned with objects deposited for the benefit of the departed. These consisted of the remains of spears of bronze, only the metal remaining (the wood handles having, of course, rotted away long since), a knife, an axe head, and a needle; besides these there was a three-legged fire-dish for cooking; this was broken and inverted over some sheep bones, no doubt, as Mr. Macalister says, the remains of a food deposit; he adds that "it is not quite safe to assume that the fracturing of the fire-dish is in accordance with the well-known custom of fracturing objects deposited in graves, that their spirits may be released and minister to the needs of the spirits of the departed."[312]

The discovery of the ruins of a temple on the Gezer site, belonging to the Israelite period,[313] revealed the gruesome picture of a number of newborn infants in large jars; the bodies were mostly put in head first; in each of the jars there were two or three small vessels, usually a jug and a bowl, i.e. food and drink for the departed spirits.[314] There can be no doubt that we have here infant sacrifices; such were offered, as is well known, by the Canaanites, Phoenicians, and Arabs; the practice is also referred to in the Old Testament (see 2 Kings iii. 27, xvi. 3, xvii. 17, xxi. 6, xxiii. 10, Mic. vi. 7, Jer. vii. 31, Ezek. xvi. 20 f., xx. 26, xxiii. 37); but it is not with this subject that we are now concerned. The jug and the bowl by the side of, or near, the body of each infant illustrate the belief that the spirit needed these things; there can be no doubt that when first deposited these vessels had food and drink in them.

Other examples are those of some Canaanite tombs excavated; these had in some cases food deposits, in others vessels for drink; the latter were large jars, pointed at the bottom, but they were all placed upright showing that originally they contained drink; in each jar there was also a small jug, obviously a drinking-vessel. "The recognizable remains of food consist of cooked fragments of mutton, identified by the bones remaining. These are placed in saucers or dishes. In the middle of one such deposit a bronze spear-head was left, perhaps to enable the deceased to cut the meat, and another bowl was inverted over the whole, presumably to keep it warm."[315] In other tombs, belonging approximately to the same period (circa 1200 B.C.) there were also found vessels with food.[316] Similar things were found in the excavations at Tell-el-Mutesellim[317] Taanach, and Megiddo[318]; Vincent gives an illustration of an Elamite tomb where the hand of the body is in a dish in the attitude of taking to food.[319]

Before we come to a brief and final word regarding the conceptions which prompted the depositing of these food vessels for the benefit of the departed, a slight reference must be made to the lamp and bowl deposits which have been found in such abundance in tombs in Palestine. This subject was briefly mentioned above (pp. 118ff.); here we may give a few examples. They have been found in various kinds of graves, arranged in different ways, but mostly the lamp is in the middle, with bowls above and below, or around. They have also been found buried under house-walls and immediately under door-jambs. A special peculiarity about the bowls is that they have been made watertight by a kind of lime having been smeared over them, a fact which leads, as Mr. Macalister points out, to the natural supposition that when first deposited they had some liquid poured into them; he says further that "this liquid most probably was either blood or grape-juice, which latter in toned-down sacrificial rites often takes the place of blood; for evidence is gradually accumulating that these foundation deposits are primarily sacrificial, and that a human victim was immolated in the original form of the rite." We have already seen that infant-bones are found buried under house-walls. The vessel with the blood or grape-juice would thus represent the sacrifice, while the lamp would symbolize the fire of the sacrifice.[320]

This is extremely ingenious; but while it may quite conceivably hold good for the lamp and bowl deposits under foundations, it is not altogether easy to accept this explanation of their presence in ordinary graves. It can, of course, be argued that in these latter cases the deposits symbolize what was aforetime a sacrifice to the dead; and in principle we do not see that any objection to this can be raised. But it is possible that a much simpler explanation will suffice; and this leads us again to the general subject of food and other deposits in graves. These consist not only of food and drink, but there are arms (whether for fighting or hunting), knives, ornaments, armlets, seals, perfumes, etc.; all things, that is to say, which were used in the lifetime of the deceased; the seals are especially instructive, since they were constantly required in a man's lifetime as standing for his signature.[321] But among the things that were much required, and, as we know, much used, were lamps; might it, then, not have been thought that the deceased, who needed all the things to which they had been accustomed when alive, would need these as much as anything, being constantly in the dark in their new abode? While Mr. Macalister may be perfectly right in his theory so far as the bowl and lamp deposits in foundations are concerned, this need not militate against their serving a different purpose in ordinary graves.

As to the reason or reasons of these grave deposits; the custom may be looked upon as a pious act of loving thoughtfulness; it was the firm belief, worldwide in its character, among men of undeveloped culture that after death life was continued under very much the same conditions as heretofore; and since the departed might well experience some difficulty in obtaining what they required, the living felt it to be their bounden duty to supply this. But, once more, we have more than once referred to the fact that the return of the departed among the living (a possibility which was fully recognized) was regarded as a thing to be prevented if possible[322]; it is, therefore, quite conceivable that by making the deceased comfortable and content by supplying him with all that he might reasonably require the danger would be avoided of his coming back to trouble the living. Both reasons may well have been responsible for the custom.

If it be asked how men in these bygone ages could have regarded it as sufficient to deposit only one supply of food, the reply must be that, probably, originally the thing was done on the principle of sympathetic magic[323]; the custom, having then once come into vogue, would have continued, as is so often the case, without further question.

Much of what has been said in the whole of this, necessarily long, chapter is open to criticism, for various opinions are held on all the subjects dealt with; but upon one point there can be no two opinions, namely the intense belief in immortality to which all these rites and customs bear witness.

The Doctrine
of Immortality

XII

IMMORTALITY
THE NORMAL LOT OF MAN

In all that has been said the fact which stands out most prominently is the deep-seated belief in the continued life of men after death. In whatever different ways that life may have been conceived of, whether it was some counterpart of the body, or whether it was the soul as distinct from the body, or whether it was merely the shade, that continued to exist, the central point of the persistence of consciousness after death is of prime importance. This is taken for granted in such a way, and is believed to be demonstrated so obviously, that it stands on the same level with the recognition of the fact that men live in the ordinary way.

I. The Origin of the Belief in Continued Existence after Death

We may pause for a moment to consider how it came about that men should have believed that in some form or other they continued to live after death; for this belief is universal; as far as the available evidence permits us to judge, it has been held all the world over from all time since man became a thinking being. In considering in the briefest manner the reason for this universal belief our purpose is to observe the common ground, and then to note how from this common ground Semitic, and more especially Israelite, belief diverged and struck out on a line which in some important respects became individual.

What was it, then, which first gave rise to the belief that men continued to live after they had finished their ordinary life on earth? Since this belief arose, in the first instance, among men in a primitive stage of culture, we must expect it to be based upon arguments of a *naive* character; and the generally accepted theory of the leading authorities on the subject is well illustrated by the answer of a native of Australia to the question as to whether he believed that his "soul" (*yambo*) could leave his body; he replied; "It must be so; for, when I sleep, I go to distant places, I see distant people, I even see and speak with those that are dead."[324] That is to say, that, owing to dreams early man came to believe that there was a part of himself, different from and independent of his body—since it could leave the body and go to "distant places"—which could meet with and converse with people who were alive, as well as with those who were dead. To primitive man what we call a dream proved that the dead were still alive. In writing on this subject Frazer says; "The savage…finds a very strong argument for immortality in the phenomena of dreams, which are strictly a part of his inner life, though in his ignorance he commonly fails to discriminate them from what we popularly call waking realities. Hence when the images of persons whom he knows to be dead appear to him in a dream, he naturally infers that these persons still exist somewhere and somehow apart from their bodies, of the decay and destruction of which he may have had ocular demonstration. How could he see dead people, he asks, if they did not exist? To argue that they have perished like their bodies is to contradict the plain evidence of his senses, for to the savage still more than to the civilized man seeing is believing; that he sees the dead only in dreams does not shake his belief, since he thinks the appearances of dreams just as real as the appearances of his waking hours."[325] From the point of view of uncivilized man it is, therefore, not difficult to understand why he believed that those whom he knew to have died were, as a matter of fact, still alive. But this belief must, at a relatively early stage, have occasioned some very natural questionings on the part of uncivilized man. The sight of the dead body of a friend, together with the occasional appearance of the same friend in dreams, must sooner or later have resulted in the speculation—vague, unformulated, inarticulate, though it may have been—as to how these two were related; why should the body of the friend have fallen to corruption and have become less and less like his former self while every now and again he appeared as his normal self? The mystery must have been very baffling; but the explanation was found in the doctrine of the "external soul." We have had occasion to speak of this and to point out the references to it in the Old Testament,[326] so that there is no reason to dwell upon it here. It may or may not have preceded belief in the continuation of life after death, for our present purpose it does not matter; but as, according to this doctrine, the soul could slip in and out of the body, it would have explained to the satisfaction of uncivilized man the relationship between the dead body of a friend and his appearance in his normal self in spite of death; i.e. it simply meant that the friend had quitted his body permanently. But another question had to be answered: how came it that the body part of man succumbed to death? It was evident that something untoward must have happened which ought to be accounted for. The ordinary life of man was that which was natural and normal to him; since that had been disturbed, it meant that something unnatural and abnormal must have happened. This reasoning may appear absurd enough to modern ears, but that to uncivilized man it was one of great seriousness is proved by the large variety of reasons given why men die, and by the myths which are in existence to account for death and to explain how it came about. A mass of evidence on these points has been gathered by Frazer, who shows that many savages in different parts of the world believe that men die because of sorcery, otherwise they would go on living indefinitely; others believe that death is brought about by evil spirits; it is exceptional when they attribute death to natural causes.[327] Very interesting, again, are the many myths which are told concerning the origin of death; here, too, Frazer supplies us with details in profusion.[328]

Death, then, was looked upon as something abnormal, which did not exist originally, and which ought not to have been the lot of man. This, so far as the evidence points, has been the general belief among practically all races. Of the earliest beliefs of the Semitic race on this subject we have no direct evidence; but one may justifiably infer that the early Semites did not differ in this fundamental belief from the rest of mankind; and this is raised to a practical certainty by the fact that the Old Testament contains indubitable remnants in regard to it.

II. The Old Testament Story of the Garden of Eden

The present forms of this story are comparatively late, but they contain conceptions on the subject of Immortality which go back to a hoary antiquity. The clear presence of some advanced ideas to be found in these extant forms of the story shows that later thinkers have been at work on them, but clearly they were not concerned to obliterate the marks of antique thought still preserved in them.

It must strike every reader of the second and third chapters of Genesis who reads these passages with any attention that of the two special trees mentioned as growing in the Garden of Eden, namely the Tree of Life and the Tree of the Knowledge of Good and Evil, it is the latter which occupies the prominent position in the narrative. Nevertheless, there are two passages towards the end of the narrative which show quite clearly that it is the Tree of Life which is, in reality, the more important. These two passages are iii. 19 and iii. 22–24. The former runs thus; "In the sweat of thy face shalt thou eat bread, till thou return unto the ground; for out of it wast thou taken; for dust thou art, and unto dust shalt thou return." The other is as follows; "And the Lord God said, Behold, the man is become as one of Us, to know good and evil; and now, lest he put forth his hand, and take also of the Tree of Life, and live forever; therefore the Lord God sent him forth from the Garden of Eden, to till the ground from whence he was taken. So He drove out the man; and He placed at the east of the Garden of Eden the Cherubim, and the flame of a sword which turned every way, to keep the way of the Tree of Life." The two central points here are that man is to return to dust, and that he must be kept from the

Tree of Life lest he should eat of its fruit and live forever, in which case he would not return to dust. So that, according to these two passages the Tree of Life is really the more important of the two trees. Indeed, the mention of a second tree overweights the story; and the surmise can scarcely be considered overbold that in its original form only one tree figured in the garden. This one tree would have been the Tree of Life; the mention of the Tree of the Knowledge of Good and Evil presupposes an advance in religious-ethical ideas, and therefore belongs to later times. But both forms of the story, the original and the augmented, have an aetiological purpose; each is intended to explain why it was that death came and disturbed the normal lot of man. We shall return to these two in a moment; but it will be instructive first to glance at one of the Babylonian forms of the story. If we had nothing but the developed form of the Genesis story before us we should still be impelled to discern the greater importance of the Tree of Life. But in one of the very much earlier Babylonian forms of the story it is told of how in "the fields of the blessed," corresponding to the Garden of Eden, there was a wonderful plant which bore fruit, and whosoever ate of this fruit remained young for ever and ever. That clearly corresponds to the fruit of the Tree of Life. There is only this one tree spoken of in this earlier form of the story. It then goes on to tell of how the man was about to eat of this wonderful fruit, but was prevented from doing so by the serpent, who seized it and ate it himself. That this Babylonian story was originally told in order to account for the existence of death is clear. A parallel story to this, and originally dependent upon it, is, therefore, to be seen in Genesis; for there, too, the story is told in order to account for the existence of death. In this latter the dwelling of Adam and Eve in the Garden of Eden was, on the face of it, meant to have continued indefinitely. Death is not thought of, and therefore not mentioned, until an abnormal state of affairs has been brought about through the instrumentality of the serpent; so that it is evident that Immortality, not the existence of Death, was regarded as man's normal state.[329]

According to the Babylonian form of the story just referred to, the existence of death is accounted for by the fact that the serpent appropriated to itself the fruit of immortality, and thus prevented man from eating it. According to the Genesis story, the serpent causes the fruit of the wrong tree to be eaten; we should have expected that the story would have gone on to say that the serpent ate the fruit of the right tree, i.e. of the Tree of Life, and thus appropriated immortality to itself; and it is quite possible that an earlier Hebrew form of the story may have done so; but while this cannot be affirmed with certainty, we do know that the Babylonian form of the story, from which the Hebrew form was ultimately derived, contains this detail, and it is an important one; for there is an extraordinarily widespread belief among primitive peoples in the immortality of the serpent because it periodically sheds its skin.[330] It was firmly believed that every time the serpent shed its skin its life was renewed; and by this means it was able to throw off its decaying part, and was thus assured of perpetual youth. If, as there is no reason to doubt, the Semites and with them the ancient Israelites, in common with so many other peoples, shared this belief, the choice of the serpent as the instrument of robbing man of immortality is seen to be significant.

We are thus tempted to hold that the beginnings of a Hebrew doctrine of Immortality took a form somewhat like this; man was originally intended to be immortal; but he became subject to death; and the reason for this was that the fruit of the Tree of Life, which was meant for him, was by subtlety taken and eaten by the serpent, who thus appropriated to itself the gift of immortality intended for man.

The consideration of the next step in the development of this doctrine we must postpone for a little, because another point which bears upon it suggests itself here.

We have seen that death was looked upon as something abnormal, and that it had to be accounted for since man was originally intended to be immortal. If we now inquire why it was that man should have been thought to have been destined for Immortality, it is because the answer will be seen to have a direct bearing upon the subsequent development of the doctrine of Immortality among the Hebrews.

III. WHY MAN WAS BELIEVED TO HAVE BEEN ORIGINALLY IMMORTAL

Uncivilized man was concerned with seeking to account for the origin of death, since, to his ideas, unceasing life was meant to have been the normal lot of men. But with the advance of civilization speculation takes a farther step. While the belief in man having originally been intended to be immortal still holds good, the universality and inevitability of death impresses men more and more, and the stress comes to be laid rather on the question as to the reason why man was originally immortal. The gradual steps which led up to this speculation are obscure, but of one thing there can be no doubt, and that is that the development of belief in supernatural beings had a great deal to do with it.

We are mainly concerned with the Hebrews, and therefore to some extent with the Semites generally. In one of the Babylonian creation accounts it is said that when man was created, a "pair" was created, and this pair was created with the blood of the Creator.[331] Now when one remembers that, according to the very ancient Semitic conception, it was in the blood that the life resided,[332] one can easily understand that the divine, and therefore immortal, life which resided in the blood of the deity would be transferred to any being in whom this divine blood was implanted. And man thus created would be regarded as immortal. For, that the gods were immortal was taken for granted; that was looked upon as their nature, regarding which no question arose.

In one of the Genesis creation stories (ii. 7) it is said that the Lord God "breathed into his [man's] nostrils the breath of life." As the late Prof. Driver said; "Man's pre-eminence…is implied in the use of the special term *breathed* (וַיִּפַּח), which is not used of the other animals, and which suggests that in his case the 'breath of life' stands in a special relation to the Creator, and may be the vehicle of higher faculties than those possessed by animals generally."[333] But it means more than this; it means that the breath breathed in by a Creator who was immortal conferred thereby on man the faculty of becoming immortal.

And once more, in the other Genesis account of the Creation (i. 26, 27) it is said; "And God created man in His own image, in the image of God created He him." This word "image" comes from the root (עלם) of which the cognate Arabic root means "to cut off"; it is conceivable that there was present the underlying, undefined idea of part of the original having been in a certain sense cut off[334]; and if so, the part would, of course, partake of the nature of the whole, according to the antique conception of the Hebrews. At any rate, in all the three accounts referred to the immortality of man would be accounted for because of the mode of his creation; a part of him partook of the divine, and therefore immortal, nature.

In connexion with these old-world ideas regarding the mode of man's creation—viz. by means of the divine blood, according to the Babylonian account, by means of the divine breath, according to the Hebrew one—it is worthwhile recalling that the Old Testament has two significant expressions for describing the process of dying which evidently reflect very ancient conceptions; they are firstly, "to pour out the blood" (Deut. xii. 23, 24); and secondly, "to breathe out the soul" (Jer. xv. 9; cp. Gen. xxxv. 18, 1 Kings xvii. 21, 22, Job xi. 20, xxxi. 39). Both expressions contain the idea of letting the essence of life go free. This being the divine part of man, it continued to exist even though the body returned to dust. For, however small the divine portion in man might originally have been, it was divine life, and this was immortal. It is also conceivable that we have in the Old Testament one or two faint reflections of a belief that at one time even the body itself continued to live indefinitely; this is suggested by the notice in Gen. v. 24 that Enoch never died—"he walked with God; and he was not, for God took him"; and by the legend attached to the name of Elijah, that he never died, but went up to heaven in a fiery chariot and horses.

IV. A Religious-Ethical Development

We surmised above that the beginnings of a Hebrew doctrine of Immortality took the form that man was originally intended to be immortal, but that he became subject to death because of the subtlety of the serpent in preventing him from eating of the fruit of the Tree of Life. This whole idea is, upon the face of it, very primitive, and reflects a very *naive* mental outlook. It will be objected that this is not quite true as an account of the Genesis story, and that we are not, therefore, justified in regarding this as a *Hebrew* form, even in its beginnings, of a doctrine of Immortality. We sympathize with the objection; though, in view of the evidence of the Babylonian account, and the well-established influence of Babylonian thought upon the Hebrews, we are unable to regard it as valid. However that may be, let us now take the story in the present Old Testament form in which the Tree of Life is put into the background, and the central importance is assigned to the Tree of the Knowledge of Good and Evil. Even so, the story is none the less told in order to account for the origin of death; only now death is accounted for by an act of disobedience on the part of man to his Creator; "and unto Adam he said, Because thou hast hearkened unto the voice of thy wife, and hast eaten of the tree, of which I commanded thee, saying, Thou shalt not eat of it: cursed is the ground for thy sake; in toil shalt thou eat of it all the days of thy life...in the sweat of thy face shalt thou eat bread, till thou return unto the ground; for out of it wast thou taken for dust thou art, and unto dust shalt thou return" (Gen. iii. 17–19). The point of prime importance here is the *reason* on account of which death was brought into the world, viz. disobedience to a divine command; this reflects a great advance in the doctrine of God among the Israelites, which, as we shall see more fully in the next chapter, conditions the development of belief in Immortality. It also presupposes the existence of a sense of sin unknown to the Hebrews of earlier ages. In this form of the story the serpent is, in reality, quite superfluous; and no fruit from the Tree of Life would have availed under any circumstances; the fact that these find a place here shows clearly enough that an old story has been utilized and adapted.

The development which this form of the story presents did not proceed further; disobedience to the Creator's command, i.e. sin, was the reason on account of which death came upon all flesh. This is the teaching of the Targums, the Apocrypha, and the Pseudepigrapha; it is also, though in a somewhat modified form, the teaching of the Rabbis.[335] It is also that which underlies what St. Paul teaches in Rom. v. 12–21.

But this constitutes only one department, as it were, of the doctrine of Immortality in the Old Testament; and before we come to consider the development in other directions it will be well to summarize what has been said in some earlier chapters.

XIII

THE DEVELOPMENT OF BELIEF

I. A Summary

A slight summary of the ground so far covered regarding the direct teaching on Immortality will be useful before we consider the final development of belief in Immortality in the Old Testament.

The belief, implicit if not formally expressed, that Immortality was originally intended to have seen the normal lot of man existed in an early stage of Israelite religion; it was always the popular belief, and it is more than probable that even the official exponents of religion in later days believed this in a vague kind of way.

Then, in a still early stage of belief, when it had become realized that Death, and not Immortality, was the normal lot of man, it was believed that owing to the fact that among the constituent elements of which man was made up one part was of divine origin, *this* part of man could not perish, whatever might happen to the rest of him. According to the popular belief this part of man continued, after death, to live under conditions more or less similar to those under which he had hitherto lived; only, as is always the case among men in a comparatively primitive stage of culture, the belief as to *where* the departed lived and *how* exactly they lived was vague and undefined. What, according to the popular belief, was certain was that those who had departed hence were possessed of knowledge and power greater than those of men on this earth. Hence the existence of Ancestor-worship, and of the Cult of the Dead in general.

With the introduction and gradual development of Jahwe-worship a new stage was reached. The regard for and veneration of the departed involved practices which were incompatible with a true belief in Jahwe. It became, therefore, the duty of the religious leaders to ban Ancestor-worship and all communication, or supposed communication, with the dead. And one of the most efficacious means to this end was what was regarded as a reformed teaching regarding the abode of the dead, *Sheol*. The departed, so it was taught, do not remain on earth, nor do they hover in or around the graves where their bodies lie; but they go at once to the dark, silent underworld, and from that city of the dead they are unable ever to emerge again. They have neither parts nor passions, they are the mere shades of what they once were; and therefore they can have no thought of men on earth. What folly, then, to have recourse to these, "to seek unto the dead," in times of need or stress; the Lord God, Jahwe, alone can help, and alone must be worshipped. Moreover, Jahwe has nothing to do with the departed in *Sheol*; His interest is in living men, not in the dead who cannot worship Him. It was taught that Ancestor-worship and the Cult of the Dead was not only folly, but that it also involved unfaithfulness to Jahwe; it was just as bad as paying homage to idols.

The evidence of the Old Testament, corroborated by much that has been brought to light by recent excavations in Palestine, as well as by present-day custom and belief in Syria, all show that the official exponents of religion were only partly successful in their efforts.

The fact is that, at bottom, the popular belief had in it something that was true, however much the people went astray, as they certainly did, in their practices. Two centuries before the beginning of the Christian era, the traditional belief, as it had become, regarding Sheol had been discarded by many, though the traditionalists still clung to it; a new belief concerning the world to come and the departed had taken its place. The immemorial popular belief was vindicated in so far that the departed were no more thought of as "Shades," but as living spirits in the enjoyment of a fuller life than when on this earth. It is this developed belief, and the reasons of its rise, that we have now to consider.

II. THE RESULTS OF THE EXILE: RELIGIOUS INDIVIDUALISM

It is quite clear that so long as it was believed that God was not concerned with the spirits of the departed gathered in *Sheol*, the hope of Immortality could not develop. True, the popular belief regarding the departed was less dark than the official teaching; but whatever there was of truth which underlay the popular conceptions, there is no getting away from the fact that they were wholly divorced from religion. There was no thought of God at all in connexion with their ideas about the world of the Hereafter; their beliefs and practices tended to become mere morbid superstition. The chasm between the *official* teaching of God enlightening the world of the living with His presence, while the world of the Hereafter was dark and hopeless owing to His absence there—the chasm between this and the *popular* belief that adequate help could be obtained in this world from the dead, and that in the world of the Hereafter men were as fully alive as they ever were on this earth, could only be bridged, and either side be put right, by a more developed doctrine of, God. This development of doctrine came with the belief that God was concerned with the spirits of the departed. And this belief arose, under God, as the result of *religious individualism*. Here we must make a slight digression in order to make our meaning clear.

The religion of Israel had, from the time of the monarchy, always been of a pronouncedly *national* character. Jahwe was the God of Israel, that is, a national God, just as the surrounding nations had their national gods; He was the God of the land of Israel.[336] So that the nation was, in its corporate capacity, the religious unit. The individual was absorbed in the nation; the individual derived whatever importance he may have had from the fact that he was one of the items which went to make up the nation. In himself the individual was almost negligible. The relationship, therefore, between the individual and God was almost entirely subordinated to that between the nation and its national God. That is true as a whole, but there are exceptions to the rule. In the case of the patriarchs, of Moses and Aaron, and further, in such cases as David, and Hezekiah, and the prophets, it is clear that the individual relationship to God could scarcely have been more intense. But it must be remembered that in all these cases, whether patriarchs, religious leaders, saintly kings, or inspired prophets, we are dealing with very special personages, who, moreover, in a real sense, *represented* the nation. Such exceptions only set in more pronounced relief the normal position, viz. that the relationship with God in early Israel was a national, not an individual one.

As long as the nation existed this national relationship continued. But with the Exile, and the consequent dissolution of Israel as a nation, a new relationship between God and man came into being. Indeed, this was already heralded when to the clear-sighted vision of the prophet Jeremiah the approaching downfall of the nation became evident. It is true that Jeremiah's individualism did not lead him to a fuller belief in Immortality, but it was part of the foundation upon which others built in later years. It was, above all, the psalmists, as will be shown, who sounded the true notes of a real hope of Immortality, for in some of their writings is seen the fruition of Jeremiah's teaching on religious individualism.

With the disappearance of the nation, as such, then, the individual came to his own. We shall see presently how this religious individualism gave a decisive impetus to the development of belief in Immortality; but we must first touch briefly upon one or two other matters which resulted from the Exile, and which contributed to bring about this development.

III. THE RESULTS OF THE EXILE: A DEVELOPED CONCEPTION OF GOD

Owing to absence from the home-land through the Captivity, worship in many a hallowed center ceased[337]; above all, the worship in the central sanctuary at Jerusalem. The effect of this was significant. We have already pointed out that Jahwe was thought of as the God of the land; according to the belief hitherto held, the worship of the God of the land could not be offered excepting in his land. When, however, the people were carried away from their land and were forced to worship their God in a foreign land—unless they were to give up their ancestral faith altogether—the result was that their conception of God underwent a great change; they came to the realization that Jahwe was not tied to any particular Centre, and that He could be worshipped anywhere. That meant a mighty step forward towards the belief that Jahwe was the God of all the world, and therefore of all men, not merely the God of Israel. Such a development in the conception of God, enlarging the sphere of His influence and power, as it did, to an almost unlimited extent, was certain before very long to affect the belief regarding the relationship between God and the departed.

IV. THE RESULTS OF THE EXILE: SPIRITUAL WORSHIP

Another result of the Exile was the cessation of the sacrificial system. There was no possibility of offering up the daily sacrifices in the land of their captivity; and therefore the worship of the people had to take a more *spiritual* form. It is difficult in these days to grasp what it must have meant at first to the people to be deprived of their ancient form of worship so significant in their eyes, so realistic, and so indispensable, as they conceived. However, what must have been to them a very bitter experience had, nevertheless, to be gone through; and they came out of it all the better. They learned the truth so pointedly expressed by one of their own teachers, who puts into the mouth of God the words:

> *Should I eat the flesh of bulls,*
> *Or drink the blood of goats?*
> *Offer unto God the sacrifice of thanksgiving,*
> *And pay thy vows unto the Most High* (Ps. 1. 13, 14).

Spiritual sacrifices, that is to say, were seen to be even more acceptable to God than those material sacrifices which had hitherto been regarded as

an integral part of the worship of Jahwe. That was an immense step forward in spiritual religion; and, things being as they were, it is difficult to
see how this could have been brought about otherwise than through the
Exile. And here again one can see the indirect effect that this must soon
have had upon the doctrine of the future life; for it was the deeper insight
into the spiritual nature of God which facilitated the belief in His solicitude for the spirits of men hereafter; and the more spiritual the worship
the fuller the apprehension of the divine nature.

V. The Effect of the Exile upon the Belief in Immortality

Here, then, are three matters of very great importance, and the effect
brought about through them in the whole conception of God can easily
be realized:—A new relationship to God, in which each individual was
able to recognize that he had a personal part; a new belief concerning
God, as One, not of a nation, but of the whole world; a new conception
regarding the worship of God, namely, a spiritual form asserting its supe-
riority over a materialistic form.

It needs but few words to show that when a real, intimate, and personal relationship between God and the individual is established and
experienced, the conviction must soon become overpowering in man
that this relationship cannot be severed by the death of the body; or, in
other words, that God's interest in His highest created beings cannot be
restricted to this world. Then, again, the immensely widened conception
of God, which recognized Him as the God of the whole world, and not
merely of one corner of it, how this must have affected the ideas hitherto held regarding His personality and nature! A truer conception of the
divine nature must inevitably, even if indirectly, have led to the conviction
that this world was a sphere all too small for the exercise of His power and
righteousness and benevolence. And finally, the giving place of materialistic to more spiritual forms of worship would of necessity bring with it
more spiritual ideas of the Object of that worship; and it stands to reason
that the more spiritual the conception of God the clearer the apprehen-

sion of the truth that His relationship is with the *spirits* of men; and this as a matter of course reacts upon the belief regarding the relationship of God with the spirits of men in the world of the Hereafter.

These converging tendencies of belief, while working only indirectly, would, from the nature of the case, work none the less effectively in developing the hope of Immortality. And they were the results of the Exile. So that it is not difficult to understand why it was the Exile which was the great turning point in the Israelite belief in Immortality. But the importance and significance of all these things center in the fact that they helped to bring about, and witnessed to the existence of, a higher and fuller doctrine of God. Here, after all, lies the kernel of the whole matter; given that foundation, the spiritual edifice that can be built upon it is illimitable in its scope. But then, again, the fuller the realization of the power and majesty and righteousness of God, the more intense becomes man's sense of his unworthiness in His sight; to apprehend God in any degree quickens the sense of sin in man. Both, the fuller apprehension of the nature of God and the deeper sense of sin in the individual, were developed in consequence of the Exile; and both, in course of time, deeply affected the whole belief and doctrine of Immortality. It came to be realized and acknowledged, above all through the initial inspiration of Jeremiah, that the Exile was the result of national sinfulness, and therefore a vindication of the justice and righteousness of God.

Bearing in mind the thought tendencies referred to, we will now illustrate by quotations from the Old Testament the steps in the development of the doctrine of Immortality.

VI. THE FIRST STEP[338]

The realization of the *possibility* of a fuller life hereafter is a preliminary step which precedes belief and conviction; but even the realization of this possibility does not come all at once; it can only be led up to by degrees. There will be trains of thought which arrest, but do not at first lead onwards; there will be adumbrations which *suggest* development of belief, and stop short there; there will be flashes of light which illuminate the horizon, but which at first appear so bright that they blind, and the seer closes his eyes. We get the signs of all these things in the Old Testament, and they are very instructive.

One of the trains of thought referred to, and which may well have been one of the factors which in course of time suggested the possibility of a fuller life hereafter, was that of the memory of a man living after him in his seed. This was undoubtedly the chief reason for the desire of a "seed" which is so often met with in the Old Testament. It was regarded as a reward for the righteous to leave a plentiful seed because their memory would live after them in their posterity. As a reward for the God fearing man it is said in Ps. xxv. 13; "His soul shall dwell at ease [in reference to this life], and his seed shall inherit the land." So, too, in Ps. cii. 28 (29 in Hebr.); "The children of Thy servants shall continue, and their seed shall be established for ever." Perhaps the most striking passage in this connexion is Ps. cxii. 1–6; "Blessed is the man that feareth Jahwe, that delighteth greatly in His commandments. Mighty in the land shall his seed be; the generation of the righteous shall be blessed. Wealth and riches are in his house, and his righteousness standeth for ever. Light ariseth in the darkness to the upright.... For he shall never be moved; the righteous shall be had in everlasting remembrance"; see also Ps. cxxxii. 1–12 and Isa. lvi. 5. Among the various passages in "The Wisdom of Ben-Sira" (*Ecclesiasticus*) in which this thought occurs, xli. 6–13 is worth quoting in part; "From the son of the ungodly power shall be taken away, and want shall continually abide with his seed. An ungodly father do the children curse, for because of him do they suffer reproach.... Nothingness is the body of a man, but the name of the pious shall not be cut off. Have a care for thy name, for that abideth longer for thee than thousands of sparkling treasures. Life's goods last for limited days; but the reward of a name for days beyond count." Passages of similar import could be multiplied; they witness to an underlying idea of a man living on, as it were, in his seed after his death. Though it was but the memory that was meant, still the name of the righteous departed continued to be a living thing, while at the same time the belief was present in the continuance of the existence, in a nebulous form it might be, of those whose memories were held in veneration. Such thoughts, one cannot help feeling, were the forerunners of something fuller.

VII. THE SECOND STEP

Next we will give instances of passages which contain adumbrations—they are nothing more—of what was to come. In Ps. ix. 13 (14 in Hebr.) it says; "Have mercy upon me, O Jahwe; behold my affliction which I suffer of them that hate me; thou that liftest me up from the gates of death." The meaning here simply is that, owing to the persecution of his enemies, the psalmist had been brought into the direst peril of death; he had been, as one may say, on the threshold of the grave, or at "the gates of death," as the psalmist puts it; but through the mercy of God he had been delivered. That is all that the verse means; but one can readily understand that with the developing conception of God and His power, and with the growth of spiritual religion—both of which received, as we have seen, such an impetus during and after the exilic period—the thought of God's power to save *from* death would soon merge into the higher thought of God's power to save *in* death.[339] If man could enter those gates, why not God? Or, again, take the well-known and sadly misinterpreted passage, Ps. xvi. 10; "For thou wilt not leave my soul to Sheol, thou wilt not suffer thine holy one to see corruption (*Shachath*)"; there the psalmist is expressing his trust in God who will not abandon him to Sheol, nor suffer one who is faithful to Him to go to corruption. But he is referring to some present stress; he does not mean that he will never have to go down to Sheol. Nevertheless, the conviction of God's power to succor men in this world must, with the growth of spiritual religion, sooner or later have led men to wonder whether He could not succor them in the next world too. Another passage which is often thought to contain a fuller meaning than is actually the case is Ps. xvii. 15; "As for me, let me behold Thy face in righteousness; let me be satisfied, when I awake, with Thy form." Here

the psalmist, strong in the belief of his own integrity, prays with sancti-
fied audacity that he may be privileged, as Moses was, to see the form of
God in theophanic vision; the reference is to Num. xii. 6–8, where these
words are put into the mouth of God; "Hear now My words, If there be
a prophet among you, I, Jahwe, will make Myself known unto him in a
vision, I will speak with him in a dream. My servant Moses is not so; he
is faithful in all My house; with him will I speak mouth to mouth...*and
the form of Jahwe shall he behold.*" The words of the psalmist witness to an
intense reality of individual relationship with God; but there is no reference in them to anything beyond the grave. He is a persecuted servant of
God, and longs to be comforted and strengthened with the vision of God;
so he prays that when he awakes from his troubled sleep of anxiety he may
both in mental and realistic vision behold God. But though there is no
reference to the future life here, one can easily see how the yearning for the
vision of God on awakening from troubled sleep would soon lead to the
hope of the vision of God on awakening from the sleep of death. There
are other passages similar in kind to the three quoted; but it is unnecessary
to give further examples; these are sufficient to illustrate the truth that the
realization of the possibility of a fuller life hereafter can only be led up to
by degrees; and that there will be trains of thought which arrest, but do
not at first lead onwards. Such trains of thought are to be found in such
passages as those quoted.

VIII. The Third Step

Now we come to another step in the upward direction. This shall be illustrated first by Ps. xxxix. 3–7 (4–8 in Hebr.); "My heart was hot within me
[namely, because of the incongruity of the fact that the righteous suffer and
the wicked are in prosperity]; while I was musing the fire kindled [what
he had been musing about was the apparent futility of the very short span
of man's life on earth]; then spake I with my tongue; Jahwe, make me to
know mine end, and the measure of my days, what it is; let me know how
frail I am. Behold, Thou hast made my days as handbreadths; and mine

age is as nothing before Thee; surely every man at his best is a mere breath. Surely every man walketh about in semblance [he means that man's life here is such a trifle that there is hardly any reality about it]; surely they worry themselves for nothing [lit. for a breath]; he heapeth up (riches), and knoweth not who shall gather them. And now, Lord, what is it that I am waiting for?—My hope is in thee!" This is a very striking passage; the pith of it is this; life here on earth must, in the sight of God, be such a trifling thing; it offers comparatively so little; men worry themselves about getting money and making themselves comfortable; but what is the point of it all? Everything passes so quickly and lasts such a short time. Then the psalmist suddenly looks at it all from his personal point of view; what is it that I—I, the servant of God—am waiting for? Is there no expectation for me, who trust in God, after this short span of life? Then there is a pause, as though he were trying to argue the matter out; the old Sheol belief is strong within him, it is what he had always been taught; he is puzzled; "what is it that I am waiting for? I cannot say; at any rate, this I know, that my hope is in God."[340] And there he leaves it.

Now we turn to another passage, somewhat similar in spirit, only it goes yet a little farther; Job xiv. 13–15 this must be quoted in full; it is preceded by a long passage in which the same thought of the shortness of life and its apparent futility again occurs, and it ends with the note of dark hopelessness; "So man lieth down, and riseth not; till the heavens be no more, they shall not awake, nor be roused, out of their sleep." Then comes the new thought, a speculation; "Supposing that Sheol were not the end of all things! What if after a long sojourn there man should live again! Ah, if that were so, I should not mind how long I had to wait there, so that at long last my God released me. I should look upon it as God's hiding place for me, where He would keep me in secret until His wrath were past; for in the end God would surely call me forth, He would show His love for the work of His hands." The passage runs thus; "Oh that Thou wouldest hide me in Sheol, that Thou wouldest keep me secret, until Thy wrath be past; that Thou wouldest appoint me a set time—and then remember me! If a man die, can he live again? All the days of my hard service would I wait, till my release should come. Thou wouldest call, and I would answer Thee; Thou wouldest have a desire to the work of Thine hands." There is no certitude here; it is but the vague yearning of a bruised heart; If only things were so! These, then, are two passages which illustrate what we have described as adumbrations which *suggest* development, and stop short there.

IX. THE FOURTH STEP

And then we come to yet another step. For this only one illustration must suffice; perhaps it is the only one available. It occurs in the book of Job (xix. 21–27). In the middle of one of his speeches Job abruptly breaks off, and implores his friends to cease worrying him; their wearisome arguments, having as their object to prove to Job that all his sufferings are due to his own sins, have become intolerable to this man, convinced as he is of his own integrity. He implores them to be still; and he expresses the wish that there might remain for all generations some indelible witness proclaiming the fact that he is innocent and not the guilty sinner that his friends declare him to be; he longs that the words which he has spoken affirming his innocence might be written down in a book, or better still, might be inscribed in the rock, as a challenge to all the world; he cries out:

> *Have pity on me, have pity on me, oh ye my friends;*
> *For the hand of God hath touched me.*
> *Why do ye persecute me as God,*
> *And are not satisfied with my flesh?* [i.e. with calumniating me].
> *Oh that my words were now written down!*
> *Oh that they were inscribed in a book!*
> *Oh that with an iron pen and lead*
> *They were graven in the rock forever!* (xix. 21–24).

Then it is that the tremendous thought flashes upon him that there is a Witness whose word is stronger and more abiding than ever the rock-hewn record; and that He will at the last vindicate His servant's innocence:

> *But I know that my Vindicator liveth* [i.e. He who will
>   vindicate my innocence],
> *And that He shall stand up at the last upon the dust* [i.e. in
>   Sheol, where Job will soon be lying];
> *And after my skin hath been thus destroyed* [he points to the
>   ravages of the disease from which he is suffering[341]],
> *Yet apart from my flesh shall I see God,*
> *Whom I, in my own person, shall see,*
> *And mine eyes shall behold, and not (as though He were) a*
>   *stranger* [God will be his friend].
> And then, as though overwhelmed by this vision of the future, he
>   whispers:
> *My innermost soul faints with yearning!* [lit. "My reins are
>   consumed within me"; the "reins," or "kidneys," were
>   regarded by the Hebrews as the seat of the deepest human
>   emotion].

Here, in truth, was a development of conception. What God saw well to refuse on earth—i.e. the declaration of the sufferer's innocence—He will proclaim hereafter. The dark underworld shall not always retain the soul; without the body it shall see God.

Here was one of those flashes which illuminate the horizon, but which at first appear so bright that they blind, and the seer closes his eyes! Never again throughout this wonderful book of Job is the subject touched upon. But the thought had been expressed; and others, by divine guidance, would think of it, and the hope of Immortality would grow.

X. The Final Stage of Development

Now we come to the last stage. This is represented most graphically by two passages from the Psalms. And here we shall find that the truth, already mentioned, is illustrated that it is through a developed and more spiritual doctrine of God that a fuller belief in Immortality is reached.[342]

In proportion to the deeper knowledge of God and the fuller apprehension of His goodness and righteousness and power, so is the living truth realized and appropriated that the life beyond the grave is better and richer than life on this earth. The full conviction that God's interest in man is not restricted to this world, but that in the world to come His solicitude and care are no whit less than here that was the truth grasped at last by one or two of Israel's devoutest thinkers; this made the hope of Immortality something different from what it had ever been before. One of them thus expressed this new understanding of the personality of God, and therefore the new hope of Immortality (Ps. cxxxix. 7–12):

> *Whither can I go from Thy Spirit?*
> *And whither can I flee from Thy presence?*
> *If I ascend up into heaven, Thou art there,*
> *And if I make my bed in Sheol, behold Thou art there!*
> *If I lift up my wings[343] towards the dawn,*
> *If I dwell in the farthest sea,*
> *Even there Thy hand will take hold of me,[344]*
> *And Thy right hand will grasp me…*
> *Even the darkness hideth not from Thee,*
> *And the night shineth as the day.*

God's presence in the land of the Hereafter; that was what was wanted to make the hope of Immortality something quite different. No more could Sheol be thought of as the enclosed city, dark and silent and dust-laden; no more could men in the land of the Hereafter be thought of as lifeless Shades, without hope and memory, without the knowledge of God, and without capacity for praising and serving Him. The presence of God is there too; it is not dark, but light.

Belief in the omnipresence of God had forced this psalmist to the certitude of God's presence in the land of the Hereafter. Belief in the righteousness and justice of God led another psalmist to a similar certitude.

In Ps. lxxiii. the writer reiterates the difficulty that had troubled many a pious thinker in Israel; how to reconcile the righteousness and justice of God with the notorious facts of life, wherein the God-fearing man suffers adversity and persecution, whilst the ungodly sinners are in the enjoyment of all that they desire?

And as for me, my feet were almost gone,
My steps had well-nigh slipped;
For I was envious at the arrogant,
When I saw the prosperity of the wicked.
For they have no worries,[345]
But perfect and settled[346] *is their strength;*
They are not in trouble as (other) men,
Neither are they plagued like (other) men.
Behold, these are the wicked,
And "being always at ease, they increase in riches
    (verses 2–12).

Then there follows a kind of hypothetical statement; for the purpose of his argument the psalmist assumes the position which most men would have taken up—but wrongly:

Surely in vain have I cleansed my heart,
And washed mine hands in innocency!
For all day long have I been plagued,
And chastened every morning (verses 13, 14).

But then come the vigorous words which show that he had only been speaking hypothetically:

If I had said, "I will speak thus,"
Behold, I should have dealt dishonestly [lit. treacherously]
With the generation of Thy children (verse 15).

And he then goes on to describe the utter destruction of the wicked at their latter end, i.e. beyond the grave; while, in contrast to this, he says in regard to himself:

Nevertheless, I am continually with Thee,
Thou holdest me by my right hand;
Thou guidest me by Thy counsel,
And afterward Thou wilt take me to glory.
Whom have I in heaven (but Thee)?
And having Thee [lit. "being with Thee"], *I desire nought else*
    on earth.

It is the quiet definiteness, the calm firmness of conviction, such as appears nowhere else in the Old Testament quite in the same way, that is so striking here; "And afterward Thou wilt take me to glory." Moreover, the passage is specially instructive because the thought development shows itself in two directions. First, regarding the doctrine of God; the apprehension of God is fuller, for it is realized that His power holds sway in the world to come; that His love for man is equally as great in the Hereafter as here on earth; and that His righteousness and justice are vindicated, for the apparent inconsistencies of life are rectified in the world to come. Then, regarding the future life and hope of Immortality, the passage witnesses to the conviction that it is glorious, and that in the land of the Hereafter God is man's portion for ever.

Thus we have reached the zenith of the Old Testament teaching on Immortality. We say this advisedly, and in spite of the fact that there are two passages in the Old Testament in which a doctrine of the resurrection is distinctly taught; for although these two passages witness to a further development of doctrine, their *religious* content falls below that of Ps. lxxiii. The first of these is Isa. xxvi. 19; the whole of this chapter belongs, according to most authorities, to about the year 300 B.C. or a little earlier. This difficult verse, the Hebrew text of which has quite evidently undergone some revision, should be read thus; "Thy dead men [i.e. of Israel] shall arise; the inhabitants of the dust shall awake, and shout for joy; for a dew of lights is thy dew, and the earth shall bring to life the shades."[347] Distinct as the reference to a resurrection is here, the context shows clearly that there are underlying materialistic conceptions; these make the passage, spiritually, inferior to the psalmist's words, which are so expressive of his deep devotion to God and which tell that his joy and hope of Immortality are what they are only because all is centered in God. Concerning the Isaiah passage, Charles clearly shows its trend when he says that "the writer, who speaks in the name of the people, looks forward to the setting up of the kingdom, with a strong city, whose walls and bulwarks are salvation, and whose gates will be entered by 'the righteous nation'; and since the nation is but few, the righteous dead shall rise and share the blessedness of the regenerate nation."[348] True, there are some spiritual conceptions here, too; but the passage lacks the note of the Godward relationship, without which the chord sounding the hope of Immortality loses its real beauty.

The other passage, Dan. xii. 2, belongs to a period some century and a half later; it is probably based on the one just considered; "And many of them that sleep in the dust of the earth shall awake, some to everlasting life, and some to shame and everlasting contempt." Here one sees a great development, inasmuch as there is a differentiation in their condition hereafter between the righteous and the wicked. Striking, too, is the teaching of the resurrection of the evil as well as the just. In the preceding verse there is a distinct reference to the setting up of the Messianic Kingdom which is to be heralded by the resurrection; this is sufficient to show, knowing what we do about the conceptions of the Messianic Kingdom at this period, that we are no longer on the same spiritual height of the Isaiah passage, let alone Ps. lxxiii. "Without any consciousness of impropriety the writer of Daniel can speak of the resurrection of the wicked. Thus severed from the spiritual root from which it grew, the resurrection is transformed into a sort of eschatological property, a device by means of which the members of the nation are presented before God to receive their final award."[349]

We believe it is, therefore, true to say that although these last two passages do witness to a further development of belief in one direction, inasmuch as they teach a doctrine of the resurrection, they are, nevertheless, not on the *religious* level of the two passages cited from the Psalms. It is in these that we must recognize the zenith of a belief in Immortality in the Old Testament.

NOTE

The biblical quotations illustrative of the development of belief which have been given in this chapter are of different dates; but strict chronological sequence in the case of particular texts is almost impossible where there is so much uncertainty. One must reckon by *periods* where it is a question of following out the development of belief in Immortality; for this is necessarily gradual. We have dealt here with the period dating, roughly, from the Exile to about 200 B.C. Within that period there were fluctuations, though the general tendency was towards fuller development of belief. The exact date of a text, even were it possible to give it, is therefore not of great moment; what *is* important is that it should belong to the period in question. And this, according to the best authorities, is the case with the texts quoted. The quotations given do not profess to be exhaustive.

Notes

1. *The Religion of the Semites*, p. 2.
2. I.e. so far as we can gather from present-day savage beliefs what these are likely to have been.
3. Acts xvii. 23.
4. Here we have an example of a further use of *nephesh*, viz. "oneself"; the words above are equivalent to "to make atonement for yourselves."
5. See further on this, Chapter XII.
6. *The Books of Samuel*, p. 156 (first edition).
7. See Frazer, *Folklore in the Old Testament*, vol. ii. pp. 506 ff. (1918).
8. *Gizeh and Rifeh*, pp. 14 ff. (1907).
9. From a root *kasa*, of which the cognate Assyrian root means "to take captive" Ephraim Syrus translates the word by "charm" (Oxford Hebrew Lexicon).
10. We have quoted the R.V. as it stands, but the text, which is obviously corrupt in some places, needs emendation (see Cornill, *Das Buch des Propheten Ezechiel*, pp. 251 f. [1886]). The corruptions do not, however, alter the general sense of the passage.
11. There are some other ways in which *nephesh* is used, e.g. as the seat of the appetites, emotions, will (this last usually when coupled with "heart"); and a few times it is used of one who was alive and is now dead, e.g. Num. v. 2, vi. 6, ix. 6, 7; Lev. xix. 28, xxii. 4; Hag. ii. 13.
12. It was definitely taught in later times, see *Wisdom*, viii. 19 f., xv. 8, 2 (4) *Esdras*, iv. 35 f.; *Syr. Apoc. of Baruch*, xxx, 2, 3; *Slav. Enoch*, xxiii. 5. It is also taught in Rabbinical literature.
13. We are here only concerned with the word as applied to men, not to God.

14. See, e.g., Exod. x, 13, 19, Hos. iv. 19, Am. iv. 13, Mic. ii. 11, etc. etc.

15. Robertson Smith, *The Religion of the Semites*, p. 40, cp. also Wellhausen, *Reste arabischen Heidentums*, p. 178.

16. This subject is connected with that of the need of burial, on which see below, pp. 177 f.

17. See, for example, Jevons, *Introduction to the History of Religion*, pp. 51 ff.

18. See Robertson Smith, *op. cit.*, Lectures viii.–xi.; Curtiss, *Primitive Semitic Religion Today*, chaps. xiv.–xviii.

19. Edited by K. Kohler in *Semitic Studies in Memory of Alexander Kohut*, it is a Jewish-Essene pseudepigraph of uncertain date, but undoubtedly embodying material which is pre-Christian.

20. For details regarding the belief that the life of the deceased lies dormant in his bones, see Tylor, *Primitive Culture*, ii. pp. 150 ff.; Jevons, *Introduction to the History of Religion*, p. ·5G; Spencer and Gillen, *Northern Tribes of Central Australia*, pp. 530 ff.; Frazer, *The Golden. Bough*, "Spirits of the Corn and of the Wild," ii. pp. 259 ff.

21. Robertson Smith, *The Religion of the Semites*, pp. 168-172 (1894).

22. See further, Stade, *Biblische Theoloqiedes alten Testametues*, i. pp. 48 ff. (1905); A. von Gall, *Altisraelitische Kultstatten*, passim (1898).

23. Pietschmann, *Geechichte der Phonieier*, pp. 155 ff. (1889); W. von Landau, *Die Phonizier*, pp. 5 ff., in "Der alte Orient,"ii. 4 (1901).

24. O. Weber, *Arabien vor dem Islam*, pp. 2 ff. in "Der alte Orient," iii. I.

25. The *shayatin* (lit. "satans") probably owe their existence in the Arab system to Jewish influence.

26. Morris Jastrow, jun., *Die Religion Babyloniens und Assyriens*, i, 355 ff. (1902).

27. F. Weber, *Judische Theologie auf Grund des Talmud und verwandter Schriften*, pp. 245 ff. (1897).

28. See further Wellhausen, *Reste Arabischen Heidentums*, p. 150 (1897); Noldeke, in Hastings' *Diet. of Rel. and Ethics*, i, 669 f.; Baudissin, *Studien zur Semitischen Religionsgeschichte*, i. 279 ff. (1876).

29. O. Weber, *Die Literatur der Babylonier und Assyrier*, pp. 148, 167 (1907).

30. Wellhausen, *op. cit.*, p. 155; Noldeke, in Hastings, *op. cit.*, i. 670

31. Jastrow, *op. cit.*, p. 350; 0. Weber, *op. cit.*, pp. 148, 165.

32. See further, J. Weiss's art. "Damonen,"in Herzog's *Realencyclopadie*, iv 408 ff.

33. O. Weber, *op. cit.*, p. 148.

34. See further, F. Weber, *op. cit.*, p. 255; and Kohler's art. on "Demonology," in the *Jewish Encycl.*, iv. 514 ff.

35. Wellhausen, *op. cit.*, p. 150.

36. O. Weber, *op. cit.*, p. 148.

37. F. Weber, *op. cit.*, p. 254; Kohler, *op. cit.*, iv. 516.

38. Wellhausen, *op. cit.*, pp. 149 f.; Robertson Smith, *op. cit.*, p. 120; Noldeke, *op. cit.*, i. 669.

39. O. Weber, in *Der alte Orient*, VII. iv. 16.

40. Jastrow, *op. cit.*, p. 281.

41. T. B. *Kiddushin*; 81 *a*.

42. T. B. *Baba Kamma*, 21 *a*.

43. See for other details, F. Weber, *op. cit.*, pp. 252 ff.; Bousset, *Die Religion des Judenthums*, p. 333 (1903).

44. Cp. the belief of the Phoenicians that the lion was the incarnation of a demon (Pietschmann, *op. cit.*, p. 193).

45. Robertson Smith, *op. cit.*, p. 129 note.

46. Wellhausen, *op. cit.*, pp. 152 ff.; Robertson Smith, *op. cit.*, pp. 120 f., 133; see also Lagrange, *Etudes sur lee religions semitiques*, pp. 317 ff. (1903).

47. Jastrow, *op. cit.*, p. 281, and compare the representation of these hybrid monsters in Babylonian religious art.

48. It is said in T. B. *Pesachim*, 112 *b*: "Do not stand still when a bull comes from the field, for Satan dances between his horns."

49. Midr. *Sifre*, 138 *b*; Midr. *Bereshith Rabba*, c. 22; T. B. *Shabbath*, 55 *b*.

50. F. Weber, *op. cit.*, pp. 252 ff.

51. Wellhausen, *op. cit.*, p. 149; Robertson Smith, *op. cit.*, PP12.0 ff.

52. Noldeke, *op. cit.*, i. 670.

53. See further, F. Weber, *op. cit.*, pp. 254 ff.

54. See Deut. xxx. 17, Ps cvi. 37, *Baruch* iv. 7.

55. Baudissin, *Studien zur Semitiechen Religionsgeschichte*, i. 282 (1876).

56. *Reste arabischen Heidentums*, p. 153. For other parallels see Kittel, *Studier: zur Hebraiechen Archaologie*, pp. 171 ff. (1908).

57. *Op. cit.*, pp. 119 f.; cp. Wellhausen, *op. cit.*, pp. 149 f.

58. Cp. Baudissin, *op. cit.*, i. 137.

59. See also Lev. xvii. 7, 2 Kings xxiii. 8 (reading "high places of the *Se'irim*").

60. Cp. Baudissin, *op. cit.*, i. 140.

61. I.e. Ps. lxxiv. 14, where the text is obviously corrupt; but some ancient myth seems to be referred to concerning the *Ziyyim* feeding on Leviathan.

62. Cp. "the howling wilderness," Deut. xxxii. 10, for the thought, but the root is a different one. Among the Arabs the wilderness is said "to speak," by which is meant the mysterious humming, buzzing noise characteristic of the desert, which they ascribe to demons.

63. *Assyrisches Worterbuch*, s.v,

64. Cp. Septuagint of Mic. i. 8, Jer. l. 39 (xxvii. 39).

65. See also Zeph. ii. 14, a somewhat similar passage, in which the words for animals are conjecturally translated; these animals are likewise looked upon as being the incarnations of demons.

66. According to Jewish tradition the meteor-stone was called "the arrow of Lilith."

67. Hence the belief of some scholars that the name is derived from the Sumerian *lil*, "storm"; this, however, hardly agrees with the idea conveyed in Isa. xxxiv. 14.

68. See further, Jastrow, *Die Religion Assyriens und Babyloniens*, i. 278 ff., 319. An illustration of an Assyrian demon which may have been a representation of Lilitu is given in Jeremias, *Das Alie Testament im Lichte de, alten Orients*, p. 342.

69. Another harmful Babylonian demon, seep. 31.

70. O. Weber, *Damonenbeechsuorunq bei den Babyloniern und Assyrern*, in "*Der alte Orient*," vii. 16.

71. Cp. F. Weber, *Judische Theologieaul Grund des Talmud. und verwandter Schriften*, p. 254.

72. M. Jastrow, *op. cit.*, pp. 332, 342-345.

73. Wellhausen, *op. cit.*, p. 135.

74. The Prayer Book Version, "Let Satan stand at his right hand," is quite misleading.

75. *Primitive Culture*, .426 (3rd ed.).

76. Curtiss, *Primitive Semitic Religion Today*, passim.

77. Hastings' *Encyclopedia of Religion and Ethics*, iv. 615 *a*.

78. *Op. cit.*, p. 179.

79. Doughty, *Arabia Deserta*, i. 240 f., 449.

80. = the Hebrew *Shedim*.

81. M. Jastrow, *Die Religion Babyloniens und Assyriens*, i. 281.

82. M. Jastrow, *op. cit.*, i. 355. Elsewhere it is said that *Shedu* walks in front, *Lamassu* behind a man as his protectors. *Shedu* is also spoken of as "the guardian-spirit of life."

83. They are taken mainly from M. Jastrow in his great work already cited; but see also King's *Babylonian Magic and Sorcery*; O. Weber, *Literatur der Babylonier und Assyrier*.

84. Jeremias, *Das alte Testament im Lichte des alten Orients*, pp. 232 f.

85. Cp. Job i. 6, ii. I, xxxviii. 7.

86. Robertson Smith, *The Religion of the Semites*, p. 445.

87. Cp. the important passage in this connexion I Kings xxii. 19-22, "I saw Jahwe sitting on His throne, and all the host of heaven standing by Him on His right hand and on His left...."(See the whole passage.)

88. The word is also used of an ordinary human messenger.

89. This phrase has an entirely different meaning from the same phrase belonging to post-exilic literature, when it means an intermediate being between God and man.

90. Although the form of the Hebrew for "God" in these cases is plural, So that one might translate lit. "the messenger of the gods," just as we translated "the sons of the gods," yet this would not be justified here, because the passages in which "the messenger of J." and "the messenger of God" occur reflect monotheistic teaching; and what were "gods" has now become "God," though the ancient plural form is retained. Moreover, in all these passages "God," though plural in form, is equivalent to Jahwe.

91. Cp. Ps. viii. 5 (6 in Hebrew), where we should probably read: "Thou madest him but little lower than gods," i.e. angels; see also Ps. lxxxix. I, 6, xcvii. 7, cxxxviii. I.

92. Gen. xix. offers some difficulties, and has evidently been subjected to some revision, inadequate it is true; for "the two angels" in verse 1 presumably refer back to xviii. 22, where "the men" are spoken of; and these men are those mentioned in xviii. 16, who in turn are the same as the "three men" in xviii. 2, one of whom is Jahwe (see xviii. 13, 14, 17, 20). See also xix. 14, 16, 18, 21, 24, which show a mixing up of the plural (referring to the "two men") and the singular (referring to Jahwe).

93. Much stress, owing to the special circumstances portrayed, cannot be laid on Job iv. 18:"Behold, He putteth no trust in His servants; and His angels He chargeth with folly," see also xv. 15.

94. Furtwangler in Roscher's *Lexikon*, art. "Gryps."

95. *Encyclopredia Biblica*, .745.

96. Cp. Ezek. xxviii. 13–16, a difficult passage, the text of which is evidently not in order.

97. For the greatly developed doctrine in the late passage Isa. xxvi. 19 see below.

98. Taken from G. A. Cooke, *North Semitic Inscriptions*, pp. 26, 30.

99. Used figuratively of those who are in Sheol and those who are dead

100. Cp. the Babylonian belief that in the realm of the dead no ranks are recognized, see below, p. 81.

101. The present Hebrew text reads: מֵעֲרָלִים נֹפְלִים אֶת־גִבּוֹרִים יִשְׁכְּבוּ וְלֹא as emended on the base of the Septuagint we should read: מֵעוֹלָם הַנֹּפְלִים אֶת־גִבּוֹרִים יִשְׁכְּבוּ וְלֹא the emendation so far as the consonants are concerned is therefore slight. Cp. also Ezek. xxvi, 20, "Then will I bring thee down with them that descend into the pit, *to the people of old time*."

102. Reading צְנוֹחָם instead of עֲנוֹחָם.

103. On this see further below.

104. See further below.

105. See further below.

106. See further below.

107. It should be noted that even in this post-exilic passage the "reformed" teaching as to the silence of the dead (Ps. cxv. 17) is contradicted.

108. Though even so, knowing as we do the predilection of the Hebrew writers for word-plays, it is strange that in Isa. xiv. 10 the writer does not use the word *raphah* for "to be weak" if he intended to imply that Rephaim came from this root.

109. *Zeitachrift fur die alt. teat. Wisscnschaft,* I 918, p. 135.

110. *Ibid.*, p. 138.

111. Herder, *Vom Geist der hebrai'schen Poesie*, i. 368.

112. See further on this Enoch viii.-xvi.; *Jubilees* v.; *Pirke de Rabbi Eliezer* xxii., cp. *Wisdom* xiv. 6; from these one gets a good idea of what was believed in the ancient times of those giants being cast down into the netherworld. In this connexion it is worth remembering that according to the Babylonian conceptions regarding the underworld it is ruled by a lower order of gods; see further on this below, p. 80.

113. Lagrange, *Etudes sur les religiona Semitiques*, p. 273; the thought had struck the present writer before he came across this passage. One is also reminded

of the healing waters which, according to Babylonian belief, existed in the realms of the dead; see below.

114. *Encycl. Bibl.* i. 496 f.

115. It is worth pointing out that Og, in whose kingdom these Rephaim were believed to have existed, is connected with some strange old myths. In the document known as the *Gelasian Decree* (fifth or sixth century A.D.) "concerning books to be received and not to be received, one of the latter which are mentioned is called "the Book of Og, the Giant who is said by the heretics to have fought with a dragon after the Flood"(see M. R. James, The Lost Apocrypha of the Old Testament, in "Translations of Early Documents," pp. xiii. 40, 41). Dr. James says: "It is a constant Rabbinic story that he (i.e. Og) was one of the antediluvian giants, and that he escaped the Flood by riding on the roof of Noah's ark, being fed by Noah". . .; see further *Eisenmenger's Entdecktes Judenthum*, and Baring Gould's *Legends of Old Testament Characters.*

116. Cp. Josephus, Antiq. VII iv. I, xii. 4. See also 2 Sam. xxiii. 13, 14 (= 1 Chron. xi. 15, 16).

117. *Encycl. Bibl.* ii. 2071.

118. An Aramaic word for "fire-place," see Robertson Smith's illuminating and convincing note in *The Religion of the Semites*, p. 377 (2nd ed.).

119. This is recorded, in the Babylonian Talmud (*Erubin* 19*a*), as the teaching of the disciples of Jochanan ben Zakkai (*circa* A.D. 75). See further, Enoch liv. 1-6, xc. 24-27.

120. But see further bellow.

121. Jeremias *Holle und Paradies beiden Babyloniern*, in "*Der alte Orient,*" i. pp. 16, 17. See also, by the same author, *Das alte Testament im Lichte des alten Orients*, pp. 1 0, 46.

122. Jeremias, *Holle . . .*, p. 14.

123. Jastrow, *Die Religion . . ,* i. 157.

124. Cp. Delitzsch, *Das Land ohne Heimkehr*, pp. 14 ff.

125. Jeremias, *Holle . . .*, p. 15. Jastrow, *op. cit.*, ii. 958.

126. See further the chapter on Necromancy.

127. Jeremias, *Holle . . .*, p. 22.

128. Jensen, *Assyrisch-babylonische Mythen und Epen*, p. 560; Zimmern in Schrader's *Die Keilinschriften und das alte Testament* (3rd ed.), p. 397.

129. See Ezek. viii. 14, and cp. Isa. xvii. 10, 11, lxv. 3.

130. Frazer, *Adonis, Attis, and Osiris*, pp. 6, 7; see also *The Scapegoat*, p. 398; both volumes belong to *The Golden Bough*.

131. Jeremias, *Holle . . .*, pp. 22 f.

132. Wellhausen, *Reste arabischen Heidentums*, p. 185.

133. In *The American Journal of Semitic Languages*, xiv. 170; but other Assyrian scholars deny that such an Assyrian equivalent exists so far as is known.

134. Cp. 2 Sam. xii. 23. "...Can I bring him back again? I shall go to him, but he shall not return to me."

135. The Hebrew text of the last sentence is corrupt, it reads: וַיִּרְדּוּ לַבֹּקֶר יְשָׁרִים בָּם. "And the upright shall have dominion over them in the morning"; these words give no sense unless a strained and unnatural interpretation is put upon them; it is better to amend the text thus: יֵרְדוּ לַקֶּבֶר: בַּמֵּישָׁרִים, "they shall go down to the grave with the upright"; this involves no change in the consonants and agrees better with the context. All, good and bad, go down to Sheol, but the righteous shall be redeemed from it (see the next verse).

136. Cp. "The river of oblivion," Lethe, the river of Hades, out of which the souls of the departed drink and forget all about their life on earth, according to ancient Greek belief.

137. Cp. Prov. xx. 27, "Sheol and Abaddon are never satisfied"; see also Prov. i.11 and Hab. ii. 5. In Prov. xxx. 15, 16 it is said: "There are three beings that are never satisfied, yea, four that say not, Enough: Sheol . . ."

138. This is a difficult sentence to translate; the rendering above is literal; and it is based upon an emedation of the Hebrew text, reading חִשַּׂכְתָּ "thou hast kept back," for חָשַׁקְתָּ "thou hast loved." The Revised Version translates *Shachath* by "pit"; but this is apt to cause confusion to readers of the English text only.

139. Here the Revised Version renders the word properly, the only time!

140. The Revised Version renders the word inconsistently; in Job xxvi. 6, Prov. xv. 11, by "Abaddon," but in Job xxviii. 22, Ps. lxxxviii. 11, as "Destruction," and *vice versa* in the margin.

141. The chapters on Necromancy and Mourning and Burial Customs should be read in connexion with this subject.

142. *Introduction to the History of Religion* (3rd ed.), p. 189.

143. On these see below.

144. But see Tylor's words below.

145. *Op. cit.*, pp. 190–198.

146. *Primitive Culture*, ii. II 3.
147. Hastings, *Encycl. of Religion and Ethics*, i. 438; Jastrow, *op. cit.*, i. 36, 55, 169 £., ii. 122, etc.
148. See Frazer, "The Golden Bough": *The Magic Art*, i.285 ff., ii. 29 ff.; *Adonis, Attis, Osiris*, i. 46; *Spirits of the Corn and of the Wild*, ii. II I ff. Hastings' *Encycl. of Rel. and Ethics*, i. 425–466.
149. Jeremias, *Holle und Paradies . . .*, p. 11.
150. Hastings' *Encycl....*, i. 440.
151. This was also the case among the Arabs, see Wellhausen, *Reste ...*p. 184.
152. I.e. the evergreen terebinth.
153. *Judges*, in the Intern. Crit. Com., p. 273.
154. Curtiss, *Primitive Semitic Religion Today*, p. 65.
155. *Op. cit.*, pp. 75 ff.; see the whole of chaps. vii, viii.
156. *Op. cit.*, pp. 85 f.
157. *Op. cit.*, pp. 89 ff.
158. In the Mishnah (*Aboda Zara*, i. 3) this is looked upon as an act of idolatry: "Every death at which a burning takes place there is idolatry (practiced)…" This is usually taken to refer to cremation, but it is not necessarily so; the word for "a burning"(שׂרפה) is the same as in 2 Chron. xvi. 14, xxi. 19.
159. The singular form of "Elohim" occurs, it is true, but only fifty-seven times in the whole of the Old Testament.
160. *Antiq.*, XVIII, ix. 5. Cp. the action of Rachel when leaving her father's house on a journey.
161. The chapters on Necromancy and Mourning and Burial Customs should be read in connexion with this subject.
162. There is probably also a reference to this in Lev. xxi. 6, where it is said that the offerings of bread are for Jahwe, i.e. not for the dead, see context.
163. *Hastings' Encycl....*, iv. 445 *b*; for a similar thing among the Greeks see Farnell, *Greece and Babylon*, p. 209.
164. *Reste....*, p. 183.
165. A fragment of a drinking-cup, belonging to circa 500 B.C., was discovered at Tell-el-Hesy (Lachish) by Prof. Flinders Petrie bearing the inscription לְהָסֵךְ ("for pouring out a drink oblation"). This may or may not have been used in the way that Asshurbanipal did; but the expression occurs in Jer. xliv. 19, 25, where mention is made of pouring out drink-offerings to the queen of

heaven. Curtiss mentions a drink offering of coffee poured out in honour of a dead sheikh (op. cit., p. 183). See further Robertson Smith, The Religion of the Semites, p. 235. In this connexion many will recall what is said in the *Iliad*, xxiii. 218 ff.

166. *Op. cit.*, i. 240 f., 450 f.

167. *Op. cit.*, pp. 169 ff.

168. *Op. cit.*, p. 208.

169. See further below.

170. R. A. Stewart Macalister in the "Report of the Excavation of Gezer "in the *Quarterly Report* of the Palestine Exploration Fund, 1903, pp. 14–19. See also Mr. S. A. Cook's remarks on the finds in the necropolis of St. Louis on the site of the ancient Carthage of the Phoenicians, *Quarterly Statement*, 1906, p. 159.

171. In the *Wisdom of Solomon* xvi. 15 we have the following distinct reference to the Cult of the Dead; "…For a father afflicted with untimely grief having made an image of a child quickly taken away, now honoured him as a god that once was a dead human being, and delivered to those that were under him mysteries and solemn rites."

172. In Hastings' *Encycl.…*, iv. 335 *b*.

173. In Hastings, *op. cit.*, iv. 445 *a*.

174. *Reste . . .*, p. 177.

175. On this see further below.

176. "The Law of Holiness," known by the symbol H.

177. *Op. cit.*, pp. 323 ff.

178. Robertson Smith, *The Religion of the Semites*, p. 443.

179. In Hastings' *Encycl. of Rel. and Ethics*, i. 439.

180. Jeremias, *Das alte Testament im Lichte des alten Orients*, p. 288.

181. The text is mutilated here.

182. Jeremias, *Holle und Paradies bei den Babyloniern*, p. 20.

183. This would, of course, only have been part of the ritual, for there would have been a "medium "of some sort (one of the order of special priests referred to) who may be supposed to have taken some special part in addition to that of the professional mourning men and women.

184. Jeremias, *op. cit.*, p. 21.

185. Cp. Jastrow, *op. cit.*, i. 269.

186. On these see next section.

187. I.e. Mount Zion, see verse 8 (end).

188. Peake's *Commentary on the Bible*, p. 44.

189. The words are put into the mouth of God.

190. We are not forgetting the retrograde action of Manasseh; but this, like Saul and the witch of Endor, is an exception to the rule as far as those in high place are concerned.

191. The R.V. rendering, "a woman that hath a familiar spirit," is ambiguous.

192. Hastings' *Encycl. of Rel. and Ethics*, iv. 811

193. See Below.

194. That these stages are not clearly marked in the Old Testament will not cause surprise.

195. This would not prevent their also being set up in houses.

196. *Das Leben nach dem Tode*, pp. 35 ff.

197. Jastrow, *op. cit.*, ii. 957.

198. Wellhausen, *op. cit.*, p. 185.

199. Muller in the *Encycl. Bibl.*, ii. 1218; Erman, *Die oegyptische Religion*, pp. 88 ff.

200. Cp. the Greek representation of Death as one with black Wings.

201. Cp. the Greek ποτάομαι, ἀναπτερόω, etc.

202. Frazer, *The Golden Bough*, "Taboo and the Perils of the Soul," p. 33,

203. In Hastings' *Encycl. of Religion and Ethics*, iv. 426 *a*.

204. There are admirable and concise accounts by H. R. Hall (Egyptian), G. Sergi (Greek) and in Hastings, *op. cit.*, iv. pp. 458–464 and 472–475.

205. Maspero, *Histoire ancienne des peuples de l'Orient clasaique*, i. 689; cp. Jensen, *Die Keilinachriften und daa alte Testament* (3rd ed.), p. 603.

206. Jeremias, *Das alte Testament im Lichte des alten Orienta*, p. 360; *Holle und Paradiea*, p. 9.

207. Wellhausen, *op. cit.*, p. 177, 181; Goldziher, *op. cit.*, pp. 244 ff.

208. Philologua, iii. 212 (Dummler).

209. Gruppe, *Griechische Mythologie und Religumageschichte*, ii. 911 ff. Frazer, "On Certain Burial Customs as Illustrative of the Primitive Theory of the Soul," in the *Journal of the Anthropological Institute*, xv. 64 ff.; *Adonis, Attis, Osiris*, ii. 264.

210. Cp. 2 Kings xix. 1; on the other hand, in 2 Kings vi. 30 the sackcloth is seen to be under the ordinary clothes!

211. "On Jes dechirait moins pour revetir le sac plus promptement que pour professer qu'on ne voulait pas d'autre parure que ce vetement grossier," *op. cit.*, p. 276.

212. The two rites are certainly not always mentioned together in the Old Testament, see, e.g., Gen. xxxvii. 29, Lev. xxi. 10, 2 Sam. i. 11, Jer. xli. 5.

213. See, e.g., Frazer, in the art. in the *Journal of the Anthrop. Inst.* already alluded to; Gruneisen, *Der Ahnenkultus und die Urreligion Israels*, pp. 95 ff.; Beer, *Der Biblische Hades*, pp. 16 f.; Marti, *Das Dodekapropheton*, p. 49; and many others.

214. Marti, *op. cit.*, p. 51, is disposed to regard this as the more probable.

215. Curtiss gives a photographic illustration of one of these on p. 91 of his book referred to above.

216. *The Religion of the Semites* (2nd ed.), pp. 335 f.

217. For references to the former rite, see above.

218. E.g. Josh. vii. G, Joel ii. 12, etc. etc.

219. Chardin, *Reisen*, vi. 250, referred to by Nowack, *Hebrdische Archaologie*, i. 193. Strange to say, the custom was in vogue among some Christians up to comparatively late times. Gregory of Nyssa deplores its existence (*Jewish Quarterly Review*, v. 238), and in the Narrations of St. Nilus (Migne, *Patr. Graec.*, lxxix. 660) we are told of a Christian woman who would not exhibit the usual signs of mourning because of the cruel way in which her son had been put to death; οὐ κατέσχισα χιτῶνα καὶ γυμνὰ χερσὶν ἔτυψα στέρνα, οὐκ ἐσπάραξα καὶ ὄνυξιν ἠφάῶνισα τὸ πρόσωπον; quoted by Krauss, *Talmudische Archiiologie*, ii. 480.

220. Krauss, *op. cit.*, ii. 7 L

221. *Journal of the Anthrop. Institute*, xv. 1 ff., 64 ff.

222. Quoted by Torge, *Seelenglaube und Unsterblichkeitshoffnung im alten Testament*, p. 194.

223. See above.

224. Lev. x. 6 is probably also a reference to this custom, "Let not the hair of your head go loose" (or according to another reading, "Uncover not your heads"), being preparatory to cutting it off; cp. xxi. 10.

225. Jeremias, *op. cit.*, p. 360.

226. Wellbausen, *op. cit.*, pp. 181 f.

227. See, e.g., *Iliad*, xxiii. 135–141.

228. See the references given above.

229. Hastings, *op. cit.*, iv. 431 f.

230. *Op. cit.*, p. 326.

231. Among other passages see 2 Sam, xxi.10, Isa. xv.3, Jer. vi.26, xlviii. 37, Ezek. xxvii. 31.

232. Jensen, *Keilinschriftliche Bibliothek*, vi. 400.

233. Jeremias, *op. cit.*, p. 360; Delitzsch, *Das Land ohne Heimkehr*, p. 39.

234. Hastings' *Encycl. of Rel. and Eth.*, iv. 439 *b*.

235. Wellhausen, *op. cit.*, p. 181.

236. Schwally, *Das Leben nach dem Tode . . .*, pp. 35 ff.

237. The fact that it was retained by the prophets would have caused it to be regarded with veneration, cp. Isa. xx. 2 ff. We are also reminded of the use of leaven among the Israelites.

238. Hastings, *op. cit.*, iv. 439 *b*.

239. *Op. cit.*, p. 192. Cp. Lagrange, *op. cit.*, p. 276.

240. Wellhausen, *op. cit.*, p. 177.

241. Hastings, *op. cit.*, ii. l 13a (Canney); Frazer, *Folklore in the Old Testament*, iii. pp. 76, 298.

242. Jastrow, *op. cit.*, iii.826; Jeremias, *Holle . . .*, p. 10.

243. *Op. cit.*, pp. 280 f.

244. Wellhausen, *op. cit.*, p. 163.

245. The interpretation of this mourning custom suggested above was reached by the writer independently of Robertson Smith, *op. cit.*, pp. 413 ff., and Schwally, *op. cit.*, p. 15.

246. Wellhausen, *op. cit.*, p. 182.

247. Lucian, *De Luctu*, xxiv.

248. Frazer, *Adonis, Attis, Osiris*, i. 272; *Journal of the Anthrop. Inst.*, xv. 92; Westermarck, *Folklore*, xviii, 403.

249. Lagrange, *op. cit.*, p. 279.

250. Hastings, *op. cit.*, v. 760 *b*.

251. Hastings, *op. cit.*

252. *Op. cit.*, pp. 21 ff.

253. *Op. cit.*, p. 434

254. Cp. Josephus, *Bell. Jud.* III. ix. 5; "...the lamentation did not cease in the city before the thirtieth day, and a great; many hired mourners, with their

pipes, who should begin their melancholy ditties for them"; cp. 2 *Macc.* iii. 19 ff., 3 *Macc.* i. 18, *Wisd. of Sol.* xix. 3. See also Budde, *Die hebriiische Lei'chenklage* in the "Zeitschrift des Deutschen Paliistinavereins," vi. 187 ff.

255. Not *all* the lamentations, however, in the Old Testament are composed in this measure; e.g. the laments in 2 Sam. i. 19–27, iii. 33, 34 · are in a different measure.

256. *Op. cit.*, p. 275, he adds; "*Il ne faut point ici chercher mystere.*"

257. Benzinger in the *Encycl. Bibl.* iii. 3221 *a.*

258. Hastings, *op. cit.*, iv.446 a. Herodotus, i.198, says of the Babylonians that "their funeral lamentations are like those of the Egyptians."

259. *The O.T.in the Light of the Historical Records of Assyria and Babylonia*, pp. 477 f.

260. Jeremias, *Dae alte Testament . . .*, p. 361; *Holle ….*, pp. 9, 10; Delitzsch, *Dae Land ohne Heimkehr*, pp. 35, 36.

261. *Op. cit.*, ii. 826.

262. Wellhausen, *op. cit.*, pp. 177, 181, 182; Goldziher, *op. cit.*, p. 244, 260.

263. Torge, *op. cit.* p. 180.

264. For details regarding funeral rites, etc., among the Greeks the most helpful work is Rohde, *Psyche; Seelencult und Unsterblichkeitsglaube der Griechn* (1890); see also Lucian, *De Luctu*, passim.

265. *Op. cit.*, pp. i. 222 f.

266. Cp. with what was said above about flute-playing and its effect upon the departed spirit.

267. For example, see Hastings, *op. cit.*, iv. 503 *a.*

268. From the Mishnah we get the following reference to the subject in *Shabbath* xxiii. 4; "If a Goi (i.e. a Gentile) brings [mourning] flutes on the Sabbath, an Israelite shall not mourn with them unless they are brought from a place near by" (i.e. within what is called the *Techum* or "Sabbath limit," an area two thousand cubits in any direction).

269. See further, Krauss, *op. cit.*, ii. 64 ff.

270. *Op. cit.*, p. 277.

271. Nowack, *Hebriiische Archiiologie*, i. 195.

272. Bertholet, *Die israelitischen Vorstellunge n vom Zu8tand rntch dem Tode*, p. 4.

273. E.g. *Iliad*, xi. 453, cp. Rohde, *op. cit.*, i. 23 note.

274. Hastings, *op. cit.*, iv. 411 ff.

275. *Hebraische Archuologie*, i. 187 f.

276. This was done by the Jews in the Talmudic period; Krauss, *op. cit.*, ii. 55.

277. See the immense number of details on this subject in Elworthy, *The Evil Eye; An Account of this Ancient and Widespread Superatition.*

278. See Hastings, *op. cit.*, iv. 426 *a.*

279. Cp. Schwally, *op. cit.*, p. 8.

280. See further, Wellhausen, *op. cit.*, p. 109.

281. Jacobs in the *Jewish Encycl.*, vii. 515 *a.*

282. Thurston in the *Catholic Encycl.*, vii. 665.

283. Cp. the circumambulation of the Arabs round the *Ka'aba,* Wellhausen, *op. cit.*, pp. l0 ff.

284. Gaster, *Daily and Occasional Prayers*, I.

285. Wellhausen, *op. cit.*, p. 178.

286. Krauss, *op. cit.*, i. 55.

287. Jeremias, *Holle,* . . ., p. 9.

288. Wellhausen, *op. cit.*, p. 178.

289. On the text of this passage see above.

290. Krauss, *op. cit.*, p. 56.

291. Jeremias, *Holle* …p. 9.

292. Welllmusen, *op. cit.*, p. l78.

293. These two passages may, however, refer to death by burning.

294. In 1 Sam. xxxi. 12 it is said that the dead bodies of Saul and his sons were burned; but the words are omitted in the parallel account in I Chron. x. 12; and see also 2 Sam. xxi. 12–14, where it is said that the bones were buried in the sepulcher of Kish. It is highly probable that the text is corrupt, and a very slight emendation would bring the passage into line with Old Testament teaching, viz. by reading וישׂפרו (=וימפרו) "and they mourned "(cp. Gen. xxiii. 2, I Kings xiv. 3) instead of וישׂרפו "and they burned." The same text-corruption seems to be present in Amos vi. 10, only here it is the whole passage which is incomprehensible as it stands.

295. Jeremias, *Holle* . . ., pp. 10, 13; Jastrow, *op. cit.*, i. 372.

296. On the other hand, Langdon says that "cremation and body-burial existed side by side from the earliest times," in Hastings, *op. cit.*, iv. 444 b.

297. In reference to the fact that only the "bones" are mentioned here see above, pp. 20 ff.

298. Judging from what may sometimes be seen in the East to-day, ordinary graves may on occasion have taken this form too; thus travelers have seen dead bodies in the desert covered over with a heap of stones; each passer-by adds to the pile by throwing a stone on to it; cp. also Wellhausen, *op. cit.*, p. 180.

299. Quoted by F. Weber, *Juedische Tlieologie . . .*, p. 338.

300. *Op. cit.*, pp. 285 f.; on the subject generally see also Charles, *Eschatology; Hebrew, Jewish, and Chrstian* (1899), pp. 31 ff.

301. Jastrow, *op. cit.*,i. 371 f., see also pp. 359, 365 ff.

302. Delitzsch, *op. cit.*, pp. 35 f.

303. Of an entirely different character are, of course, foundation sacrifices and the like; for example, during the excavations at Taanach Prof. Sellin came across the remains of about thirty children near the base of a tower; and under the houses were also discovered the remains of infants and adults "who had been hurried when the houses were built." Macalister also came across infants' bones under house-walls, and sometimes built into the walls themselves in the Gezer excavations (cp. l Kings xvi. 34); see *Pal. Expl. Fund, Quarterly Statement*, 1903; pp. 224, 273. These examples are Semitic, and perhaps Israelite, but the most remarkable is one found in the second stratum (pre-Semitic) of the Gezer excavations; this is the skeleton of an adult, a woman of advanced age, who had been deposited in a hollow under the comer of a house (*Quarterly Statement*, 1904, pp. 16 f., where an excellent illustration shows how perfectly the skeleton is preserved).

304. *Pal. Expl. Fund, Quarterly Statement*, 1902, pp. 347, 356, 1904 pp. 119f., cp. Vincent, *op. cit.*, pp. 24 f.; see also, for the same among other peoples, Frazer, *Folklore in the Old Testament*, iii. pp. 13 ff.

305. Delitzsch, *op. cit.*, p. 35.

306. *The Excavations at Babylon*, pp. 271 f.

307. Quoted in a German translation by Bertholet, *Die israelitischen Vorstellungen vom Zustand nach dem Tode*, p. 13, but he does not give the name of the poet.

308. Wellhausen, *op. cit.*, pp. 178 f.

309. See further, Nowack, *op. cit.*, i. 190 ff

310. In the Greek Version xxx. 18 reads; "Good things poured out upon a mouth that is closed are as messes of meat laid upon a grave," but this, though

bearing witness to the custom, is a misreading of the Hebrew; "...are like an offering placed before an idol."

311. *Quarterly Statement*, 1903, pp. 12 ff.

312. *Ibid.*, p. 16.

313. *Q.S.*, 1903, pp. 32 ff.

314. Similar things were found during the excavations at Tell-el-Hesy (the ancient Lachish) and at Taanach; an excellent picture of the jugs is given on p. 121 (1903).

315. *Q.S.*, 1904, p. 326.

316. *Q.S.*, 1905, pp. 31 ff., see further 309 ff., 318 ff.

317. *Q.S.*, 1905, p. 79.

318. Vincent, *op. cit.*, p. 232.

319. *Op. cit.*, p. 230, see also pp. 269, 275, 276, 281.

320. See *Q.S.*, 1903, pp. 306 ff.

321. See further, Nowack, *op. cit.*, i. pp. 261 ff.

322. Excepting for special reasons and through the medium of properly qualified persons; see the chapter on Necromancy.

323. I.e. the principle of thought that "like produces like, or that an effect resembles its cause," Frazer, *The Golden Bough*; "The Magic Art and the Evolution of Kings," p. 52.

324. Howitt, "On Some Australian Beliefs," in the *Journal of the Anthropological Institute*, xiii. 189.

325. *The Belief in Immortality* . . ., i. 27, cp. Tylor, Primitive Culture (4th ed.), i. 397 ff.

326. Pp. l5 ff.

327. *Op. cit.*, i. p. 31.

328. *Op. cit.*, pp. 59 ff.

329. Here it will naturally be objected that if it was necessary for man to eat of the fruit of the Tree of Life in order to gain immortality, it cannot be said that immortality was the normal lot of man, since this was only conditional upon his eating the fruit. But the answer is that this was the Semitic way in which the matter was put; part of the normal let of man was that he should eat of the fruit of the Tree of Life; the normal thing would have been for nothing to have intervened between the time that he was created and the time when he should have eaten of the fruit. In the various other accounts among other

peoples it is always something that intervenes and prevents the normal process.

330. Frazer, *Folklore in the Old Testament*, i. pp. 49 ff., where many examples are given.

331. Cp. the teaching of the Koran, xcvi. 2, where it is said that God created man from clotted blood.

332. See above for references.

333. Genesis, p. 38.

334. Cp. the idea of the woman having been made out of part of the man.

335. For details, see Oesterley and Box, *The Religion and Worship of the Synagogue* (2nd ed.), pp. 255 ff.

336. Cp. Judges xi. 24, where it is said that Chemosh is the god of Moab, and I Kings xi. 33; "…Ashtoreth the goddess of the Zidonians, Chemosh the god of Moab, and Milcom the god of the children of Ammon."

337. The reform of Josiah (2 Kings xxii., xxiii.) in about 621 B.C. was *nominally* supposed to have done away with all local sanctuaries and all cults which were incompatible with the pure worship of Jahwe; but that this was not the case actually is clear enough from the subsequent history, see e.g. Ezek. viii. 14; Isa. lxv. 1–7.

338. Regarding the dates of quotations given in these sections see the Note at the end of this chapter.

339. See also Ps. xxx. 3 (4 in Hebr.)

340. This is probably also the purport of Ps. xlix. 15 (16 in Hebr.).

341. There is no mention of "worms" in the Hebrew. The disease described was the worst form of leprosy, called *elephantiasis*; the skin becomes black and folded, resembling the hide of an elephant, and, together with the flesh, gradually falls off.

342. This is more fully dealt with in the present writer's book, *Life, Death, and Immortality; Studies in the Psalms*, pp. 156 ff.

343. So the Septuagint and Syriac against the Hebrew; this only involves a change in the Hebrew points, not in the text.

344. This rendering (instead of "will lead me") is based on a single letter in the Hebrew text; it suits the sense and the context better.

345. The Revised Version renders; "For there are no bonds (marg. "pangs") in their death"; this assumes the correctness of the Hebrew text as it stands, which is quite obviously corrupt.